Southern Humboldt Indians

The Press at Cal Poly Humboldt
Cal Poly Humboldt Library
1 Harpst Street
Arcata, California 95521-8299
press@humboldt.edu
press.humboldt.edu

Copyright © 2022 Jerry Rohde
Second printing, 2024

This book is licensed under a Creative Commons Attribution-NonCommercial-4.0 International License.

Cover Photo: Albert and Sally Smith at Briceland, Ray Jerome Baker, photographer (CPH, colorized by JR).

Original copyright holders retain all copyright over images used in this book, and are thereby excluded from provisions granted by Creative Commons license.
Cover design and layout by Maximilian Heirich
Interior layout by Maximilian Heirich

ISBN: 978-1-947112-79-7

Southern Humboldt Indians

Jerry Rohde

The Press at Cal Poly Humboldt

History of Humboldt County People and Places series

Both Sides of the Bluff
Southern Humboldt Indians
Southwest Humboldt Hinterlands
Southeast Humboldt Hinterlands

Table of Contents

Expressions of Gratitude..vi

Acknowledgements vii

A Reader's Guide to Using this Book..ix

Key to Photo Credits... x

Preface.. xi

Introduction xiii

I. Finding the Lost Story of the Southern Humboldt Indians.................... 1

II. Earlier People, Earlier Place... 27

III. Three Tragedies 45

IV. Southern Humboldt Tribal Groups 75

Sources 133

Endnotes... 141

Epilogue.. 153

About the Author.. 154

Expressions of Gratitude

A number of people generously gave their time and expertise to help me create this book. The late Susie Van Kirk frequently shared her vast knowledge of Indian families and Indian tribes, while also providing a sensitive perspective from which to write this type of history. The late Victor Golla warmly responded to my questions about Indian dialects and vocabularies, offering information for which he was the only possible source. Sally Anderson was very helpful in updating my knowledge of current linguistical research. Carly Marino, Joan Berman, and Edie Butler all excelled at connecting me with items in the Humboldt State Library's Special Collections. Nick Angeloff, Bill Rich, Jamie Roscoe, Janet Eidsness, and Erica Cooper all offered their extensive knowledge as practicing archaeologists. David Heller, Laura Cooskie, and Ann Roberts conveyed often obscure but important information they had collected about the local Indians. Carolyn Mueller, Barry Evans, and Jan Anderson excelled in editing parts of an often complex text. Kyle Morgan and Maximilian Heirich of the HSU Press navigated, with commendable expertise, the turbulent waters of the publication process. Lastly, my wife Gisela stedfastly supported and supplemented every phase of the book's development by providing her editing expertise and empathetic enthusiasm as my thoughts were cast into words.

Acknowledgements

This book is a geographical history of the early-day Indians that inhabited what is now called southern Humboldt County. These peoples' land was forcibly taken from them, without recompense, during the California Indian genocide. Much of the information contained within these pages uses testimony from 19th century Indians to establish the names, boundaries, and histories of the Indian tribes and tribal groups that had occupied and claimed the land within this area. None of this southern Humboldt land has ever been returned to the descendants of the early-day people who were members of what are commonly called the Bear River, Mattole, Sinkyone, Wailaki, Lassik, and Nongatl tribes. Instead, all of their territory was taken by the federal government when California became a state in 1850. Surveys were then made and land laws established that allowed these lands to come into the possession of what are now known as settler colonists, almost all of whom were white. This process has seldom been described in print.

From the 1900s to the 1940s, numerous interviews with early-day southern Humboldt Indians were conducted by researchers, who, with one exception, were white. Most of the interviewees were present at the time of white contact and some were alive even before then. They possessed, and transmitted, indigenous knowledge based on their own experience. The researchers who collected this information were linguists or cultural anthropologists whose work was influenced by the values and perspectives of the settler colonist culture and by the academic paradigms of the disciplines in which they operated. Chapter 1 of this book is devoted to describing and evaluating the work of the individuals who conducted these interviews.

Most of the information collected by these researchers now exists in two forms: the field notes of the interviews and the published accounts based upon the interview materials. In published accounts the authors, by the act of writing, took control of the indigenous knowledge the Indians had provided. In doing so they could present the interview information through lenses of their own choosing, while sometimes drawing patently incorrect conclusions or ignoring facts that did not fit with the goals for their work.

Published accounts can thus be unreliable, misleading, or both. The unaltered field notes of the interviewers offer a much better chance for accuracy. They either captured verbatim statements from the Indians or presented brief summaries of what they said. Many times these statements were recorded in the field as the interviewer and interviewee were moving from place to place through tribal territories. A hundred years later, we have little knowledge of the questions interviewers asked, nor do we know if the interviewers selected which responses they would record. Cultural bias may sometimes have influenced the interview process. Mindful of this, I have placed my greatest faith in the accuracy of Pliny Goddard's work and have used his interview information whenever possible. We know that he spent extensive time with at least five southern Humboldt Indians and filled several notebooks with information they gave him. It appears he had exceptional rapport with all five and received from each of them substantial geographical and historical information. In the case of Van Duzen Pete, Goddard's Nongatl interviewee, I have in three instances provided local archaeologists with site-specific accounts from the field notes. In all three cases the information was found to be absolutely accurate.

As the author of this book, I recognize that I have been educated within and affected by the settler colonists culture of the United States. I make no claims, as an older white male, as to how this has influenced what I have written. I will say however, that over the last 14 years I have written 16 reports about the Southern Humboldt Indians for the Bear River Band of the Rohnerville Rancheria, a federally recognized tribe that has ancestral connections with the Indians from this area, and that all 16 were accepted with no criticism or requests for revision. These reports formed the foundation for this book.

In one area I have knowingly altered ethnographical materials. In preparing photographs for this book I have colorized all black and white images, including those of people. I am aware of concerns about the possible effects colorization may have on our perception of the person or persons whose images appear in the photographs, but I do not believe that this process has a negative impact. In fact, colorization may offset the deleterious effects of the original rendering of a full-color subject into a black and white image. My feeling is that presenting full-color images helps us to connect more deeply with the persons in the photos, and forming such connections is one of the main purposes of this book.

A Reader's Guide to Using this Book

Certain aspects of this book need explanations. They are collected here for the convenience of readers. First, there is a lack of agreement about the orthography of Indian names, which were, and are, often rendered by various ethnographers in different ways. When reproducing these words here, the following rules were followed: 1. When used in a direct quote, the word(s) are reproduced as given by the ethnographer, except that accent marks and other linguistical symbols are normally not included. 2. When not part of a direct quote, proper nouns are capitalized and hyphens replace spaces that were sometimes used to separate syllables of a word. 3. If two ethnographers diverged greatly in their rendering of a word, both versions are given, with the second version placed within parentheses.

Second, endnotes and indexing do not follow traditional patterns. Endnotes, which are located at the end of each chapter, offer only partial citations. They provide the author's last name, year of publication, and page numbers of the cited material. To obtain the full bibliographical reference, readers should then consult the "Sources" section at the end of the book. This method, while involving slightly more work on the part of the reader, greatly reduces the amount of space required for the endnotes and eliminates the confusion often caused by the use of such old-style reference terms as "ibid." and "op. cit."

Third, some the sources I cite are not available to the general public. Pliny Goddard's field notes contain a wealth of primary source material, but granting access to some of it is problematic, since certain sections reveal the location of sensitive tribal sites. Many years ago copies of the Goddard notebooks were obtained by myself and the Cultural Resources Facility (CRF) at Humboldt State University. Anthropology students subsequently read through the notebooks and transcribed geographical and historical information, which then appeared in parallel files opposite the original notebook text. I then reviewed the students' work, made corrections, installed key-term search devices, and provided comments about the text. These unique files were then housed at the CRF offices. At a meeting of senior CRF staff (myself and three archaeologists) it was decided that because of their sensitive nature, we would treat these new files as if they were a report about an archaeological site. This would mean that access would be restricted to CRF staff, tribal representatives, and archaeologists and scholars who needed, as professionals, to view the notebooks. Readers who want to gain access to these documents should contact the Cultural Resources Facility at https://crf.humboldt.edu .

Key to Photo Credits

The photo captions use initials to designate the sources. I colorized numerous black and photos using both the colorization feature at myheritage.com and Photoshop Elements 2021, and I have noted this at the end of the relevant captions.

AMNH = American Museum of Natural History

APS = American Philosophical Society

ARC = Archaeological Research Center, Department of Anthropology, California State University, Sacramento

BL = UC Berkeley, Bancroft Library

BLM = Bureau of Land Management

CEFP = California Ethnographic Field Photographs UC Berkeley, Phoebe A. Hearst Museum of Anthropology; the photographer is Pliny E. Goddard

CPH = Cal Poly Humboldt Library Special Collections

DPR = Department of Parks and Recreation, State of California, the Resources Agency

DTC = Don Tuttle Collection

EDC = Ethnological Documents Collection of the Department and Museum of Anthropology, University of California, Berkeley, 1875-1958. UC Berkeley, Bancroft Library

FM = Fritz-Metcalf Photograph Collection, UC Berkeley, Bioscience & Natural Resources Library; the photographer is Emanuel Fritz

GH = Gordon Hewes

GR = Gisela Rohde

HCHS = Humboldt County Historical Society

HIC = Alfred L. Kroeber, *Handbook of the Indians of California*

IA = Internet Archive

JNL = J. N. Lentell, Map of Humboldt County, 1914

JR = Jerry Rohde

LC = Library of Congress

MCNAP = Merriam (C. Hart) Collection of Native American Photographs, UC Berkeley, Bancroft Library; the photographer is C. Hart Merriam

MVHS = Mattole Valley Historical Society

PBS = Public Broadcasting Service

SMH = Sterling M. Holdreige

Preface

Tell me what were their names,
Oh what were their names. . . .
> - Woody Guthrie

In a sense, this book is about the discovery and disclosure of names. When we learn the name of someone or something, a relationship changes. What had been vague becomes precise. What had been abstract becomes real. What had been distant becomes close. We seek, and need, the enhanced connection these changes create.

Making these connections is a main purpose of this book. If we look back to a time before there was a Humboldt County, we find people and places that, for the most part, we cannot name. Starting in 1850 a cultural curtain was swiftly drawn across the past, so that the people who were then arriving in the area—the whites—soon saw little, and understood less, of what had been here before them. The people they were displacing—the Indians—were suddenly called "D*ggers," a term meant to belittle those to whom it was applied and to elevate the status of those who used it. The places where the Indians dwelt—their villages—were quickly destroyed, usually before the destroyers had even bothered to learn what these locations were called. New names came upon the land. The burnt Wiyot village of Djorokeg-ochkok became the town of Humboldt City, and when the "City" soon failed, the place waited a century for its next name, King Salmon. Jack Woodman, a Sinkyone Indian captured as a boy, was given the last name of his enslaver. A massacre site in southern Humboldt was commemorated by the offensive name Squaw Creek, as if killing the victims were not enough and the perpetrators needed also to insult them.

But the old names, and what they stood for, were retained by the people who had bestowed them, and starting in 1903 some of the names and the stories about them were finally recorded. Most of this information, however, has never seen print.

Now, however, important parts of these accounts appear in this book. More than a century after they had spoken, these early day Indians will be heard. All of us who make Humboldt County our home deserve to have access to this information. We deserve to know the many, many names of the tribal groups that were once here and to learn the story of these groups. And we deserve to know the names of the Indian elders who transmitted these names and told these stories, just as we deserve to know the stories about the elders themselves. We deserve to know all this because we *need* to know it. Only with this knowledge can we go forward as a community and begin to heal the wounds of the past, for only the truth will heal.

This book is but a small thing in the vastness of the world around us. But if it can bring forth at least a part of the truth about what has happened here at a certain time in the past, it will have succeeded in its purpose.

Introduction

This book is the second volume in a series now called the "History of Humboldt County Peoples and Places." It tells part of the story of the place we call southern Humboldt County, and it tells about some of the people who once lived there. It is also a sort of prelude to later parts of that story, for much of *Southern Humboldt Indians* focuses on the area as it was in about 1850. Why? Because that was the last time the multi-millennial culture of the local Indians was fully intact. After the white arrival on the North Coast, which began in April 1850, Indian life was soon drastically disrupted. In southern Humboldt the disruption became almost total destruction, as entire tribal groups were either erased or so completely fragmented that they no longer existed as cohesive units. Villages were wiped out, and tribal boundaries had no meaning because there were no longer any tribes to bound.

A half century later, ethnographers began the long-overdue task of trying to piece together what southern Humboldt was like in the time leading up to the Indian genocide of the 1850s and 1860s. From 1903 to the early 1940s these researchers collected statements from local Indians who could remember the terror that once beset them, and who could sometimes also recall the peaceful times before that. These recollections have left us a priceless record, and they form the heart of this book.

Why are these accounts so important? Because they are the most reliable reports we have about the southern Humboldt Indians' past. They represent history from the perspective of the victims—by people whose voices are seldom heard. Their stories were told simply and, perhaps remarkably, without rancor. They reflect the precise recollections of southern Humboldt people, places, and events before and immediately after the arrival of the whites. They tell us a truth that was seared into the memories of those who survived the Humboldt Indian holocaust.

While *Southern Humboldt Indians* can be read in its own right as a monograph on the history and geography of these people, it is also intended to be used in conjunction with the next two volumes in the series, which will be titled *Southwest Humboldt Hinterlands* and *Southeast Humboldt Hinterlands*. Together this pair of books will cover the history of all of southern Humboldt County from 1850 to approximately 1964, the year of the last major rearrangement of the area, which was caused not directly by human action but by that year's epochal Christmastime flood. Many of the accounts in these two later volumes rest upon the foundation provided by the current book.

All of the volumes in this series follow a similar format. Primary source material is used whenever possible. When secondary sources are used, their accuracy has been vetted as thoroughly as my skill permits. Virtually all factual statements receive an endnote that provides the source of the information. Sometimes additional endnotes are used to provide details that, while important, are placed there to avoid disrupting the flow of the main text. Sidebars contain short accounts of particular subjects that can best be read as self-contained stories.

This book is meant for two audiences: for the general reader who is interested in Humboldt County Indian history, and for archaeologists, ethnographers, and other researchers who need detailed, primary-source information for their reports and field work. There are four chapters, as follows:

Chapter I, "Finding the Lost Story of the Southern Humboldt Indians," follows the trail of the first, and best, account of the local Indians' story, the numerous notebooks of U C Berkeley anthropologist Pliny E. Goddard. All but unknown to other ethnographers, and almost entirely unread, Goddard's work languished in the dungeon of archival obscurity for a century before it escaped into the sunlight of recent research. Earlier scholars, lacking access to these notebooks, often failed to produce fully accurate reports about the southern Humboldt Indians, although a few conducted interviews with knowledgeable elders that added to the compilations created by Goddard. I have evaluated the efforts of these other southern Humboldt ethnographers and described what I believe are the strengths and limitations of their work. Thus, when perusing subsequent chapters in this book, readers can better assess the reliability of information provided by C. Hart Merriam, John P. Harrington, Edith Van Allen Murphey, Gladys Ayer Nomland, Martin Baumhoff, Alfred L. Kroeber, and other relevant researchers.

Chapter 2, "Earlier Peoples, Earlier Place," first describes the situation of southern Humboldt Indians in the spring of 1850. The activities of the people of the different tribes are sketched but not analyzed, the goal being to impart some sense of what the lives of these many groups of Indians were like prior to the arrival of the whites. There follows a summary of the southern Humboldt Indian genocide, where for most of two decades white vigilantes and various military forces murdered, massacred, and in other ways attempted to eliminate the Indian presence from the region.

Chapter 3, "Three Tragedies," provides detailed accounts of three different aspects of the Humboldt Indian holocaust. In one instance, a small group of white civilians attacked an unsuspecting village near Briceland, killed many Indians quickly, and then pursued survivors all the way out of the county to distant Island Mountain. The second account describes the army's role in the destruction of the southern Humboldt Indians, including the implementation of its policy of killing male Indians on sight and, far too late to have much effect, the eventual prohibition of such acts. The chapter's last section describes the tragic conflict between two Indian tribes caused by the duplicity of certain army officers. The two subsequent southern Humboldt books will include other such incidents in the context of the places where they occurred.

Chapter 4, "Southern Humboldt Tribal Groups," briefly tells the story of more than 50 independent collections of southern Humboldt Indians, explaining how these people identified not with a large unit called a "tribe," but with a much smaller entity that I and others call a "tribal group." This perspective provides a description vastly different from that found in most earlier writings on the subject. It relies chiefly on the Goddard notebooks. The interviews he conducted between 1903 and 1908 represent the golden age of southern Humboldt ethnography, for Goddard created a remarkable rapport with Indians from throughout the area and recorded in detail the accounts they provided. When we read the statements collected from his many interviews, we suddenly behold a place where dozens of distinctly separate groups of Indians each claimed a precisely defined piece of land, living in what were generally peaceful, if not always friendly, relationships with neighboring groups. We read the words Goddard heard and transcribed into his small, well-worn notebooks, and voices long silent again speak. They tell us of a time beyond imagining, but a time we know was real, for our knowledge comes from the testimony of the people who were actually present.

Chapter I

Finding the Lost Story of the Southern Humboldt Indians

On September 14, 1903—a Monday—Pliny E. Goddard was in the heart of southern Humboldt County, not far from the bustling tanbark town of Briceland. He opened a brand-new "Bank Stock" notebook and prepared to start an interview. Across from him was a handsome, middle-aged Indian with a strikingly robust, well-trimmed mustache. Goddard asked a question and then began to write as George Burtt answered.[1]

Burtt was about 45 years old. His parents, Los-ki-ta and Betsy, had come from the upper Mattole River, probably from the village of Lenillimi,[2] several miles northwest of Briceland. One day they had left the Mattole and taken the trail that led northeast to Elk Ridge. There they turned north and crossed over the austere rocks and grasslands of Clark's Butte, finally leaving the ridge to drop northeastward into the canyon of Lo-lun-ko, the stream the whites later called Bull Creek. Part way down the canyon they stopped at the village of Kahs-cho-chin-net-tah, and there they stayed. It was here that a son, Ah-dah-dil-law, was born.[3] A few years later he would take the white man's name of George Burtt.

Goddard's interview with Burtt was brief. It first involved learning the Indian names of some nearby geographic features: "Sin-ki-ko," the South Fork Eel River; "Xa-cho," the main Eel River; "Lo-lun-ko," Bull Creek; and "Ca-na-ko," Salmon Creek.[4] Just eleven syllables, but they defined much of the area where Ah-dah-dil-law spent his early life.

A few more words and they were done for the day. On Tuesday, George was gone and in his place stood Briceland Charlie, older and much shorter than Burtt, wearing a narrow-brim straw hat. Charlie started off by giving the names for many animals—"cac," grizzly bear; "sa-tco," fisher; "ltci-tco," ground squirrel—and then went on to trees, shrubs, and other plants. He provided many names of places and of other Indian tribal groups. Shelter Cove was called "tan-a-dun" and the Indians there were the "tan-a-dun ki-a." Goddard's notebook was filling up.[5]

On they go—colors, everyday phrases, how to hunt for a female grizzly bear.[6] Goddard was receiving a crash course in the vocabulary and culture of Charlie's people. Although he didn't know it at the time, he had just started what would become the most extensive documentation of the southern Humboldt Indians.

Goddard, along with Alfred L. Kroeber, served as faculty for UC Berkeley's brand new anthropology department.[7] His position allowed him to spend his summers making expeditions into the geographical—and temporal—California backcountry, finding and recording Indians whose memories often stretched back to, and beyond, the days of white arrival. Much of the time Goddard worked with the Indians from southern Humboldt, which eventually resulted in the publication of monographs on the Bear River (Nekanni) and Wailaki tribes, along with the compilation of a vast col-

George Burtt, left, and Briceland Charlie, right, at Briceland, 1903 (CEFP, colorized by JR).

lection of unpublished material, including maps, notecards, and hundreds of photographs. Of greatest significance, however, was a set of at least 35 notebooks, filled mostly with word lists and mythlike stories, but interspersed with invaluable accounts of significant people, places, and events.

In these early years funding for Berkeley's anthropology department came from Phoebe Apperson Hearst,[8] widow of millionaire mine owner George Hearst. This endowment ended in 1908, and Kroeber and Goddard clashed over the future of the department, which Goddard wanted reorganized to focus on linguistics. Kroeber wanted no such change; he prevailed, and in 1909 Goddard left the university and took a position at the American Museum of Natural History in New York.[9] Most of his material on the California Indians remained at Berkeley.[10]

In May 1911 Goddard wrote his former colleague. The letter was not intended to heal their fraught relationship:

Dear Kroeber:

Now I am not sorry I have delayed my comment on your paper on the "Languages North of San Francisco." Your latest paper gives me a still better opportunity for expression. I think you are to be congratulated on attaining the goal of your many years of striving. I am sure that even you alone, or aided by Dixon,[11] will never be able to produce a paper based on less information or in a field in which you are less qualified to write or bearing a more ridiculous proportion to the problem. . . .

P.S. - I had a toothache last night.

By the time of Goddard's "toothache" letter a new ethnographer was working with the southern Humboldt Indians. It wasn't Kroeber or another Berkeley scholar, but rather a recently retired biologist who had made a mid-life career change. Starting in 1910 and for nearly 30 years thereafter, C. Hart Merriam was the primary ethnographic researcher in southern Humboldt and, in fact, in the entire state.[12] Like Goddard, Merriam published little, but between them they left the largest legacy of information about the northwestern California Indians that will ever exist. (See Appendix A at end of chapter.)

Other researchers followed. Some published substantial reports. Some confined their work to the compilation of notes. None approached Goddard and Merriam in collecting significant accounts, but their efforts are worth reviewing. (See Appendix B at end of chapter.)

In 1928 another promising ethnographer arrived in southern Humboldt, when Gladys Ayer Nomland commenced fieldwork as a Berkeley graduate anthropology student. She recorded interviews with elderly Indians from the Sinkyone, Bear River, Mattole, and Mawenok[13] tribes preparatory to writing monographs about each group. By 1935 three of Nomland's main informants had died and she ended up publishing monographs on only the Sinkyone and Bear River tribes.[14] She also created manuscripts for the Mattoles and Mawenoks but they never reached print, and, worse yet, these works have been lost. Nomland developed detailed descriptions of the Indians' lives, but her efforts were compromised by a problem she was only partly aware of—the unreliability of her informants.

Nomland's work with the southern Humboldt Indians ended in 1931.[15] Her hope was to obtain accurate accounts of the cultures of several tribes, but by then it was sometimes too late. When Pliny Goddard had come to southern Humboldt and filled his notebooks, he had interviewed Indians with still-keen minds who had been alive at the onset of white contact, but Nomland arrived 25 years later and time had taken its toll. Some of Goddard's informants, such as Briceland Charlie, Albert Smith, and Van Duzen Pete, had died. Some, like George Burtt, she apparently failed to locate. And one woman was interviewed when her information was no longer reliable.

Although Nomland was able to find new sources, this led to new problems. For example, Nora Coonskin, Nomland's Bear River informant, was born in 1871,[16] a generation after the time of white contact. The world she lived in had been transformed by the Indian holocaust of the 1850s and 1860s. She grew up on Bear River but was married to a Wiyot and adopted many of that tribe's ways. The information she provided Nomland had been handed down by her parents. Nomland admitted that Coonskin "had been separated from her own people so long that much of her account is vague and some things she has entirely forgotten, so that her account is, at best, fragmentary."[17] Goddard, who also published a monograph about the Bear River tribe, received much of his information from a man known only as Peter, who had been born about 1837.[18] He was Nora's uncle.[19] Peter had grown up in a way of life and had witnessed events that Nora had only heard about.[20]

Southern Humboldt Indian tribes and locations of main informants: AS = Albert Smith, BC = Briceland Charlie, GB = George Burtt, ID = Ike Duncan, JD = Joe Duncan, JW = Jim Willburn, KP = Kitty Prince, LY = Lucy Young, NR = Nick Richard, P = Peter, S = Sally Bell, SS = Sam Suder, VDP = Van Duzen Pete (JNL, colorized by JR).

Worse yet, Nomland also encountered difficulties with her Sinkyone sources. She stated that Jenny Young had been subjected to "white influence since a child; information unreliable...." It was a similar story with Sally Bell, who had been "reared by white settlers" and by the late 1920s was described as "blind and senile...."[21] Despite this, Nomland chose to include Bell's account of "the massacre at Needle Rock," wherein Bell claimed that "some white men" murdered her mother, father, grandfather, and baby sister. It is a graphic, chilling story that has been anthologized[22] and is required reading in certain Native American literature courses.[23]

But it may not be entirely true. When Goddard interviewed Bell in September 1907 she was more than 20 years younger than when Nomland recorded her massacre story. She provided Goddard with information that conflicted with what she later told Nomland. At one point Goddard quoted Bell about a massacre on the coast north of Shelter Cove. Bell said that at this location there ". . . used to be lots of Indians. Saw [rifle?] shells after they were all killed. *Her father was killed by Indians* (she thinks) when she [was] little."[24] [Emphasis added.]

If what Bell told Goddard is correct, then her father was *not* murdered at Needle Rock, and this tarnishes the accuracy of the account she gave to Nomland. But the massacre story was published, and then republished, and has now been in print for over 80 years. It has, in fact, become a cornerstone of the Indian genocide literature. The earlier statement Bell gave to Goddard, on the other hand, has resided within the obscurity of his field notes and has never been published, as far as can be determined, until now.

If Nomland had concerns about the veracity of Bell's and Young's accounts, she had none about the information she received from Jack Woodman, the Sinkyone whom she called "her only reliable informant." She burnished the luster of his recollections by claiming that he was "born and always lived in own culture at Briceland."[25] Once again, however, Goddard's notes provided contradictory information. His interviewee Briceland Charlie gave a very different account of Jack's life:

> Jack Woodman born at kon tel kyo dun Myers [Flat]. Never lived on reservation. Was taken by John Marshall at Phillipsville. He sold him to George Woodman of Long Valley [in Mendocino County] who was pretty mean.[26]

Jim Willburn, another Goddard interviewee, provided additional information:

> A man named Woodman used to buy all the Indian boys they would bring him. They used to keep them in pens. When the Indian women used to come up to see them [the boys] one man used to set hounds on them.[27]

Small wonder, then, if Jack Woodman had blanked out the memory of his childhood.

Perhaps because of Woodman's prolonged absence from his homeland, Charlie indicated that "he knows some stories but not many."[28] Charlie's statements call into question Woodman's credentials, as given by Nomland, and thus render his information suspect.

Although Goddard's accounts contradicted what Nomland wrote about Sally Bell and Jack Woodman, it is almost certain that Nomland never read them. At the time of her research Goddard's notebooks still resided in the archives of Berkeley's anthropology department, perhaps only a few steps away from the halls she must have trod as a

Future Nomland informant Jenny Young, Briceland, 1903 (CEFP, colorized by JR).

graduate student. Alfred L. Kroeber was on duty in the department in 1909 when Goddard left his notebooks and other materials at Berkeley and moved to New York. And Kroeber was there when Nomland conducted her inquiries into some of the same tribes that Goddard had researched. Yet it appears that Kroeber never informed Nomland of this very near, and very dear, resource.

If Kroeber's behavior in this situation seems strange, his actions (or lack thereof) regarding another graduate student, Martin Baumhoff, appear absolutely shocking. In 1955 Baumhoff was charged with preparing a monograph covering part of C. Hart Merriam's ethnological data, the papers of which had come to Berkeley in 1950. Baumhoff's work was to be conducted under the joint supervision of Kroeber and R. F. Heizer, a member of the anthropology department's faculty.

It was decided that Baumhoff would focus on Merriam's work with the California Athabascan Indians, which included all the southern Humboldt tribes, along with the Kato, Hupa,

Finding the Lost Story

Whilkut, and Yuki. It quickly became apparent that it was advisable to include the closely related unpublished work of Goddard in the assessment, and with this dual focus, Baumhoff went to work.[29]

But soon Baumhoff ran into trouble. In the departmental archives he found a map, hand drawn by Goddard, with what appeared to be a stream and a series of numbers, from 1 to 51, marked at various locations on the stream and the surrounding area. There was a word near top of the map, which Baumhoff learned from other Goddard documents referred to a branch of the Nongatl tribe. He searched in vain for a key to the map that would tell him what the numbers meant. Finally, knowing that it was an important, if incomprehensible, document, he included it in his report with one of the most bizarre captions ever published: "*Presumed* Nongatl villages in the Bridgeville region."[Emphasis added.][30]

And there were more gaps in the university's Goddard collection, some of which Baumhoff soon became aware of—and some that he didn't. He contacted other institutions that he thought might have Goddard material but came up empty. Finally, in frustration, he inserted a disclaimer into his introduction: "It is clear, on the basis of internal evidence, that there is or was more Goddard material than is now accessible to the present author."[31]

Most of the missing material Baumhoff postulated was contained in the set of notebooks that Goddard left at Berkeley when he resigned from the university and went east. In this collection were the 35 notebooks pertaining to southern Humboldt and northern Mendocino tribes and another 22 relating to tribes in the northern part of Humboldt County.[32] For 38 years they reposed in the archeology archives at Berkeley, apparently untouched and unread—even though at least several students—including Gladys Nomland, Harold Driver, and Frank Essene—would have greatly benefitted from learning what was in them.

Finally, in 1946, someone took notice.

It was the year of Kroeber's retirement from Berkeley,[33] but before he left he gave the Goddard notebooks to the American Philosophical Society in Philadelphia to become part of the Society's Franz Boas collection.[34] Boas had been a pioneer in the development of the discipline of anthropology and Kroeber had been one of his students.[35] It is unclear if Kroeber had the authority to de-accession the Goddard documents, and if the anthropology department kept a record of the transaction, Baumhoff never found it. He also never found the field notes, even though the one person who should have recalled where they were—Kroeber—was the co-supervisor of Baumhoff's project.[36]

Kroeber.

Kroeber's work with the southern Humboldt Indians is not summarized in this account because no such work is exists. The Kroeber Papers, archived at Berkeley, contain zero notebooks on the southern Humboldt tribes.[37] His notebook 45 does include three lines that refer to the "South Fork Eel River Athabascan," indicating that Kroeber bought from these Indians (for 50¢) two objects that he used for illustrations in his handbook.[38] This publication, the monumental Handbook of the Indians of California, contains 13 pages on the Indians of southern Humboldt, all of it (except for drawings of the 50¢ objects) derived from information other than his own.[39] Despite his lack of knowledge about the subject, Kroeber decided there were five southern Humboldt tribes—the Mattole, Sinkyone, Wailaki, Lassik, and Nongatl. In the preface to his Handbook, Kroeber reveals his attitude towards both the history of the California Indians and of the Indians themselves:

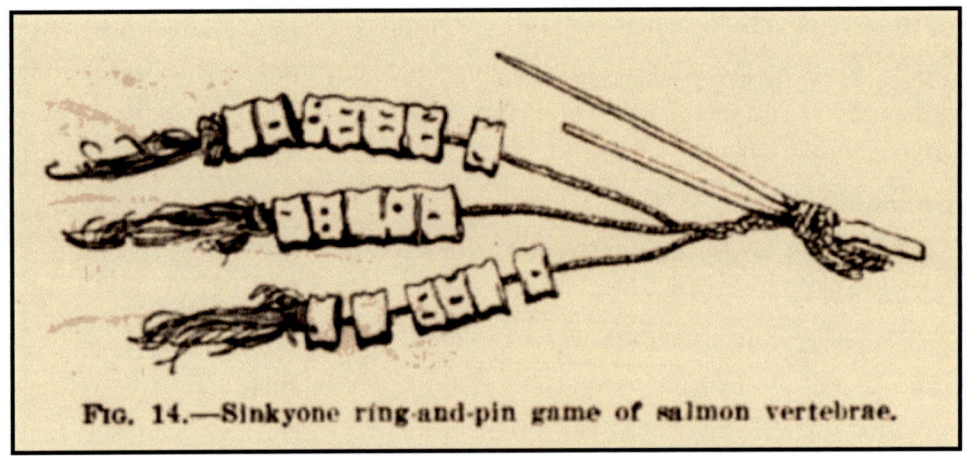

Half of Kroeber's early research on the southern Humboldt Indians. One of two objects purchased from them on September 17, 1902, for 50¢ (HIC).

This book . . . is not a history in the usual sense of a record of events. The vast bulk of even the significant happenings in the lives of uncivilized tribes are irrecoverable. For the past century our knowledge is slight; previous to that there is complete obscurity. *Nor do the careers of savages afford many instances of sufficient intrinsic importance to make their chronicling worthwhile* [Emphasis added].[40]

Small wonder, then, that Goddard and Kroeber clashed, given Goddard's insistence on recording accounts of the "careers of savages."[41]

In 1958 Baumhoff's work was published by the University of California Press as *California Athabascan Groups*. In it, Baumhoff added a sixth southern Humboldt tribe, the Bear River or Nekanni, which he believed was a distinct entity that should be separated from the Mattole tribe, within which it had previously been subsumed. Baumhoff also subdivided some of the other tribes into smaller units that he called "bands" or "subgroups."[42] The monograph was a noteworthy achievement, for it utilized unpublished material from both Merriam and Goddard, contained cultural information about the various tribes, and described their boundaries. It immediately became the standard ethnogeographical account of the California Athabascan Indians and has remained so ever since.

Having Baumhoff as a resource made life much easier for educators, agency personnel, archaeologists, ethnographers, and others who needed to know the boundaries of tribes, the names and locations of villages, and related information about the Indians of northwestern California. Many types of projects—including road and highway improvements, housing developments, utility line extensions, small hydro plant installations, and other proposed land alterations—require the creation of various environmental review documents. For decades, the archaeological surveys and ethnographical studies that comprise parts of these reviews relied on Baumhoff as a foundational work in building their assessments. Even researchers with the best intentions failed to realize that *California Athabascan Groups* was a flawed document that could lead to false conclusions and hamper field work. (See sidebar 1.)

But now, with the availability of Goddard's notebooks, and with other ethnographic information more easily accessible, Baumhoff's monograph no longer needs to serve as the main resource about the California Athabascan Indians. It is now possible to view the ethnography of southern Humboldt County from a vastly different perspective. We can, far better than before, behold a place inhabited by many distinct but interconnected groups of people, each with their own name and clearly defined territory. We can discover a small but vibrant collection of knowledgeable elders, persons who vividly told the story not only of their own tribal group but also of individual Indians, including themselves. We can view a map with many dots upon it and now know what each dot stood for—a place with a name and often a story attached to it. We now can read thousands of pages, and thousands upon thousands of words, that contain a story that for over a century was unavailable.

Words are magic. We have only to read what these southern Humboldt Indians said to realize it.

1. Finding the Lost Stories

In the fall of 2001 Humboldt State University's Cultural Resources Facility (CRF) was engaged to survey a location of interest in southern Humboldt. As a course project, HSU students from an archaeological field methods class participated, under faculty supervision, in examining the area. The students arrived at the site, were arranged in a line that spaced them several feet apart, and then began walking through the area, probing the ground with various hand tools.

Humboldt State University anthropology students begin their survey of a site in southern Humboldt, 2001 (JR).

It was not long before one student uncovered some interesting objects—pieces of "fire-affected" rock and what appeared to be part of the type of refuse heap that archaeologists call a midden. These were startling discoveries, since the area had been the subject of previous archaeological surveys that had found no such significant material.

CRF completed its examination of the area and then prepared a report, part of which was an ethnographical review. The main sources used in the review were Baumhoff's monograph and selections from C. Hart Merriam's collected papers. At the time, no one at CRF, including the author of the review, was aware of the existence of the Goddard notebooks. The review attempted to determine which Indian tribe was associated with the area, but after several pages that tortuously navigated through the Baumhoff and Merriam material, the document concluded that no definite tribal affiliation could be determined.

So things stood for several years until the author of the review happened to find a reference to "Field notes in California Athabascan languages/Pliny E. Goddard." It happened that copies of the notes were preserved on five rolls of microfilm that had been created by the American Philosophical Society. The review author obtained access to copies of the microfilm, began to look at the first roll, and was transfixed. There, displayed on the microfilm reader, was the Rosetta Stone of northwestern California ethnography.

On the screen, scrawled on lined paper in Goddard's sprawling but legible hand, was page after page, book after book, of the story of the southern Humboldt Indians. Here were vocabularies, folkloric tales, and—sprinkled intermittently—descriptions of the geography and accounts of the history of all the area's tribes. Here were the recollections of people who had been alive at the time of white arrival, who could remember the villages and the ways of life that had existed before the Humboldt Indian holocaust. Here often were their exact words, taken down by Goddard as they were spoken. Here was a chance to follow those words as they led back through the decades to a time that had been lost to living memory but could now come alive once again.

The story of a people had been fragmented, but now, with the words of Joe Duncan, and George Burtt, and Briceland Charlie, and Van Duzen Pete, and all the others, there was a chance to join the story together again. Now we learned how the Sinkenes of Salmon Creek hunted elk by chasing them for five, ten, or even twenty miles.[43] Now we discovered that the Nongatl tribe built rectangular houses, like tribes to the north, rather than the conical structures of tribes to the south.[44]

We still did not know everything, but we knew enough that people who had been mere names to us had now, with their lost words at last there to be read, been allowed to make part of the broken story whole again.

At last researchers had a tool they could trust to take them back to the past. Reading the notebooks was like listening to a tape recorder—here were entire sentences, or even paragraphs, of direct quotations from the Indians.

Then came the question, how reliable was it? Did the Indians whom Goddard interviewed trust him enough, like him enough, to tell the truth? It took a while for the results to come in, for locations that were described in the notebooks (and sometimes even mapped) had to be visited and the descriptions confirmed by archaeologists. The first confirmation was already at hand—mention of Indian activity at the southern Humboldt site that CRF inspected. Then, over time, other confirmations were made—locations that when visited corresponded exactly to what Goddard had described.

Now the accounts in the notebooks could be set next to what Baumhoff had written and then used to supplement or correct his monograph. In one notebook were a series of numbers, each followed by a name and a short description.[45] The numbers corresponded to those on the map that Goddard had, in desperation, labeled "Presumed Nongatl villages." They showed that Baumhoff had presumed too much. Site 14, "se tcil bai," for example, was simply "a big rock." Site 19, "an ai tce," was a "round point of timber." Site 22, "sen dul kuk," was "a creek from north." Site 24, "L tuk ka nun din," was a white man's house." What Goddard was recording were *places*.

In the same way, a passage in "Mattole Notebook #1" changed our understanding of much of the ethnogeography of southwestern Humboldt. Goddard is interviewing Joe Duncan, who tells him, "up as far [as] John Everts [sic] were his people."[46] This meant that the Mattole tribe's territory only went to Evarts's ranch, which was about four miles upriver from Petrolia.[47] Baumhoff, however, had mapped the Mattole tribe's land extending many miles south of there, all the way to Honeydew.[48] He did so because of what he had found in the main set of Goddard documents available to him, a collection of notecards (since lost)[49] containing information about individual Indian villages. Goddard had marked the notecards for those villages along the Mattole with one of two headings: those on the lower part of the river were each listed as "a Mattole village," while those farther upriver were each called "a village of the upper Mattole people."[50] Baumhoff interpreted this to mean that the Mattole tribe was divided into two tribelets—the "Mattoles" and the "upper Mattoles," and he proceeded to map them this way.[51] What Goddard didn't make clear on his notecards was that "upper Mattole people" did not mean upriver members of

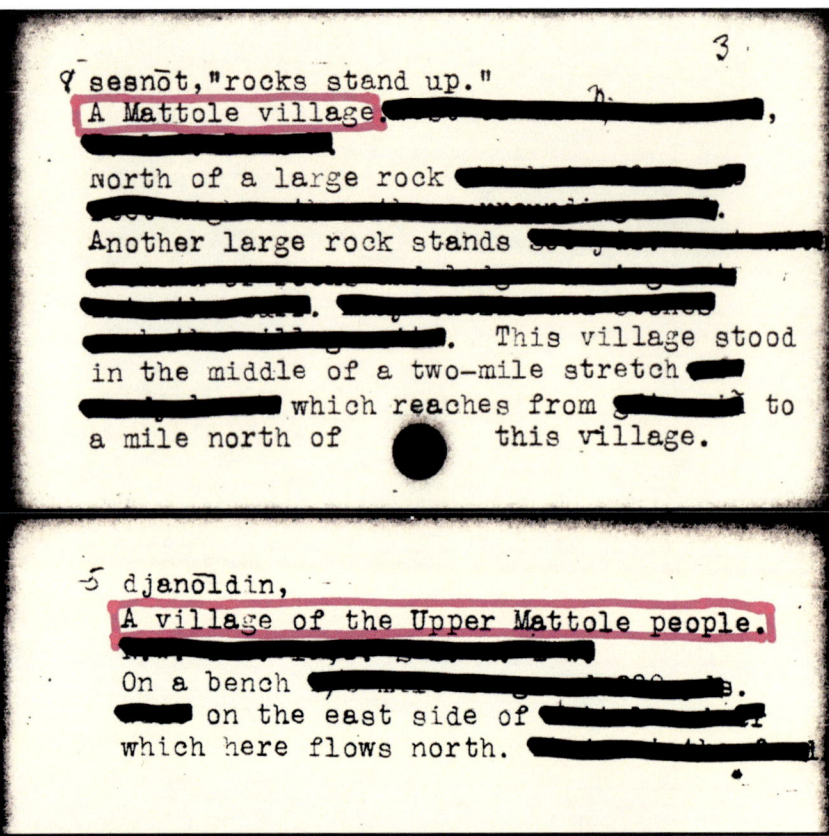

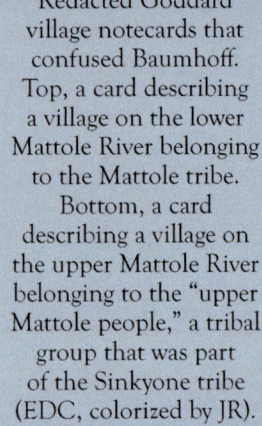

Redacted Goddard village notecards that confused Baumhoff. Top, a card describing a village on the lower Mattole River belonging to the Mattole tribe. Bottom, a card describing a village on the upper Mattole River belonging to the "upper Mattole people," a tribal group that was part of the Sinkyone tribe (EDC, colorized by JR).

the Mattole tribe, but instead referred to a separate, unnamed tribal group that lived on the "Upper Mattole" and was actually a part of the Sinkyone tribe. As Goddard put it, "all these people probably [Briceland] Charlie's kind, not Mattole Indians."[52] The effect of using this notebook information is to divide the territory Baumhoff assigned to the Mattole tribe almost exactly in half, with the southeastern portion becoming part of the Sinkyones' territory.

Nothing else would ever—will ever—tell us more about the southern Humboldt Indians than Goddard's notebooks. They include accounts by Indians from all the local tribes. They contain stories from some Indians who would soon, like Briceland Charlie, pass away, or, like Sally Bell, have their memory fail. And the notebooks almost always recorded—rather than providing a paraphrase or summary—exactly what the Indians said. They let us, more than any other source, link word to place, with all the mystery and power that such a connection makes. They take a number on a map and give that number a name, and give that name a description—a creek, a rock, or something else—and at last allow us to straighten the jumbled threads of time and place. They restore, as best as can be done, the wholeness that a holocaust had rent apart. They move across a land, drenched in sorrow and in blood, and allow the survivors to speak.

Appendix A: The Story Catchers of Southern Humboldt

I have never found any Indian of any tribe who did not amaze me by the extent of his knowledge.[53]

— C. Hart Merriam

In the April 1872 issue of the *Overland Monthly* there appeared the first installment in a series titled "The Northern California Indians."[54] The author was Stephen Powers, a former war correspondent who had recently published an account of his travels from Raleigh, North Carolina, to San Francisco.[55] By the second paragraph of his maiden *Overland* article, Powers's prose had bloomed into full floridity, as he summarized the plight of his subject peoples:

> It has been the melancholy fate of the California Indians to be at once most foully vilified and least understood. . . . To have been once the possessors of the most fair and sunny empire ever conquered by the Anglo-Saxon, and to have had it wrenched out of their gripe [grasp] with the most shameless violence; to have been once probably the happiest, and afterward reduced to the most miserable and piteous ruin, of all our American aborigines! Pity for the California Indian that his purple-tinted mountains were filled with dust of gold, and that his green and shining valleys, lying rich and mellow to the sun, were pregnant with so large possibilities of wheat! . . . It is small concern of pioneer miners to know aught of the life-story, customs, and ideas of a poor beggar, who is fatuously unwise as to complain that they darken the water so he can no longer see to pierce the red-fleshed salmon, and his women and papposes [sic] are crying for meat; and when he lies stiff and stark in the arid gully, where the white pitiless sun of California shakes above him the only winding-sheet that covers his swart body, he is not prolific in narration of his people's legends and traditions. Dead men tell no tales.[56]

But live men—and women—could, and did, tell tales, and thirty years after Powers's lament, some of those stories were finally being recorded. Among the southern Humboldt Indians, it was possible to find at least one knowledgeable survivor from several of the tribal groups, and during the ensuing decades a number of these people were located and interviewed. The accounts they gave were as fleeting as the deer moving through the forest or a flock of geese flying high overhead, for the tellers were already passing away, leaving only a growing silence. The ethnographers who visited the area became story catchers, snaring words that otherwise would soon fade to silence, the memories they contained no longer heard.

Much of the work with the Indians of southern Humboldt was done by just two story catchers. One came for a few years in the early 1900s; the other arrived a decade later and remained, off and on, for the rest of his life.

The most precise source of tribal information for the southern Humboldt area came from the first of them, Pliny Earle Goddard. In the 1890s Goddard was far from California, serving as a poorly paid principal at a series of schools in the Midwest. In 1897 he finally left both the area and his occupation to become a lay missionary at Hoopa. According to his later colleague, Alfred L. Kroeber, the trip to get there was an adventure:

There was no road into Hoopa then; Mrs. Goddard had never ridden; and Goddard piloted her and carried his seventeen months old daughter on horseback over the two days' trail through a snowstorm.[57]

It was at Hoopa that the course of Goddard's early ethnographical career was set:

> Goddard's informal, simple, direct ways won the affection of the Indians; and their life, still largely unspoiled from native days, engaged his interest. He set himself not only to note their customs but to record the language systematically, acquiring also a fair speaking knowledge of it. More and more the plan grew in him to make ethnology his life work. . . .[58]

Goddard left Hoopa to enroll at the University of California Berkeley. He became an instructor in the just-organized department of anthropology, joining Kroeber as the two members of the faculty.[59] He received his Ph.D. in 1904; it was the first such degree in linguistics ever granted by an American university.[60] In 1906 he was promoted to assistant professor. Two years later came the split with Kroeber and soon Goddard was the width of a wide continent away.[61]

Once in New York, Goddard held various positions with the Museum of Natural History until his death in 1928.[62] Kroeber subsequently

Pliny E. Goddard (AMNH, colorized by JR).

set aside past differences to write an eloquent and moving obituary for the *American Anthropologist* in which he described Goddard's method of work:

> Many of his ethnological accounts are essentially . . . personal renditions from one or two individuals; and between him and his informants there always existed a strong bond of affection. Analysis per se interested Goddard only slightly, and synthesis less. It was the data themselves, in their aura of ex-

Finding the Lost Story

perience by personalities, that drew him and that he reproduced with felicitous fidelity. Ethnologic or linguistic study therefore always meant to him field work; not so much because this secured new or exacter materials, as because it secured the only materials really worth while in their livingness.[63]

As Kroeber explained it, Goddard would focus on one informant from each tribal group:

> This resulted in a strong reciprocal identification of the two persons, especially when they went off together for weeks, with a pack mule and a white horse, to camp in the hills and seek settlement sites. In 1910, with Goddard gone to New York, I found that the University owned a mule at a pasture near Laytonville which I had to dispose of.[64]

Goddard himself described how he conducted his field work:

> Today the country drained by Mattole, Eel and Mad rivers have only a few scattering Indians—three or four where there used to be hundreds or even thousands. To all outward appearances they live as white people, with a little less work, and in rather more dirt, but the inner life of the older ones is still aboriginal....
>
> The problem is to find out what dialect was spoken in each valley, how the people lived, and what they thought about things, to save wherever possible their many folktales and myths, and the religious formulas and prayers used in their worship....
>
> The first necessity is a means of getting to the out of the way places where these

Goddard's pack mule and white horse, awaiting his return to Laytonville, 1906 (CEFP, colorized by JR).

few Indians are situated and of living near them for some weeks at a time. A gentle saddle-mule and a stout pack-horse furnish transportation and allow the extension of the trips far beyond the wagon roads. No place in the world could be more delightful for out door life in the summer than is the region just east of the fog belt. A tent is hardly necessary except for the protection of the outfit against the possible but not probable rains. There is no dew after June. The mountain side furnishes abundant feed for the saddle animals: some small stream or spring, pure and abundant water.

The confidence of the Indians has been gained by a preliminary visit or through common friends, the work of recording texts of tales and myths may be begun at once.... The note-books fill up rapidly, and stories new and old unfold. Primitive life and thought are reflected in these stories, and the language is secured in a connected form. Countless matters of interest are suggested by them. The early summer of 1907 was spent in this way with an Indian named Pete, on the upper portion of Van Duzen river, a tributary of Eel River. Besides Pete, there is one Indian from this vicinity in the penitentiary, one living on Redwood creek, where he is married, and one woman, who has a husband and family, on the South-fork of Eel River. Pete's wife is smart and enterprising. She belonged to a people on [M]ad River, speaking a different dialect. The stories were obtained in Pete's particular dialect, for which in the last few years he has had no use, since he employs the language of his wife in his home.[65]

In addition to Pete and his wife, Goddard interviewed southern Humboldt Indians from the Bear, Mattole, main Eel, and South Fork Eel rivers, collecting dozens of folk tales while also learning the locations of various tribal boundaries and numerous village sites. His notebooks contain a wealth of information that transmit the deep and rich accounts his informants provided. But once in New York, Goddard left most of his southern Humboldt work behind,[66] just as his left his mule at Laytonville. His work with the California Athabascans remained unfinished,[67] the seeds for its completion—his wealth of field notes—waiting a century and more to germinate. Today, as this is being written, copies of dozens of his notebooks are near at hand, and the information contained within them informs a substantial part of this chapter and other sections of this book.[68]

Shortly after Goddard departed from California for the East, another researcher traveled across the country in the opposite direction and more or less took over where Goddard left off. For C. Hart Merriam the journey was not only a trip, it was a transformation.

Merriam, the son of a New York congressman, began his career as a medical doctor in 1879. He left his practice in the mid-1880s[69] to devote himself to "full-time scientific work." Merriam accordingly took a position with the United States Department of Agriculture in 1885.[70] He was a founding member of the American Ornithologists' Union[71] and in 1888 was one of the founders of the National Geographic Society.[72] His early focus on ornithology gave way to a growing interest in mammals.[73] Eventually Merriam became head of the Bureau of Biological Survey, describing 71 new species of mammals and developing his "Life Zones" concept that related ecosystems to specific conditions of temperature and humidity.[74]

In 1899 Merriam was asked by railroad magnate E. H. Harriman to assemble a group of natural-

North Fork Yager Creek, a beautiful and rugged area Goddard and
Van Duzen Pete traversed when locating several Nongatl villages (JR).

Kus-tci-to, or Goat Rock, a boundary on the Van Duzen River between two Nongatl tribal groups, photographed by Goddard in 1907 (CEFP, colorized by JR).

ists for a scientific expedition to Alaska. Merriam agreed, and in doing so unknowingly secured his future.[75]

The set of luminaries that Merriam collected for the Harriman Expedition was remarkable—it ranged from ornithologist and author John Burroughs to Henry Gannett, the Chief Geographer of the U. S. Geological Survey; from Indian expert George Bird Grinnell to budding photographer Edward S. Curtis; and, as a conservationist capstone, naturalist and Sierra Club co-founder John Muir.[76] During that June and July some 50 scientists and other expedition experts explored and examined areas on and near the Alaska coast, collecting information that was published in a 13-volume record of observations and findings from the trip.[77] Harriman appointed Merriam overseer of the research and editor of the books.[78]

Harriman died in 1909. The following year his widow, Mary, after being approached by various influential individuals (perhaps including Theodore Roosevelt), "established the Harriman Trust." It allocated $12,000 per year,[79] "to be administered by the Smithsonian Institution and to provide Merriam support for research of his own choosing to the end of his days." Merriam was 55, at the height of his career, and with the endowment was

Finding the Lost Story

expected by his friends to "produce a great work on the mammals of North America."[80]

Instead he went to California to study the Indians.

Merriam resigned from the Biological Survey and, while keeping a home in Washington, DC, built a house at Lagunitas, amid the redwoods of western Marin County. He used his new residence as a "base of operations for five or six months each year as he roamed the state collecting data."[81]

Suddenly Merriam's career turned off the highway of professional-level biology that he had long traveled so successfully and bumped onto the rutted, unmapped road of amateur ethnography. Often this new route proved to be no more than a trail, leading to the whereabouts of a solitary Indian who was perhaps the last repository of knowledge about the old ways of his or her tribal group.

It was not an easy task, especially for someone who was moving from middle to old age. A photo shows Merriam at some remote location, his shock of white hair glinting in the sunlight, seated next to an Indian elder, deep in conversation, his notebook in his hand. Even getting an Indian to sit down with him was sometimes difficult, as he described in his encounter with "Old Tony Bell" in northern Mendocino County:

> On going to 'Tony' the first result was rather discouraging; he said he knew what I was there for—as he had seen me working with

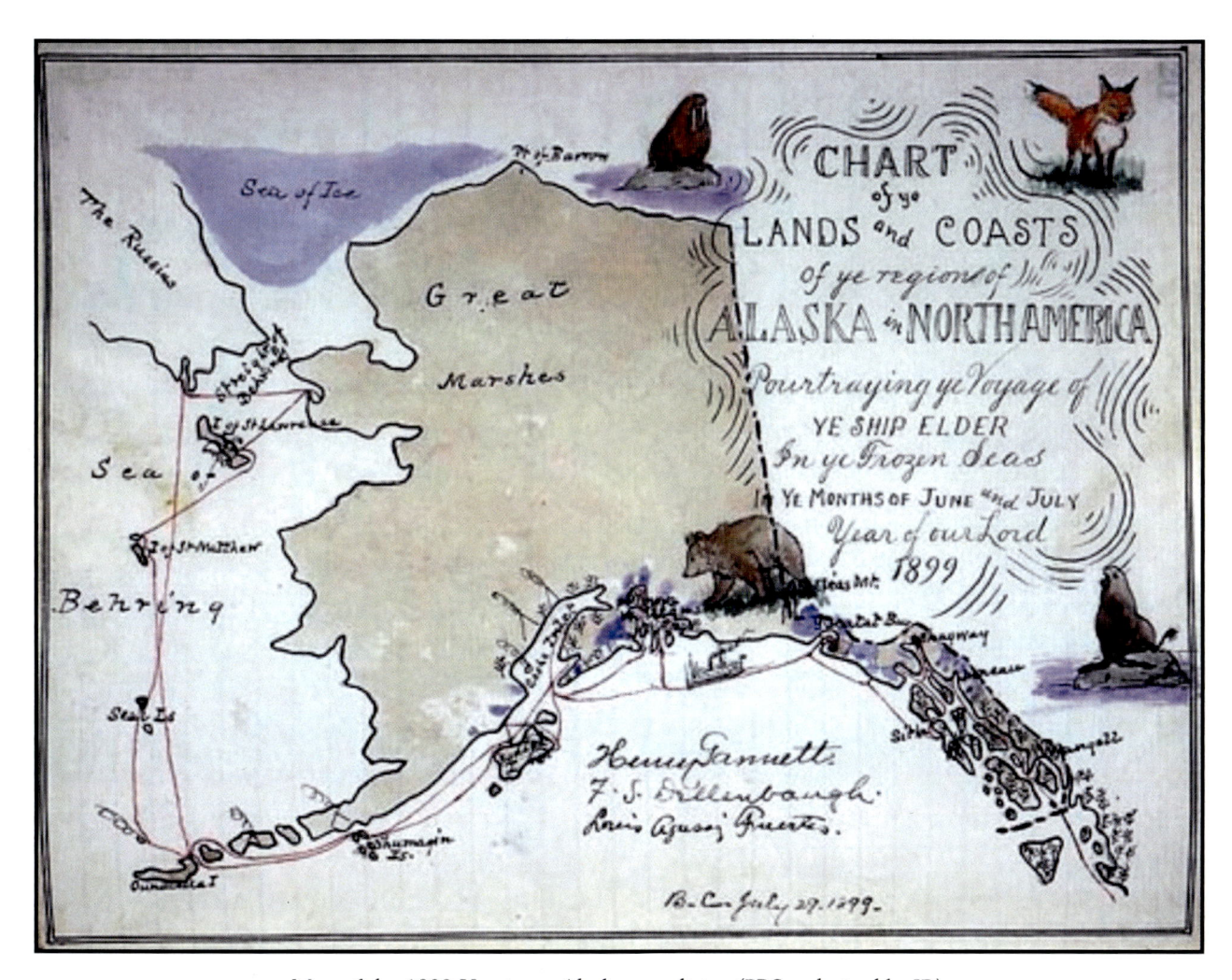

Map of the 1899 Harriman Alaska expedition (PBS, colorized by JR).

a woman [a previous interviewee]—but he would not give me a word of his language. His people had been persecuted and finally destroyed by the Whites until he was the only one left, and he did not intend to give a white person any information. Failing to make headway, I changed the subject and told him where I was camped. He replied that he knew already. I noticed that he was whittling a plug of tobacco with a very poor knife, so I handed him my knife, adding that if he liked he might keep it, which he did. Then I suggested that he had better come to my camp at suppertime and have something to eat with us. He agreed. The knife and supper proved entering wedges. I didn't press him that evening other than to ask the names of the trees among which we were camped, and of a few birds we saw or heard, but when he left I remarked that we would eat at daylight and would be glad of his company. He came, and we spent the day together. Breaking his promise of the day before, he talked freely and gave me a fair skeleton vocabulary of his language ... which during later visits (with him and with an old relative discovered by accident) was materially increased.[82]

For decades Merriam rode and drove across California, locating and then recording Indians from dozens of tribal groups. He compiled vocabulary lists on preprinted forms, took hundreds of photos, and collected thousands of pages of information. He had hoped to classify and map all of the groups in the state, but the task was enormous, and he ran out of time. After spending his last years in a nursing home, he died in Berkeley in 1942. Whatever grand survey Merriam had hoped to publish was never completed.

What prompted Merriam to take up the study of the California Indians? Some would say it was a desire to impose the scientific order of a biologist on the ethnographical chaos that prevailed at the time. But there was more to it than that. Merriam's motivation might be best explained by a short response he wrote to an insensitive article about Indians in one of Eureka's newspapers, the *Humboldt Standard*. Merriam concluded his piece by saying,

> That our treatment of Indians is a stain on civilization everyone knows. Let us even at this date try to make some amends. Let us cease speaking of an Indian as belonging to a "Digger" tribe, for there is no tribe of that name; and let us cease calling their women squaws, an obnoxious term. Let us encourage their children to come to our schools; let us afford them much needed medical attention; let us drop our air of superiority and treat them as fellow human beings; and let us try to learn from them, before it is too late, the thousand-and-one things worth while for us to know. It may be overtaxing the truth to say that we have as much to learn from them as they from us, but nevertheless, and entirely apart from their superior knowledge of the food, textile, and medicinal values of animals and plants, they can put us to shame in matters of patience, fairness, honor, and kindness.[83]

By the mid-1940s the generation of Indians that Goddard and Merriam interviewed had nearly all passed away, as had some of the interviewers themselves. But the collaborators, Indian and white, left a lasting legacy—notebooks and file folders that when opened magically offer a pathway to the past, where vibrant villages lined rivers and

C. Hart Merriam and Blind Sam Osborn, 1935 (MCNAP, colorized by JR).

streams yet unsullied by the hands of the whites, where brush shelters surrounded an oak-shaded spring on a summer hillslope, where people long since departed returned to populate some earlier landscape. And there were also the photos, showing the Indians who told the stories, their stoical and often pensive expressions echoing the content of their words. And other photos, often of a monumental rock or a vast, sloping prairie, that depicted places of a significance all but forgotten. A world was contained in these works, a world fading, year by year, farther into the dimness of the past. But here, within the photos, and the files, and the notebooks, that fading was forestalled, so that the story of a people and their places could be recalled, whenever later people took the time

Merriam photo of the South Fork Eel River, southwest of Garberville, 1925. In this vicinity three tribal group areas converged (MCNAP, colorized by JR).

to look. Took the time to move through time with the help of the story catchers and their work.

* * * * *

Sometimes the story catching transcended the main purpose of the research. When Pliny Goddard and Pete were on their 1908 trip into the eastern Humboldt back country, the experience prompted Goddard to write:

> Today has been charming, and the solitude almost absolute. We have been away a week and I have seen white men 3 times. We had a profitable trip. Pete is fine to camp with. He doesn't help much with the work. He gets all the wood, builds all the fires and normally tends the bread while it is baking. He is full of fun and always cheerful.[84]

And then there was a magical moment when Goddard received the greatest gift that Pete could offer, the four secret syllables that comprised Pete's Indian's name. Goddard wrote the word in his notebook and added, simply, that Pete "told me because he likes me."[85]

Appendix B: The Other Ethnographers

After Stephen Powers reported on the California Indians for the *Overland Monthly*, his journalistic exertions found their way into a more prestigious format. He reworked his material and in 1877 it was issued in book form as *Tribes of California*, a volume in the federal government's *Geographical and Geological Survey of the Rocky Mountain Region*.[86] It contained 18 pages on the southern Humboldt Indians,[87] but the book had severe limitations. Years later, from his lofty professorial perch at Berkeley, Alfred L. Kroeber evaluated Powers's writing thus:

> Powers was a journalist by profession and it is true that his ethnology is often of the crudest. Probably the majority of his statements are inaccurate, many are misleading, and a very fair proportion are without any foundation or positively erroneous. He pos-

sessed, however, an astoundingly quick and vivid sympathy, a power of observation as keen as it was untrained, and an invariably spirited gift of portrayal that rises at times into the realm of the sheerly fascinating.[88]

Following the publication of Powers's book readers found almost nothing, accurate or otherwise, to inform them about the Indians from southern Humboldt County. Goddard and Merriam collected invaluable information but published only a few brief articles or short monographs. They were followed by a progression of other ethnographers who studied the local Indians but seldom shared their work with the general public. Either they consigned their field notes to archival oblivion or offered a dry summation of inherently interesting interviews that was published in a scholarly journal seen only by specialists in anthropology. Rarely did the actual words of any Indian make an excursion onto the printed page.

At first, these younger ethnographers still ventured into the field, where they recorded important accounts about the various tribes, but by the 1940s the ever-turning wheel of mortality brought these opportunities to an end. Subsequent decades saw fieldwork replaced by ivory tower analyses that removed research from the realm of reality and instead lodged it on barren islands of academic abstraction.

But first, there were some exhibitions of scholarly sunlight.

John Peabody Harrington was among the sunniest and also perhaps the funniest. He was a linguistical monomaniac, obsessed with the study of Indian languages, especially those of California tribes. Between 1906 and 1954 he roamed the region, recording material about scores of languages, and working from 1915 on as a research ethnologist supported by the Smithsonian Institution. Harrington was suspicious of other ethnographers to the point of paranoia. He often hid his field notes in obscure locations rather than bringing them to Washington, where he worried that they might be pilfered.[89] In one case, after doing work on the Chimariko tribe in the New River country of Trinity County, Harrington boxed up his notes and left them with the Dailey family, at whose ranch he had stayed. Twelve years later a worried Viola Dailey contacted the Smithsonian Institution about the still-unretrieved notes and eventually heard back from Harrington, who wrote, "I wasn't concerned—I knew you'd take care of it."[90] Harrington became especially interested in the north coastal tribes and in about 1940 interviewed two Mattole Indians, Johnny Jackson and Ike Duncan.[91] They provided names of important locations and accounts of intertribal warfare and tribal boundaries.[92] Anyone who reads Harrington's exuberant, pen-slashed field notes will enjoy the ride.

In 1940 Gordon W. Hewes, a Berkeley graduate student in anthropology, interviewed several Humboldt County Indians about tribal fishing practices. He was fortunate enough to contact Nick Richard, who by then was the last living elder of the Nongatl tribe. As a result, Hewes's work contains brief but significant statements about the Indians of the Van Duzen area. This ethnographical treasure has never seen print, but instead circulates in photocopies of Hewes's handwritten notes, the detail of which displays the intense enthusiasm of youthful scholarship.[93]

Far more formal but almost equally intriguing is the work of the famed Indian photographer Edward S. Curtis, who published a chapter about one of the southern Humboldt tribes—the Wailakis—in volume 14 of his monumental *The North American Indian*. Much of the research for the chapter was probably done by his uncredited

Harrington's informant Johnny Jackson, a Mattole Indian (MVHS, colorized by JR).

associate, William E. Myers.[94] No Wailaki source is named for the narrative section of the chapter, but seven Wailaki myths are credited to North Fork John, otherwise known as Nahlse, an "Eel River Wailaki."[95]

Three researchers provided substantial information, Lucy Young. She was a Lassik Indian from the Set-ten-bi-den ke-ya tribal group, which occupied the Alderpoint area. Merriam interviewed her at Zenia in 1922, but, as was usual for him, fit most of her responses into a set of his preprinted forms.[96] This technique allowed Merriam to systematically collect a wide-ranging vocabulary in each informant's language, although it often stifled the unstructured accounts of history, culture, and geography that were allowed expression by Goddard's looser interview style. It was left to two other researchers to fully record Young's remarkable story. Edith Van Allen Murphey, who lived near Young in Round Valley, transcribed a dramatic account of Lucy's life, quoting her at length in Young's version of the English language.[97] Another researcher, Berkeley graduate student Frank Essene, also collected extensive information from Lucy, although he recast her account in his own words.[98]

Both Essene and another Berkeley graduate student, Harold Driver, interviewed local Indians in the late 1930s for two volumes in an anthropology department series inspiringly entitled "Cultural Elements Distribution." In each case, several Indian elders from various tribes were asked to respond to an exhaustive list of cultural practices, indicating which of these were engaged in by the informant's

Merriam and Harrington informant Ike Duncan, mouth of Mattole River, 1923 (MCNAP, colorized by JR).

tribe. The results were rigorously presented in page after page of tables, which were followed by a series of statements that provided details about specific activities. Some items on the list were fairly straightforward, such as the "launching ceremony" for a "dugout boat or canoe," and the type of fire pit used in the Indians' houses. In other cases, the researchers asked deeply invasive questions that could easily have been deemed offensive, such as which of four types of intercourse were practiced by the informant's tribe, or whether or not one of a pair of twins would be killed at birth.[99] The rigor of Essene's and Driver's tabulations was somewhat offset by their informants' occasional elaborations that were also recorded, such as the account of a battle between coastal tribal groups and the events that precipitated the event.

The years progressed, making it harder to form connections with the always receding past. Collection of information was replaced by its analysis. By the 1960s and 1970s certain Berkeley scholars were operating within what might be called the "ethnometric" school of anthropology, exemplified by such zealots of quantification as Albert B. Elsasser, who presented a table entitled "Coefficients of Intertribal Relationships or Similarities" in his essay on the southern Humboldt Tribes in volume 8 of the Smithsonian *Handbook of North American Indians*.[100] Elsasser's stark statistics had been anticipated by the work of Martin Baumhoff, who, in 1963, published "Ecological Determinants of Aboriginal California Populations," in which he postulated that an abstract unit called "fish miles" (the collective distance of salmon-bearing streams within a tribe's territory) accounted for the size of a tribe's population.[101] With publications such as these, the disassociation of early day Indians from any connection with the reality of their everyday lives became the product, if not the goal, of the ethnometricians, and was nearly made complete.

Hinc illae lacrimae.[102]

Chapter II

Earlier People, Earlier Place

In March 1850 the region now known as southern Humboldt County was much as it had been for millennia. The landscape was defined chiefly by five rivers and the adjacent mountainous areas that formed twisting lines of intervention. Three of the rivers flowed from south to north. Near the coast the King Range, an abrupt upsurge of rugged ridgelines, separated the Pacific Ocean from the Mattole River Valley. East of the Mattole, a long line of steep and intermittently shaded slopes rose to Rainbow Ridge and Elk Ridge, the latter punctuated by a series of picturesque buttes. Farther east another valley, that of the South Fork Eel, was in many locations filled to overflowing with groves of giant redwoods. Next came scenic Mail Ridge, with stunning views both east and west, and then the confining canyon of the main Eel, and beyond it mountainous country that ascended eastward into Trinity County. At the northern end of the region two other rivers, the Bear and the Van Duzen, flowed westward, impelled by their search for the ocean, the pair forming a fluvial dividing line that separated the southern part of the county from the north.[103]

Where redwoods did not dominate, other trees abounded. Black oak, white oak, and canyon live oak often fringed the upland prairies. Tanoak, although not a true oak, produced the acorns most valued by the local Indians, and vast tracts of these trees were found both east and west of the wide belt of redwoods.[104] Madrone and California bay formed parts of mixed woodlands, and Douglas-fir flourished where it could grow as the tallest conifer.[105]

The rivers teemed with salmon and steelhead, so many, in fact, that during spawning season streams many miles from the sea were reputedly filled bank to bank with fish.[106] Deer, elk, and bear roamed the woodlands and prairies, ready—if not willing—to become food, while many nutritious plants were available for easy gathering.[107] The climate was temperate, with lots of rain, but only the higher elevations regularly received snow. Thus southern Humboldt had long proved a nurturing place, for the most part both bountiful and benign.

And it was a place made distinct by the actions of its inhabitants. For example, if a few northern Humboldt Indians had visited southern Humboldt in the spring of 1849, they would have been startled by what they saw. The local Indians were preparing to leave their winter villages for their annual migration to the upland prairies and oak groves, when suddenly they began dismantling their houses.

These structures looked very different from those in north. They were conical in shape, rather than rectangular, with walls made from pieces of Douglas-fir bark that had been stripped from nearby living trees. The bark had been laid against a frame of poles somewhat in the manner that plains Indians used buffalo skins to clad their teepees. Now the bark and poles were carried off and stored for use in the coming winter, while family possessions were secreted in hollow redwoods or carried about until the villagers returned from the hills. All that was left were the firepits that had been at the center of each house.

Pringle Ridge, its sunlit prairie shining above the Mattole River gorge, is one of a set of serried ridges that rises toward the distant, nearly indistinct King Range (JR).

Come the fall rains of October or November, the house could be reassembled around the same pit in a day, or moved to a different location after a new pit was dug.[108]

The visitors would have found the dismantling extraordinary. For them, houses were something permanent, meant to last far beyond an individual's lifetime. In the north a house was given a name. Its walls and roof were made of sturdy redwood slabs that withstood the rigors of the centuries. Each family identified with its house, and stories told of structures that had existed since mythological times.[109] Here, in the south, no part of a dwelling lasted for long, and its location changed frequently. Decades later, archaeologists might locate a southern village site with 50 housepits. In the north, that number of pits would have indicated a huge community, but in the south they might mark the presence of perhaps eight or ten houses that over the years had migrated multiple times.

Not all the southern Humboldt Indians lived in these annually rebuilt dwellings. Van Duzen Pete told Goddard that the Kit-tel ki-ya and certain other Nongatl tribal groups had built rectangular houses with corner posts.[110] The Bear River Indians also constructed a rectangular house that was a lean-to with "broad redwood slabs leaned upright against [the] frame."[111] The Sinkyones used both the lean-to and the conical house. Gladys Nomland believed that Sinkyone territory thus represented an architectural transition zone where both the rectangular slab houses of the north and the circular houses of the south were represented.[112]

If southern Humboldt house design often diverged from that of the north, migration patterns in each area were similar. All the tribes wanted easy access to food, a situation that occurred in different places at different times of the year. In the cold, wet months the Indians lived in small villages near the rivers and larger creeks, where salmon were close at hand and where the people dwelt snugly in their various types of wood

Earlier People, Earlier Place

and bark houses.[113] In the warm, dry months they moved up to the prairies and oak woodlands, living in brush shelters as they hunted game and gathered acorns, seeds, nuts, berries, and bulbs.[114] Thus an annual round of travel was integral to their lives.

Over time the southern Humboldt Indians developed a wide array of ways to fish, gather, and hunt. Nature was generous in southern Humboldt, offering its gifts in the rivers and streams, among the woodlands and prairies. The bounty was especially lavish in the provision of three types of staple foods—fish, large game mammals, and acorns.[115] All three of these foodstuffs had the added attribute of being easily preserved. Fish and game could be dried or smoked and acorns could "be kept without treatment." Thus a reserve supply of all three were stored over the winter and consumed in the "lean time of the year," early spring, "before plant growth began and before the start of the spring salmon run."[116]

Although fish were among the foremost foods for all the local Indians, the methods of acquiring them differed by tribe. In the daytime the Wailakis took salmon with dipnets and spears, but at night they used a weir that they built across a stream by driving stakes into the streambed. They left a small opening at one end of the stream

Nongatl conical house near Blocksburg, 1903. The traditional bark cladding has been replaced by small pieces of milled wood (CEFP, colorized by JR).

The prairies and oak woodlands below Tuttle Butte (upper right-center) provided a summer hunting and gathering area for Sinkyone Indian tribal groups from the vicinity of Garberville and Dean Creek (JR).

and placed white pebbles upon the bed there. When a salmon glided through the opening it was easily seen against the white background and was quickly caught in a net.[117] The Sinkyones sometimes stretched nets across the entire stream and held them down with rocks.[118] The Bear River Indians used nets of various sizes but might vary their fishing technique by sometimes shooting salmon with a bow and arrow.[119] The Nongatls fished directly in the Van Duzen, rather than in side streams. They put a 40- or 50-foot weir across the river in the springtime to catch steelhead that were coming not upstream, but down. If they had placed the barrier there in winter, the enhanced force of the rainy season water would have washed the weir away.[120] Another inland tribe, the Lassiks, caught trout in "long-handled dip nets."[121]

Plentiful as salmon and steelhead were, the Indians did not live by fish alone. They hunted deer, and to a lesser extent elk, along with smaller game animals. Various methods were used. The Sinkyones and the Bear Rivers sometimes killed deer by driving them along a trail until one animal stepped into a noose made of twisted iris fibers. The noose was attached to a bent-over tree limb. When the deer hit the limb the noose was released. It caught the deer about the neck as it jerked upright, either breaking the deer's neck or holding it until a hunter came and cut its throat.[122] As a perquisite of office, a Sinkyone village leader received the best piece of deer meat. The hunter who had killed the animal was "entitled to skin, antlers, brains, hoofs, tendons, and share of meat." The other hunters divided the residuals.[123] Briceland Charlie, from the Sinkyone tribe, described the acquisition of elks, which was part hunting and part marathon running:

> Used to run after elk. Big one he give up about noon. Little one about 4 o'clock. Sometime little one he get away. All run after and holler. 5, 10, 20 miles then he stand still let man come up close and shoot him. He gives out he can't run any more.[124]

Elk were big and provided much more meat than deer. Mindful of the need for a reserve food supply, the Wailakis smoked whatever elk meat they couldn't readily consume.[125]

The Bear Rivers killed grizzly bears for their pelts and raccoons and skunks for their skins but did not eat the animals' flesh.[126] For the Sinkyones, deer and elk hides "were of the utmost importance for clothes, blankets, and other skin-made articles."[127] They painted the smooth side of deer skins. Both the Sinkyones and the Mattoles made rabbit skin blankets.[128]

Parts of the Mattole, Bear River and Sinkyone tribes claimed ocean frontage. The Sinkyones caught fish from rocks along the coast.[129] The Bear Rivers butchered whales that washed ashore, with everyone sharing the various resultant products. Nomland tells us that "the man who discovered the whale [an object hard to miss] had the right to select his portion of the carcass."[130] She did not mention what happened when the discoverer was a woman. The Mattole Indians called Sea Lion Rock, located north of the mouth of the Mattole, Tci-ya-tci-se. Joe Duncan indicated that it was "covered with sea lions." The Mattoles would swim out to the rock and kill them by clubbing the sea lions on the nose.[131]

When hunting, southern Humboldt Indians were on the lookout for more than game. If the Bear Rivers noticed that the acorns and buckeye nuts were ripening, they notified the village leader. Soon many Indians came to the gathering areas, where duties were determined by gender. The men

Miniature lupine (*Lupinus bicolor*) north of Honeydew, May 5, 2021. Would the local Sinkyone tribal group have considered this a sign of "spring proper" or of "summer coming" (GR).

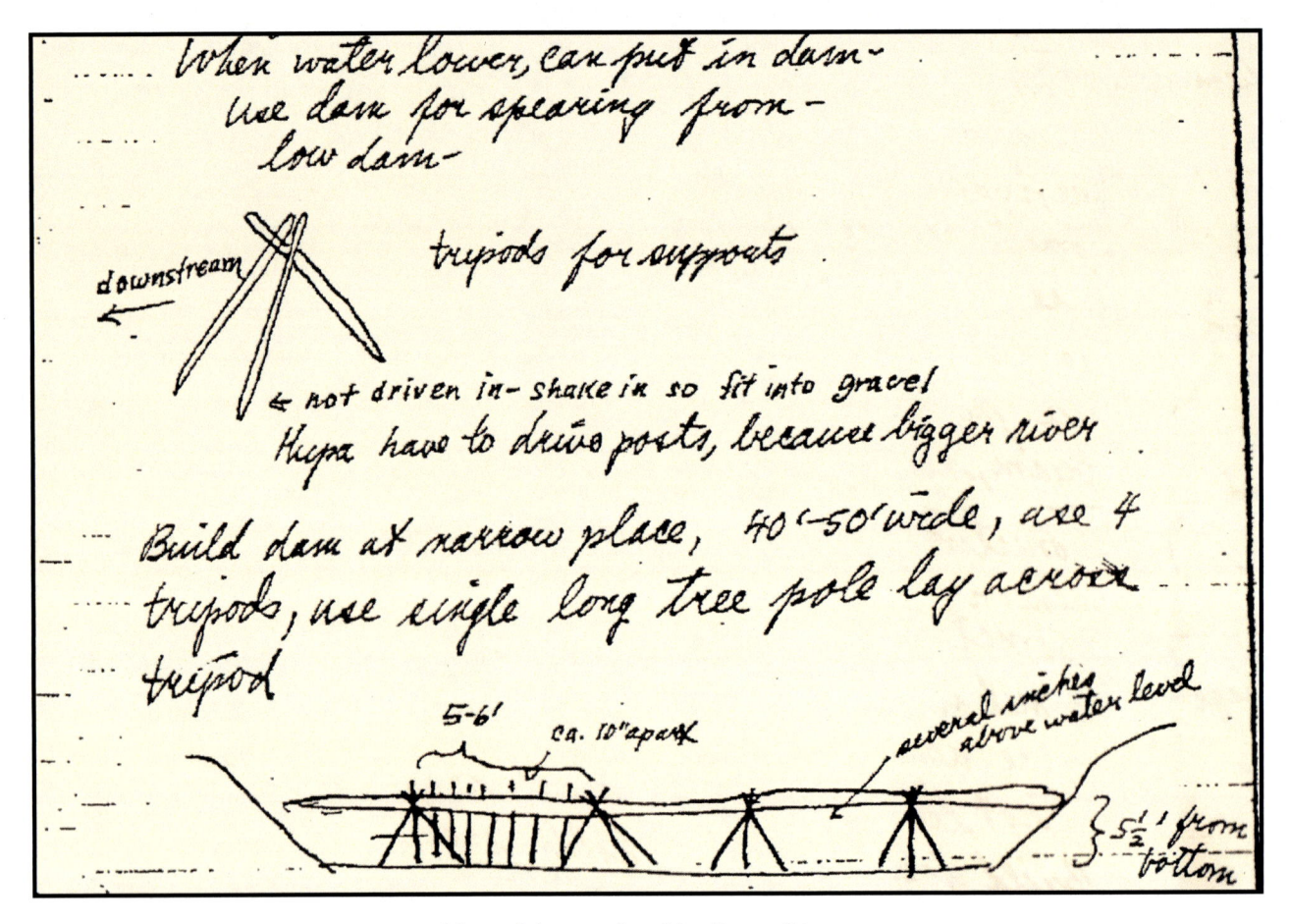

Nongatl dam used on Van Duzen River,
as described by Nick Richard (GH).

climbed the trees and shook the limbs to dislodge the acorns and nuts. The women picked up the fallen food from the ground and stored it in large conical baskets for later transport.[132] For many Indians the preferred acorn[133] came not from a true oak but from the tanoak (*Notholithocarpus densiflora*),[134] which covered vast stretches of southern Humboldt until the insatiable demands of the leather tanning industry decreed the destruction of most of the trees for their tannin-rich bark.

According to Nomland, the Sinkyones celebrated an annual "first-acorn" ceremony after the harvest. Preparing the acorns for consumption was a lengthy process: they were cracked on a mortar, "winnowed in a large, flat basket," placed in a hole in the sand, and leached with boiling water for five or six days. The acorns were then "partially parched with hot rocks," dried, packed in baskets, and stored for winter.[135] The Lassik Indians honored tanoak acorns by keeping them inside their houses while all other acorns were relegated to outside storage.[136]

When whites arrived in southern Humboldt they showed little respect for tanoak acorns. Instead they fed them in the fall to the area's semi-feral hogs to fatten them before slaughter. Frank Hammond McKee, who homesteaded near the Mendocino County line in 1871, followed this practice, which increased his ability to sell "ham and bacon to nearby stores and lumber camps."[137] According to one report, however, at least a few whites used tanoak acorns for their own food. C. Hart Merriam's wife, Virginia, no doubt encouraged by her husband, baked "excellent corn bread and pones" using a mixture of four parts corn meal to one part acorn flour.[138]

Some vegetable foods common in 1849 became hard to find after the arrival of the whites. The prairies upon which grew camas and other plants with edible bulbs were soon converted to cultivated fields or to sheep and cattle grazing ranges.[139] Berry bushes, which inhabited both forests and the edges of grasslands, stood a better chance of survival. The Indians ate several varieties of berries either raw or dried, including huckleberries, blackberries, strawberries, and salmonberries. Dried berries were cooked in acorn cakes.[140]

Many other foods, ranging from grasshoppers[141] to seaweed,[142] helped create a diversified diet. It appears that most of the southern Humboldt tribes were usually well-supplied with food, although the Lassiks, who sometimes endured long and cold winters, experienced shortages every fourth or fifth year and one winter members of the tribe reportedly starved to death.[143]

Conditions at various times of the year—most especially in relation to food availability—had fundamental consequences for the Indians' lives. The Sinkyones acknowledged this by recognizing not only the traditional four seasons but also four additional "onset" seasons. Thus "spring coming" preceded "spring proper" and so on through the year. Similarly, Sinkyone activities were coordinated by dividing the day into ten parts, each referring to a certain degree of darkness or light, so that the duration of each unit varied during the year. Their day started with "before daylight," followed by daylight, before sunup, before noon, midday, afternoon, before sunset, before dark, dark, and through the night.[144]

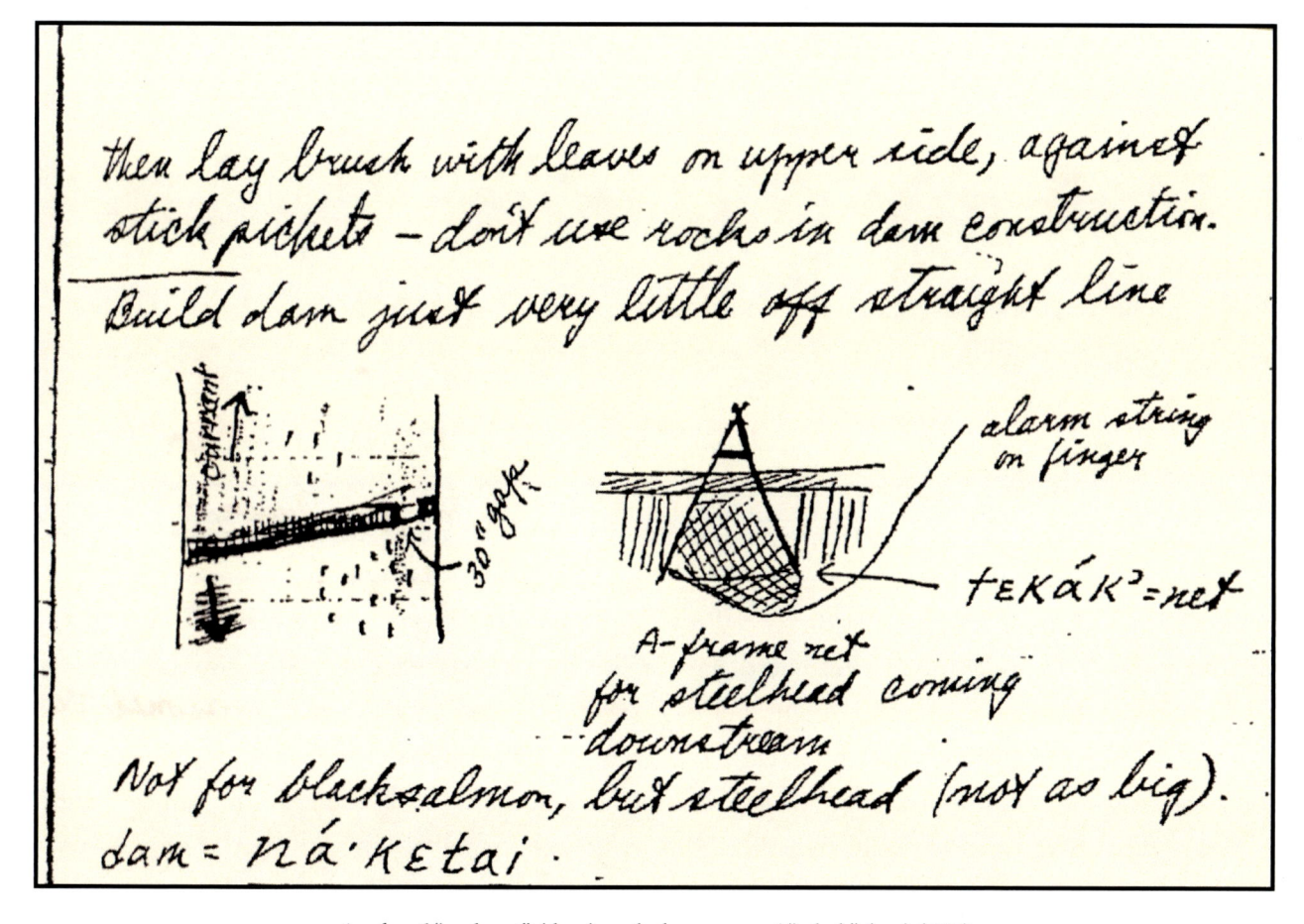

Angle of "na-ketai" (dam) and placement of "tekak" (net) (GH).

Oregon white oaks and silverleaf lupine on Mail Ridge, a hunting and gathering area near the boundary between the Sinkyone and Lassik tribes (JR).

There is no way to accurately determine how many Indians lived in southern Humboldt County before the 1850 arrival of the whites. No census of these people was conducted until half a century later, by which time murders, massacres, disease, and dislocation had erased any sense of the size of the earlier populations of these peoples. This, however, did not stop later scholars from making estimates.

The most thoroughgoing attempt was probably the 1956 effort of the Indian population specialist Sherburne F. Cook, a dedicated ethnometrician who estimated how many southern Humboldt Indians had been present 106 years earlier. Despite the lack of any reliable data, Cook nonetheless determined that there were approximately 12,250 members of the five tribes listed by Kroeber—the Mattole, Sinkyone, Wailaki, Lassik, and Nongatl.

This total was derived by taking the approximate number of square miles in each tribe's territory and then multiplying it by a hypothetical "density of persons per square mile." In southern Humboldt, Cook's densities ranged from 5.82 persons for the Wailakis to 5.72 persons for the Mattoles to 4.96 persons for the other three tribes.[145] To observers today,[146] Cook's work appears as an island of insubstantial assumptions separated by a sea of speculative statistics from the realm of reality.

But other information reveals tangible truths. The five "tribes" that Kroeber and Cook posit subsumed more than 50 smaller entities that were named specifically by the early day Indians, and which, for lack of a better term, can be called tribal groups.[147] The Indians within these groups lived in more than 180 known villages,[148] some of which still have a presence today. (See sidebar 1.)

1. Knowing about No-le-bi

One morning in July 1907 Pliny Goddard crossed the Van Duzen River and started down the Blocksburg road in eastern Humboldt County. He was accompanied by Van Duzen Pete, an elderly Nongatl Indian who lived on his namesake river. Pete was guiding Goddard through his tribe's territory and they had a big day ahead.[149]

The men rode through some ranch land and climbed the side of a high mountain ridge. They crossed "a good sized creek" that was called Luc-bai-kut. Below the trail was Un-tci-ac-tco-tes-a-dun, a place with "lots of elk" and where, according to Pete, an Indian group called the Ne-tcin-dun-kut kai-ya "used to stay in summertime." Just beyond this campsite the two men dismounted at a traditional resting place. Pete told Goddard that the Indians who came here in summer spent their winters at a village far downslope called No-le-bi. He added that these people "talk like Se-nunk," a reference to the Nongatl dialect spoken on Larabee Creek and along the Eel River.[150]

Pete and Goddard then passed around the head of a creek, "went down a ridge through a barnyard into big redwoods," and came out on a flat called Kac-tci-a-kut. Here the canyon's main creek swung around the flat, on which they found 23 housepits. Pete indicated that the Indians who had lived at this place "were taken [to the] reservation [near] Crescent City [and] died there."[151]

Following the main creek upstream, the men arrived at No-le-bi, the village Pete had mentioned earlier that morning. It derived its name from the "no-le" (the stretch of water on a stream just as it reaches a fall)[152] that was just up the main creek from the village site. Goddard "counted about 56 [house]pits," noting that the "ground [was] literally covered" with them. There was "big timber all about, but the no-le is gone."[153] The waterfall had been just east of the village on the main creek, which issues there from a long gorge and passes through a jumble of rocks and boulders.[154] On the hillside north of No-le-bi they found a rock house (a shelter of overhanging rock) called Se-nin-dus-ci-se-ye. Both the rock shelter and the village below it had belonged to the Ne-tcin-dun-kut kai-ya, but other Indians were allowed to come to the creek to fish. Goddard supplemented his description of No-le-bi with a small map that covered a page in his stenographer's notebook. He and Pete finished a lengthy day's exploration by locating one more village, Das-tan-kut, by the main creek. It had 14 pits. The men then rode back up the hillside whence they came.[155]

A century after Pete and Goddard's trip, a local timber company wanted to log a stand of redwoods just west of No-le-bi. A bit of research revealed

Main stream near No-le-bi (ARC, colorized by JR).

the existence of the village site, and the Bear River Band of the Rohnerville Rancheria, which has ancestral ties to the area, expressed interest in learning more about both No-le-bi and Se-nin-dus-ci-se-y, the rock shelter on the mountainside above the village. Soon affiliates of the Archaeological Research Center (ARC) of Cal State Sacramento's Department of Anthropology became involved, with the result that the ARC conducted field work at both sites in the fall of 2009. The accuracy of Pete's information and of Goddard's map was confirmed at that time, with nearly 50 house pit depressions being found in the exact areas marked by Goddard on his map. In June 2011 the ARC released a lengthy report on their archaeological findings at the two sites.[156] Much of this work would not have been possible were it not for the help provided by the Nongatl tribe's most noted historian, Van Duzen Pete.

Because of southern Humboldt's steep ridges and intermittently fast-flowing rivers, the various tribal groups lived in semi-isolation from one another, each inhabiting an area bounded, and protected, by these dominating natural features. Pliny Goddard, who interviewed several local Indians, summarized the ethnogeographical situation:

The northwestern portion of California contained a large number of fairly small tribes, each with a very limited range of territory. The primary cause of this diversity would appear to be the many small valleys separated by mountain ridges. Even the valleys of the larger rivers are often subdivided where they narrow into canyons.[157] There appears to have existed between the tribes almost universal hostility, so that each tribe was confined to its particular territory except for hostile excursions and occasionally trading expeditions. It appears that the women and many of the men would under ordinary circumstances pass their entire lives within the limits of a small valley and the surrounding slopes and ridges, which furnished the range for acorns and other wild vegetable foods and which were also the hunting territory of the tribe.[158]

Briceland Charlie,[159] the Sinkyone Indian from the Sinkene tribal group, told Goddard of the consequences of trespassing onto another tribe's territory:

> If Mattole, Eel river Indians or Garberville Indians come they [Charlie's people] fight them. Long way off Indian never come this place.... Long time ago can't go to Mattole. Can go Bull Creek. Don't go Van Duzzen [sic]. They kill me right there. Can't go Briceland nor Garberville.[160]

Writing in 1877 in *Tribes of California*, Stephen Powers noted the importance of the role that boundaries played in Indian life. From an early age children were taught—and needed to know—the markers for their tribal group's territory:

> ... it is necessary to premise that the boundaries of all the tribes on Humboldt Bay, Eel River, Van Dusen's Fork, and in fact everywhere, are marked with the greatest precision, being defined by certain creeks, cañons, bowlders [sic], conspicuous trees, springs, etc., each one of which objects has its own individual name. It is perilous for an Indian to be found outside of his tribal boundaries, wherefore it stands him well in hand to make himself acquainted with the same early in life. Accordingly the squaws teach these things to their children in a kind of sing-song. . . . Over and over, time and again, they rehearse all these bowlders, etc., describing each minutely and by name, with its surroundings. Then when the children are old enough, they take them around to beat the bounds . . . and so wonderful is the Indian memory naturally, and so faithful has been their instruction, that the little shavers generally recognize the objects from the descriptions of them previously given by their mothers. If an Indian knows but little of this great world more than pertains to boundary bush and bowlder, he knows his own small fighting ground better than any topographical engineer can learn it.[161]

Alfred L. Kroeber summarized the effect such strict and forbidding boundaries had on one Indian's life:

> The narrow horizon of many of the Californian tribes is illustrated by the travels of an old Sinkyone, who was born and lived and died at the mouth of Bull Creek. He recited that in the course of years he had been downstream to the Wiyot boundary, upstream to one of the South Fork tributaries still in Sinkyone territory, coastward to the Mattole River, and inland to the ridge

Deadline at the ridgetop: the main Eel River at Shively Bluff, center, ran through Sinkyone territory. Over the ridge the Nongatls claimed the Van Duzen River drainage. According to Briceland Charlie, crossing the boundary would be a fatal error (JR).

beyond which lies the Van Dusen Fork. A circle with a 20-mile radius around Dyerville would more than include this little world of his life's experience.[162]

Although confined within such borders, the members of each tribal group traveled widely and regularly within their own territory. As Kroeber described it:

> Like most of the surrounding groups, the Sinkyone were quite definite in the habit of occupying their permanent villages in the stream valley only in the winter half of the year, while in summer they dwelt on the more open mountain sides and hilltops. Thus the Bull Creek people spent the dry season at a variety of places in the hills, living on game and vegetable food. After the first rains, when Eel River and the South Fork began to rise, they came down to them to fish. After these large streams were swollen, the smaller water courses appear to have offered better facilities for taking salmon, and the heart of winter was spent in the home villages on Bull Creek. With this dependence on the food in the hills during a large part of each year, it seems that the limits of the territory of each little local group must have been accurately observed upland, as well as along the streams, and that the fixed boundaries must have given something akin to political cohesion to the people of each unit.[163]

It appears that no early day Indian offered an explanation for the vigor with which boundaries were defended. Kroeber's speculation that the strict observation of borders helped strengthen tribal group unity is one plausible reason, but it fails to explain why such an intense level of unity was needed. At least two other possibilities are pertinent. When a tribal group occupied a single watershed, such as that of Salmon Creek or Bull Creek, the ridges surrounding the drainage became the equivalent of the walls around medieval cities—once breached there was often no other line of defense, and thus maintaining the boundary was of compelling strategic importance. In other situations, such as on the Eel in the vicinity of Camp Grant, tiny tribal groups held such small pieces of land that encroachment causing even the least diminishment of their territory could be devastating. But however strong the need to protect a homeland, it is puzzling that neighboring tribal groups did not more often achieve amicable relationships with one another. As we will see in chapter 3, this failure of friendship could lead to tragic consequences.

The potential for conflict was at its highest during the warm months, when travel up the mountainsides brought each group to the ridgetops and therefore close to its neighbors. West of the Bull Creek canyon is the ridgeline upon which the Fox Camp Ranch was once situated. The ridge constituted a boundary between the Lolahnkoks of Bull Creek and a tribal group known only as the "upper Mattole people." Such borderland locations could become areas of strife, but in this case it appears that there was an ongoing amicability that prevented significant conflict. In other locations and situations, however, certain infrequent but dire events escalated into armed combat. Nomland, probably receiving her information from Jack Woodman, described what occurred if any of the Sinkyones went to "war." She indicated that

> When taking the offensive in war, the Sinkyone first held an incitement dance for five days and nights. Fighting began in the morning and continued one day only, or until the Sinkyone had killed as many warriors as had been killed by the enemy. Each side was permitted to search the field of battle and remove its dead without molestation.
>
> The only weapons were bows and arrows. Armor for the best warriors was of elk hide doubled at the neck and raised high enough so that the wearer could shrug into the collar when the enemy shot at his head.
>
> Trained warriors, so equipped, took the front rank and dodged missiles. They were flanked by other fighters who were naked or wore only loin cloths. The enemy only shot at war leaders, either because they thought that the leaders' death would disrupt their followers and so bring victory, or because a tacit agreement between the contestants made this the stereotyped form of warfare. Undoubtedly they could have slaughtered many of the unprotected warriors unless some accepted rule had intervened. The common warriors pushed against enemy ranks until one side broke, then shot at them.[164]

Not all combat, however, was conducted with such decorum. Jack Woodman and Briceland Charlie both told of a sort of war between Sinkyone Indians of the Myers Flat area and other Sinkyones from around Garberville. In one battle, all the Myers Flat men but one were killed, while in a retaliatory attack 40 Garberville men died. The Myers Flat Indians took one scalp at Gar-

A sharply defined boundary: the oak woodlands of the Nongatl tribe give way to the cloud-covered canyon of the Mad River, home of the Mawenok tribe, whose territory extended to the line of mountains in the background that includes Mad River Butte (JR).

berville and brought it back because "that made even."[165] In another incident, a party of Mattole warriors went far inland and wounded a Wailaki girl. A Wailaki war party thereupon went into Mattole territory, ambushed and killed three men and a woman, and brought back the head of one Mattole who was a noted fighter and leader.[166]

But in southern Humboldt, battles were the exception, not the rule. Merriam, who interviewed many California Indians during nearly 30 years of research, concluded that "they were unwarlike . . . and did not know how to fight."[167] Many conflicts were avoided because Indians like Briceland Charlie knew the tribal group borders and the consequences of crossing them. His knowledge wasn't randomly acquired, either. As Powers pointed out, in early childhood Indian children were trained to recognize places of great importance, among which were the boundaries that both confined and protected them.

In these and other ways, the Indians of southern Humboldt ordered their lives by following a set of shared rules and practices developed over centuries. And so they continued to live during the early months of 1850. Then, that April, there came a change.

Word reached the San Francisco area that several explorers had located a large bay far up the California coast, a place from which bold adventurers could head inland to the gold mines on the Trinity, Klamath, and Salmon rivers, and also a place where the less bold could set up businesses meant to supply the miners.[168]

Hundreds of men charted ships to take them

Earlier People, Earlier Place

north. By mid-April the vessels began landing parties on the shore of what was promptly named Humboldt Bay, and soon four small towns appeared.[169] Even earlier, the Wiyot village opposite the mouth of the bay had been burnt and the two unsuspecting Wiyot boys who had led the whites there lay dead. Murdered.[170]

Thus began Humboldt's 15-year Indian genocide, which first claimed the Wiyots who lived near the bay, but then, like a human-borne bacillus, spread inexorably to reach every point and tribal group in the region. No Indian was safe. Murders and massacres perpetrated by whites went unpunished. Parents were killed and their children sold into slavery. Young Indian women were raped and then sometimes forced to live with their rapists. Villages were left in ashes. Many Indians, not killed but captured, were taken to reservations that were little more than concentration camps. When the Indians attempted to defend themselves or retaliate, well-armed vigilante groups or military units hunted them down and killed them.[171]

By the mid-1860s the whites had what many of them wanted—possession of the Indians' homelands, and nearly all the Indians either dead or subjugated.[172] Although only a portion of the white population participated in the attacks, objectors could muster no countervailing force to stop them. And, in the end, attackers and objectors alike enjoyed the benefits of gaining control over what had been the Indians' land.

Humboldt Times, January 11, 1863

GOOD HAUL OF DIGGERS.—On Friday of last week a party of ten white men, with Jerry Whitmore at their head, came upon an Indian camp, on Bull Creek, a few miles east of the Monument. Whitmore and his party started out in search of these Indians on the 24th of last month, and kept lurking on their trail, endeavoring to find their winter quarters, until they came upon them as above stated. They came upon the ranch about 9 o'clock in the morning and found the Indians busily engaged in building houses, having eight already finished. Most of the bucks were out, it being good weather for them to kill and dry beef. There were only ten bucks in the ranch and Whitmore thinks that two got away. Five of them were killed on the ground and three in the creek, while attempting to escape. There were quite a lot of squaws in the ranch, some of whom were killed in the firing and several wounded. Four were made prisoners and brought in to Fort Humboldt where they now are with the other Indian prisoners. The diggers had two guns, one of which Whitman got from the first Indian he killed—the other was carried away. In the ranch they found quite a lot of wearing apparel, both for male and female which had been taken from various houses which have been robbed within the last six months. They also found some wheat and oats, and about 400 pounds of dried beef. They burned the ranches and what they contained, and, being out of grub themselves, returned to the settlements.

When a "good haul" meant a massacre.

No area was harder hit than southern Humboldt. Entire tribal groups were wiped out. Other groups had only a few people left. Gradually some survivors returned from the reservations or from hiding, but they found their villages destroyed, their prairies reduced to cattle range, their rivers lacking the many salmon that were now quickly caught downstream and fed into the white men's canneries. The Indians came back to a land shrouded in darkness—a darkness cast upon it by the whites.

The southern Humboldt Indians who were left were now landless. For decades either individual whites or the government owned almost all the land. Then, in 1887, Congress authorized the transfer of certain federal property to Indians in allotments from 40 to 160 acres in size,[173] and by the early 1920s at least 32 Indians owned land in southern Humboldt.[174] Meanwhile, in 1910 the government established the Rohnerville Rancheria, which provided small parcels for hitherto landless Indians who came from the southern part of the county.[175] In 1956 some 30 "Bear River Indians" were listed there as residents.[176]

By 1900 there were few reminders that 50 years earlier thousands of Indians had lived along the streams and camped among the hills of southern Humboldt. Here and there a cluster of depressions in the ground marked the site of

Much of the Bear River area was quickly taken over by whites and the land converted into dairy ranches that produced noteworthy butter.[177] A hundred and thirty years later the Green Pond Ranch displays a scattering of range cattle where earlier milk cows and earlier yet Roosevelt elk grazed upon grasslands cooled by the ocean breeze (JR).

Earlier People, Earlier Place

Indians, probably Nongatl or Lassik, near Blocksburg, circa 1903 (HCHS, colorized by JR).

a village. A few pictographs on a rockface hinted at some now-obscured message. The wide range of tanoaks shrank yearly as tanbarkers cut and peeled their trunks, heedless that with the death of the trees went the acorns that had for so long provided the Indians with so much food. At countless places a tree or "bowlder" recalled a nearly forgotten boundary that had once been fraught with danger.

But few people remained who knew the significance of such sites, and their numbers diminished yearly. New generations of Indians appeared, people who had never seen the bark houses at Kahs-cho-chin-net-tah, who had never caught an eel at Len-lin Teg-o-be, who had never watched the water rushing over the rocks at No-le-bi or No-le-din. For many of them the past was no more than a whisper upon the wind, one that grew fainter with each passing year.

Then, in 1903, Pliny Goddard arrived in southern Humboldt for the first of six summers he spent interviewing Indians throughout the region. He was followed by a progression of other ethnographers that ended with John P. Harrington and Gordon Hewes, who finished their work in the early 1940s by interviewing the last of the holocaust-era Indians, the last of the earlier people. And then there was no one left to tell of the earlier place.

* * * * *

There is a spot, in the heart of southern Humboldt on Elk Ridge near Dickson Butte, with views to the west of the Mattole Canyon and to the east of the Salmon Creek drainage. It is said that Indian trails converged here, giving access to the territories of four or more tribal groups. Some modern-day houses and other structures now speckle the forest and prairie landscape, yet the inescapable feeling is that of being back in a time before such buildings existed. It is a place heavy with the weight of memories, but the years have moved such recollections beyond the point of last recall. Like the sweep of time, the wind blows across the rocks of the ridgeline—gently or harshly, or sometimes not at all. The wind comes and goes, but the rocks remain.[178]

Chapter III

Three Tragedies

For 15 years no Indian was safe in northwestern California. Between white arrival in 1850 and the termination of the Indian genocide in the mid-1860s, the local Indians were murdered, massacred, raped, and taken as slaves. They saw their villages burned and were dispossessed of their land. They were attacked by white vigilantes, by the United States Army and by the state militia. And once, at the end of a chain of tragic circumstances, they attacked one another.

"The Last Wylackie Indian Round Up"

The lengthiest description of a Humboldt County Indian massacre tells of one that started in the Briceland area, about five miles northwest of Garberville, and killed most or all of a large village of Indians. It is crude and prejudicial in expression and self-serving. It contains factual inaccuracies and provides much information that cannot be verified, but it does not appear to minimize the extent of the killing that occurred. It was written about 80 years after the event by the son of the massacre leader.[179]

According to Frank Asbill, his father Pierce and several companions determined to punish the Indians of southern Humboldt for two attacks they had made on local whites. Neither incident, however, was as dastardly as Frank Asbill claims,[180] and the two events occurred not in close succession, as he implies, but instead almost exactly eight years apart. If either attack supplied the motivation for the massacre, it was almost certainly the first one, where a band of Indians attacked two brothers, Gilbert and Atwood Sproul, at their home on the South Fork Eel in 1861.[181]

It was probably later that year when Pierce Asbill and his cronies followed an Indian trail to the village of To-cho-be, which was located near of the future townsite of Briceland.[182] The men made a nighttime approach to the village, coming from the west, and at daylight,

> . . . as soon as they could see the silver half-dollar front sights on their two-barreled guns, they charged the unsuspecting Indians. With the explosion of black powder the Indians knew it was not the soldiers in blue, but the dreaded, long-haired men who shot and never missed. All but several old ones stampeded and left the camp. What happened to the ones left behind no one ever said.[183]

The Indians apparently fled east, following the "pepperwood gulches" along the course of Redwood Creek. Frank Asbill claimed that "for many years afterwards the bones of the Wylackies could be found along those gulches."[184] Throughout his account, Asbill referred to almost all the local Indians as "Wylackies," even though the collective name "Wailaki" properly applies only to several tribal groups that were located on the main and North Fork Eel rivers.[185]

Asbill claimed that 150 Indians reached the future site of Garberville, atop the bluff above the South Fork Eel. Here the pursuers chased two Indians to the edge of the precipice. Rather than face the oncoming whites, the pair jumped to their deaths. Asbill adds that:

> These men who went after the Indians were not barbarians by any means. They simply knew this was the only way. And that the band of outlaw Wylackies had to be exterminated before anyone could settle down peacefully, in this land.[186]

In actuality, many people had previously settled the land more or less peacefully—the Indians who had already lived there for centuries. Their relative peacefulness was disrupted only when whites like the "mountain men" arrived and began to take over the tribal territories.

The vigilantes' chase continued, as "the Indians kept on south, on the exact course now followed by the redwood highway."[187] One of the whites, Cap Hardin, "was shot in the belly with an Indian arrow." The others treated his wound and left him behind as they resumed their pursuit. Seven whites were left. The Indians continued their flight up the South Fork Eel to the future site of the Hartsook Inn,[188] where they left the canyon and turned southeast, going over Red Mountain and up over the top of Mail Ridge. When Asbill's party reached the latter location they encountered another Indian band, one that they were not interested in massacring at the time. They therefore returned to the top of Mail Ridge at Blue Rock, whence they turned north, picked up the tracks of their intended victims, and continued on past Bell Springs.[189]

Somewhere north of Bell Springs the Indians split into two groups. About 50 of them headed north onto Island Mountain, pursued by Pierce

A rock formation at the northern end of Island Mountain, near where the pursuit of the villagers from To-cho-be ended, punctuates the brooding landscape (JR).

Three Tragedies

Asbill, B. M. Cox, and William Woods.[190] The other Indians turned east, towards Round Valley. They were followed by Jim Neafus,[191] Jim Graham, and George Phillips.[192] No mention is made of the seventh member of the party.

Asbill, Cox, and Woods caught up with the first group of Indians at the headwaters of Chamise Creek, a short distance north of the Humboldt County line.[193] It is unclear what happened to the second group or how many more Indians were killed. Frank Asbill claimed, however, that "in that rough hell-hole along Chamise Creek there were many rat-gnawed bones of the Wylackies found years later."[194]

Between October 1882 and September 1884 Pierce Asbill bought the Alex Coil Ranch, which sat astride Walker Ridge in southeastern Humboldt County.[195] At the southern edge of his property was Chamise Creek, the "rough hell-hole" that decades earlier he had helped turn into an Indian graveyard.

Camp Grant, General Grant, and General Order No. 100

Those [Indians] about here are the most harmless people you ever saw. It really is my opinion that the whole race would be harmless and peaceable if they were not put upon by whites.[196]

—Ulysses S. Grant, in 1853, on the Indians of Washington Territory

On June 30, 1853, Lt. L. C. Hunt sent a report to his superiors in San Francisco regarding conditions in the vicinity of Fort Humboldt, which had been established just south of Eureka in January of that year. He claimed that the local Indians lived in a state of "quasi-hostility" towards the whites, but explained that:

. . . the occasional murders which they have committed from time to time upon the citizens passing through their country, [were] frequently, no doubt, in retaliation for the outrages of white miscreants [that] have been visited so terribly upon the heads of great numbers of them [the Indians].[197]

Hunt urged that the "humane policy" of Edward Beale, superintendent of Indian affairs for California, "be applied to these Indians," and expressed his belief "that with time and good management it will prove successful."[198] Beale had proposed a system of military reservations that would be "organized as self-supporting Indian colonies." The Indians would be invited, not forced, to come to them.[199]

Six months after Hunt submitted his report, a new officer arrived at Fort Humboldt to serve under Lt. Col. Robert C. Buchanan. He was Lt. Ulysses S. Grant. It was January, a time when "the military life at Fort Humboldt was slow and monotonous. . . ."[200] Grant had few duties but plenty of time to brood about lack of communication with his wife, Julia, who was far away in Missouri.[201] According to one account, "he soon found his best lounging spots were Brett's Saloon and Ryan's Store."[202] A perhaps apocryphal anecdote has Grant, who was a gifted horseman, connecting three buggies in a row, hitching the buggies' three horses in tandem, and driving the resulting contraption through the streets of Eureka.[203] A friend indicated that one day Grant was found to be drunk while on duty, and Buchanan offered him a choice: resign or face a court martial.[204] On April 11, 1854, Grant received his commission as captain, whereupon he submitted his resignation.[205] He left Fort Humboldt on May 7.[206] Buchanan, although strict with his command, was support-

The ghostly remains of Fort Humboldt, 1885 (CPH, colorized by JR).

ive of Beale's pacification policies, at one point requesting a supply of gifts to be used in conducting friendly parleys with the Indians.[207] A month after Grant's departure from Fort Humboldt, Lt. Hunt was sent by Buchanan into the Humboldt hinterlands. Hunt was to attempt contact with the various tribes in order "to explain in no uncertain terms the danger to [the] Indians of continuing petty annoyances to travelers between Humboldt Bay and the Trinity gold mines."[208] The lieutenant soon met a party of nine whites who were looking for the Indians that had allegedly stolen some mules and horses from them. The whites offered to accompany Hunt's detachment and the lieutenant accepted.[209]

It proved to be a disastrous decision. One of the civilians shot at an Indian boy, and this and other behavior led Hunt to think that the whites' claim about the stolen animals was simply a ruse to allow them to attack innocent Indians. Then Hunt received a report that some of the civilians, who had stayed behind the lieutenant's group, had captured several Indians. Hunt reversed direction and came upon a tragic scene; the whites had killed two Indian men and taken a woman and child prisoner. The lieutenant was shocked. "He expressed his sorrow and gave the woman and the child presents. Hunt asked the woman to tell her relatives and associates that the soldiers intended to punish only 'bad' Indians."[210] Thus ended Hunt's attempt to establish friendly relations with the native population.

The episode was part of a pattern that developed in Humboldt County. The United States Army, through its presence at Fort Humboldt, aimed to keep the peace between whites and Indians, walking a fine line as its soldiers tried to prevent either group from attacking the other and trying, also, to protect the innocent, regardless of race. It was a thankless and probably impossible task. Numerous whites wanted to take whatever they could from the Indians and were willing to injure and kill to do so. The Indians, for their part, often tried to defend themselves and, when possible, retaliate for the depredations committed against them. Hundreds of Indians and whites would be drawn into the conflict, and the troops at Fort Humboldt, however good their intentions, were too few in number to stop it.

But they continued to try. About three months after Hunt's attempt at peacemaking, another incident required the army to intervene. In September 1854 a white named Arthur Wigmore was killed by Wiyot Indians near the mouth of the Eel River. Soon a party of white vigilantes attacked a nearby Wiyot village, wounding two Indians and raping a third. Other Wiyots, fearful of further reprisals, captured one of the alleged murderers, killed him, and brought his head back to the whites on the Eel. Later two other Indian suspects were captured by soldiers and taken to Fort Humboldt. The pair reportedly "confessed the killing but aver they had provocation."[211] Lt. Col. Buchanan, still in command at the fort, held the Indians pending a request from the county sheriff that they be remanded to his care. This Sheriff Peter Lothian refused to do unless the federal government agreed to pay for the upkeep of the prisoners. The *Humboldt Times*, impatient with these maneuverings, advocated the formation of "A Vigilance Committee" that would "cooly [sic] and dispassionately adjudge . . . the guilt or innocence of a prisoner, outside of a courtroom." Buchanan, unintimidated by the call for mob rule, subsequently released his prisoners.[212] Only decades later, when the Indians' side of the story was finally told, did it become apparent that Wigmore had been killed because he attempted to murder an elderly Wiyot.[213] Had Buchanan turned the two prisoners over to the vigilantes it is almost certain the pair would have been murdered.

A sterner test for the military came a few months later, in January 1855, when miners in the Orleans area organized into militia units to attack the local Karuks. There are various versions of the precipitating event, but it revolved around the death of a miner's ox that was blamed on the Indians. What followed was the so-called "Red Cap War," so named for the leader of a branch of the Karuk tribe.[214] Five companies of white militia were raised, totaling 234 men, as fighting spread all the way to the coast. Over the next five months "a minimum of forty-five Indian people were killed" in what was later described as not a "war, but a thinly veiled annihilation campaign."[215] Further disaster was averted by the presence of a regular army unit of some 25 to 30 men[216] commanded by Captain Henry M. Judah.[217] Anthony Jennings Bledsoe, author of *Indian Wars of the Northwest* and no friend of the Indians, nonetheless provided an impartial report of Judah's peacemaking efforts in an uncharacteristic outburst of candor:

> While Captain Judah was on the Klamath he met with much opposition from a certain class who advocated the total extermination of all the Indians in that section, irrespective of location or peaceable disposition, and it was with great trouble and vexation that he managed to compromise matters by an agreement that the Indians would give up their arms and remain in their rancherias [and] were to be protected in their lives and property.[218]

Judah and his troops did wind up fighting the Indians on the Klamath, "capturing and killing Red Caps," but he dismissed two of the militia companies and finally persuaded the Indians to surrender—thus, according to one source, by "demonstrating the army's power to stop genocidal killing campaigns, Captain Judah ended the so-called war." By June 1 the fighting had concluded, although many of the surviving

Indians had been "consigned to California's new Klamath Indian Reservation."[219]

If the federal government, through actions by Judah and other officers, hoped to avoid the wholesale slaughter of Indians, they faced opposition from the many Californians who wanted the opposite outcome. As early as January 1851, California's first governor, Peter H. Burnett, fatalistically foresaw the elimination of the state's Indian population in a statement he made just before he left office:

> That a war of extermination will continue to be waged between the two races until the Indian becomes extinct, must be expected; while we cannot anticipate this result with but painful regret, the inevitable destiny of the race is beyond the power and wisdom of man to avert.[220]

The violence in Humboldt County continued during the 1850s, as certain whites attempted to fulfill Burnett's prophecy. After a three-month period in 1858 when four whites were killed and four others wounded, *Humboldt Times* editor Austin Wiley explicitly advocated the option of mass murdering the Indians:

> We have long foreseen the present state of things and have been well satisfied, and so expressed it repeatedly, that it could be averted by placing the Indians on the Reservations or by extermination: in other words, by removing them from the range they inhabit, either alive or dead.[221]

Less than a month after Wiley's editorial, California governor John B. Weller received word from the commander of the army's Pacific Division that there were insufficient federal troops available to keep the trail between Humboldt Bay and Weaverville free from Indian attacks.[222] This prompted Weller, in October 1858, to have California Adjutant General W. C. Kibbe organize a state militia unit of civilian volunteers called the Trinity Rangers at Pardee's Ranch, which was located above upper Redwood Creek. The Rangers took the field for five months, after which the state legislature granted them a "payment for indebtedness incurred by the expedition of $52,527.86." For their services, each Ranger received from $50 to $100 per month, depending on rank.[223]

This was decent money, for it meant that a private would earn about as much as a skilled worker, such as a blacksmith, carpenter, or machinist.[224] It was probably more than almost any unskilled Ranger could hope to make from any regular job, and it came with a bonus—the military status that authorized the troops to attack Indians. For a certain group of men the desire to be a Ranger must have been overwhelming.

After the Rangers were disbanded, the United States Army remained the only authorized option for persons who wanted to fight Indians for pay. However, the wage for a U.S. Army private was only about a quarter[225] of what the Rangers had received and the army wanted its soldiers to mediate, not massacre. Between 1856 and 1860 the commander at Fort Humboldt was Major Gabriel J. Raines, who "emphasized protecting and negotiating with the Indians,"[226] much in the style of Captain Judah. Those locals, like the members of the Rangers, who saw themselves at war with the Indians were confounded and angered by Raines's attitude. Bledsoe later criticized Raines because:

> His heart was too tender, his sentiments too soft, his sympathies too profound, for

Three Tragedies

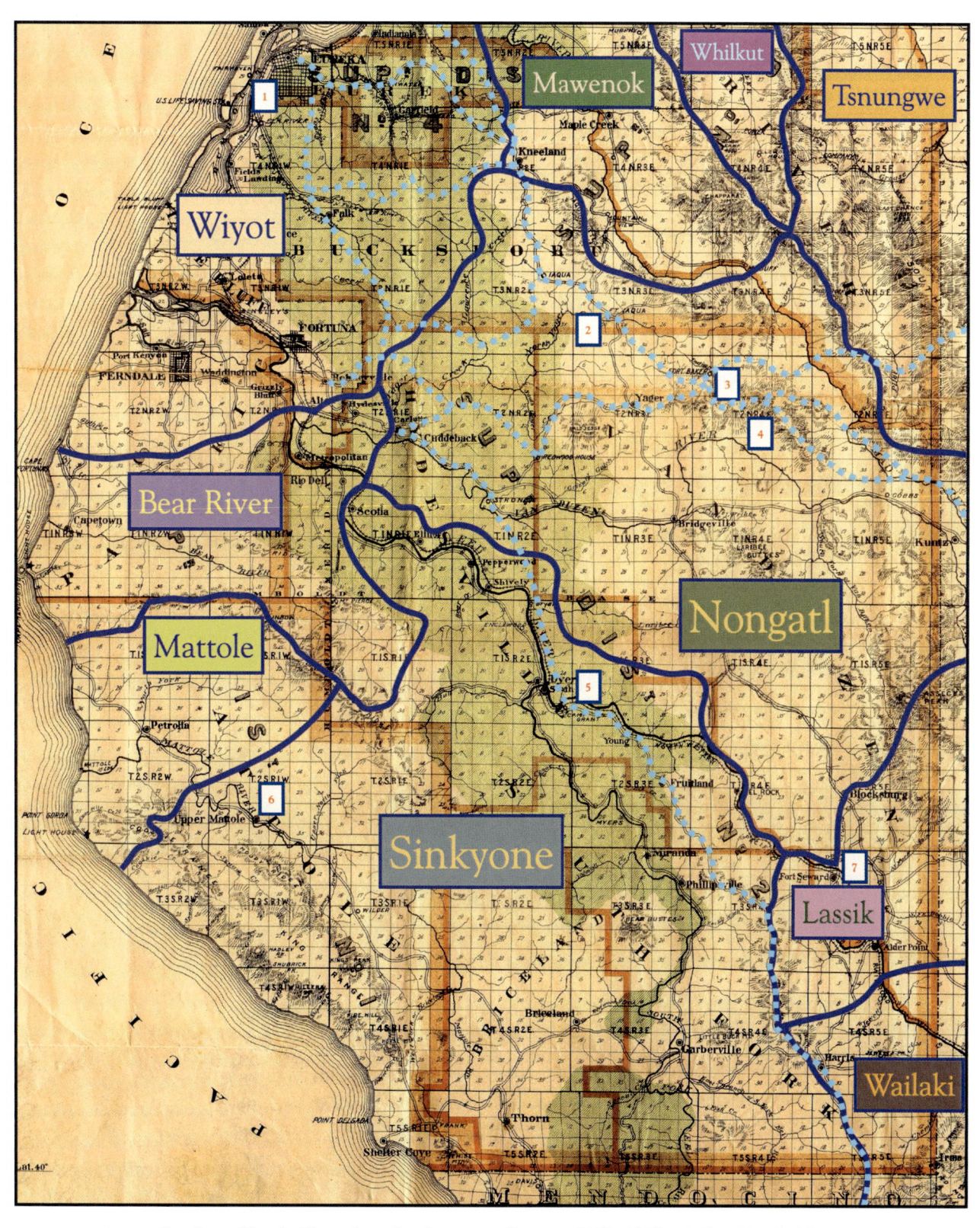

Southern Humboldt trails and military installations, 1850s-1860s: 1. Fort Humboldt; 2. Camp Iaqua; 3. Incorrect location for Fort Baker; 4. Fort Baker; 5, Camp Grant; 6. Camp Olney; 7. Fort Seward. Trails shown as light blue dotted lines (base map JNL).

any but the loftiest motives of philanthropy to find expression in his military orders. His officers were tied hand and foot by the severity of his orders. No Indian could be killed unless he was detected in the act of killing a white man, and it was a crime for a soldier to shoot at an Indian who was driving away cattle from the ranges of the settlers. Fort Humboldt was converted into a kind of hospital for sick Indians and refuge for well ones. Major Raines was unpopular with all classes of citizens. . . .[227]

So it was that local residents, dissatisfied with the army's handling of Indian incidents in the Yager Creek area, established a volunteer company in the spring of 1859. The informal group lacked state financial support, however, and soon disbanded.[228]

Undaunted, whites in the Hydesville area then formed the Humboldt Volunteers on February 4, 1860.[229] This group, led by Captain Seman Wright, went to the South Fork Eel and killed some 40 Indians.[230] No doubt mindful of the Trinity Rangers and their lucrative pay scale, local residents had petitioned Governor John G. Downey to muster Wright's volunteers into state militia service. Tired of waiting for Downey to act on the petition, a group of whites planned and executed a series of attacks against the peaceful Wiyot Indians near the end of February 1860. Included in the dozen or more massacres was the one that took place on Indian Island. As a letter to Downey from one of the volunteers' organizers, E. L. Davis, made clear, the intent of the massacres was to intimidate the governor into approving the muster of the Humboldt Volunteers.[231]

But Downey, it turned out, had already turned down the volunteers. The governor refused to enter the Hydesville unit into the state militia and the volunteers, lacking funding, soon disbanded.[232] Perhaps, thought some, the massacring of Indians would now abate. But then, in June 1860, Major Raines was replaced by Captain Charles S. Lovell.[233] Within a few months Lovell was busy attacking Indians.

In early 1861 the commander of the army's Pacific Department was brevet Brigadier General Albert Sidney Johnston.[234] On March 25 he ordered two detachments sent from Fort Humboldt to the Eel and South Fork Trinity rivers. They were to act against "predatory Indians." If the detachments found

> . . . that any depredations have been committed, or should be committed while they are in the country, they will endeavor to ascertain the party or parties, and then pursue them with the greatest activity, and when found, punish them with the utmost severity.[235]

The commanders of the detachments were given no leeway. They were not to attempt capturing the depredating Indians, they were to kill them.

At about the same time, Johnston ordered Captain Lovell out onto an Indian-hunting expedition and then asked Governor Downey to enroll 30 volunteer guides at the army's expense. At the end of March Lovell's soldiers began a four-month campaign in eastern Humboldt County that killed more than 190 Indians. The *San Francisco Herald* reported that "the troops are not engaged in 'fighting' the Indians, but in slaughtering them."[236] In military jargon, this was inflicting punishment "with the utmost severity."

Lovell had divided his force into three units, the southernmost of which was commanded by Lieutenant James P. Martin. This detachment operated on the South Fork Eel.[237] Martin was baffled and disturbed by his stark orders, stating,

> I do not know positively what depredations, if any have been committed by the Indians killed by this command. I have no means of finding out whether those that we may come upon are guilty or innocent; no communication can be held with them. Circumstantial evidence goes to show that they are all guilty. My instructions are to consider all who run on approaching them as hostile, and to fire upon them. In every case where any have been killed they ran at the first sight of the men.[238]

Martin sent this dispatch in June 1861.[239] By then, thousands of miles away, events had occurred that would rearrange the military playing pieces in California.

In April 1861 the Civil War began. It quickly caused repercussions in the western states, where most of the country's soldiers had been stationed. In fact, during the "immediate pre-Civil War period, nearly 75 percent of the United States peacetime army was garrisoned at frontier posts fighting the Indians."[240] There were only 12,984 men in the entire U. S. Army.[241] Vast numbers of new troops were required immediately, while those already in service were needed in the theater of war to provide a core of experience within the burgeoning federal force. Congress moved quickly, approving the Volunteer Employment Act in July 1861. Under this legislation soldiers would serve between six months and three years and were to receive the same pay as regular army troops.[242]

At the time, California was the most populous state or territory in the western United States, and by the end of 1861 some 17,500 Californians had signed up as volunteers. The rapidity of the enlistments enabled the army to begin sending regulars east in October 1861. On December 21 the last regular troops slated for Civil War action departed; left behind were one infantry regiment, four companies of artillery, and an ordnance detachment.[243] By then, however, the infusion of volunteers had swollen the army ranks in California to 5,900 men, "a much larger armed force than had ever existed in antebellum California."[244]

In addition to the volunteers who joined the United States Army, others signed up for state militia duty. A group from Humboldt County called the Mounted Volunteers, commanded by Captain George Werk, served for three months at the end of 1861. This unit of some 40 soldiers was supposed to supplement the short-handed federal troops; they did so for about 20 days, but then they were mustered into state service.[245] Regardless of their affiliation, the Mounted Volunteers followed the Indian-killing policy of federal army general Johnston. As subsequently reported:

> . . . the State volunteers' campaign . . . was a mere series of Indian hunts, whose only object was to slaughter, of course. The last act in this bloody drama, the fight at the head of Redwood Creek, did not much tend to prepare the Indians for subjection. The company under Captain Werk was there defeated and driven back with loss.[246]

Unlike the usual encounters between the well-armed militia and poorly equipped Indians, the Redwood Creek "fight" reportedly found the soldiers outnumbered and attacking a well-defended position. The detachment commander, Charley Huestis, was killed and six of the other ten troops wounded, two severely.[247] The Mounted Volunteers were subsequently mustered out of

Brigadier General Albert Sidney Johnston resigned his United States Army commission on April 9, 1861,[248] and subsequently defected to the Confederacy. He was the highest ranking officer to do so.[249] On April 6, 1862, while commanding Confederate troops at the battle of Shiloh, Johnston was shot in the leg and bled to death within the hour. The Union general who opposed him that day was Ulysses S. Grant[250] (IA, colorized by JR).

the service, "their task," as a report fulsomely and falsely stated, "fully and conscientiously completed."[251]

In January 1862, Col. Francis J. Lippitt took command of the army's newly created Humboldt Military District.[252] He issued orders for dealing with the Indians that differed diametrically from Johnston's:

> The purpose for which the military force in this district is to be employed is not to make war upon the Indians, nor to punish them for any of the murders or depredations hitherto committed, but to bring them in and place them permanently on some reservation where they can be protected against all outrages from hostile whites. The end in view in all your expeditions will be therefore, a friendly one.[253]

It was four years since editor Wiley had claimed that the Indians must either be placed on reservations or killed—they certainly, in his mind, could not be allowed to stay on the lands, by then so coveted by whites, that their people had inhabited for centuries. Now Lippitt was indicating that while the Indians should not be killed, they indeed must go to the reservations. Like Wiley, Lippitt saw no possibility of the Indians remaining on their own land. Furthermore, the reservations to which they would be consigned should be far, far away:

> In deciding what is to be done, the question of which are the aggressors in this chronic warfare—the Indians or the whites—is entirely immaterial. It is plain that they never can live together in peace. The Indians must all be removed for their own sakes and

for the sake of the whites, and the sooner they are removed the better. The Klamath, the Nome Cult, and the Mendocino Reservations are all too near. The Indians carried thither have all soon returned to their usual haunts—at least all the wild and more dangerous ones. . . . If they could be all transported to the Tejon reservation, or, still better, to one of the Santa Barbara Islands, they could never return hither again.[254]

Lippitt wrote this just three days after he arrived at Fort Humboldt. Despite the brevity of his exposure to the local situation, he had already formed opinions about the parties involved in the conflict:

> The state of things in this district may be summed up in a few words: There are several, perhaps many, thousands of Indians scattered through the forests and mountain gulches with which the whole country is covered. These Indians, or some of them, are constantly committing depredations on the whites, stealing or killing their stock and occasionally murdering them—sometimes for vengeance, sometimes for the sake of getting their arms or clothing. There are white men that associate with them, living with squaws, that are constantly furnishing them with arms and ammunition, and sometimes encourage and join them in their depredations and attacks upon the citizens. These Indians are not divided into any considerable tribes with responsible chiefs, but are made up of numberless rancherias[255] or villages, in many cases speaking totally different languages. There are so many of them, they are so scattered about, and so hard to find, that to bring them all in by sending from time to time small parties or independent detachments after them, it would take about as long as it would to bring in all the coyotes or squirrels. On the other hand, there are many whites that are constantly killing Indians, often making up parties for that purpose, and as they generally find them in their rancherias, they kill as many of the women and children perhaps, as bucks. Individuals and parties are, moreover, constantly engaged in kidnapping Indian children, frequently attacking the rancherias, and killing the parents for no other purpose. This is said to be a very lucrative business, the kidnapped children bringing good prices, in some instances . . . hundreds of dollars apiece.[256]

Lippitt's 1862 perspective was far different than Captain Judah's view in 1855, which had optimistically seen a chance for compromise between the Indians and the whites. Judah thought it possible for the Indians to remain in their villages, under protection of the army. It was a questionable proposition, even at the time, but seven years of continued conflict had confirmed the army's inability to attain Judah's laudable but unrealistic goal. Lippitt, like Judah, wanted to protect the Indians, but he foresaw only a harsh and unjust means of attaining that objective—isolate the potential victims at some distant and alien location where they *might* live *peacefully* but would *certainly* live *miserably*, far from their beloved homelands and at the mercy of reservation authorities. It was an expedient attempt to address a problem that was, given the realities of human behavior, unsolvable—how to have two vastly different peoples peacefully coexist when one group wanted almost everything the other group possessed.

However flawed Lippitt's plan might have been, the colonel was given almost no time to implement it. On April 7, 1862 General George

For a time the Third Infantry, California Volunteers, was stationed at Fort Baker, which was located on this lovely flat above the Van Duzen River.[257] One of its main purposes was the protection of the pack trails that crossed through Showers Pass, which was inconveniently located three miles to the north and at an elevation 2,500 feet higher. The installation was established in March 1862 and promptly proved ineffectual. It was almost as promptly abandoned in September 1863. (JR).

Wright, the commander of the Department of the Pacific, ordered Lippitt to execute captured Indian combatants:

> The late outrages of the Indians in your district require prompt, decisive action to punish them. . . . Every Indian you may capture, and who has been engaged in hostilities—present or past, shall be hung [sic] on the spot. Spare the women and children.[258]

Two days later Lippitt sent virtually the same order to his officers.[259] At the time, the federal government's "Articles of War," which dated from 1806, did not expressly prohibit the killing of prisoners of war. But later, on April 24, 1863, a year and two weeks after Lippitt's order, President Abraham Lincoln signed General Order № 100, otherwise known as the Lieber Code,[260] article 56 of which stated:

> A prisoner of war is subject to no punishment for being a public enemy, nor is any revenge wreaked upon him by the intentional infliction of any suffering, or disgrace, by cruel imprisonment, want of food, by mutilation, death, or other barbarity.[261]

A year earlier the murdering of prisoners of war had of course already been a "barbarity," the only difference being that the federal government had yet to recognize it as such.

Three Tragedies

But the promulgation of General Order N⁰ 100 apparently had no effect on the army's policy of killing male Indians.[262] If anything, the situation in northwestern California became more dire in June 1863, when Lippitt turned over command of the Humboldt Military District to Lt. Col. Stephen G. Whipple, the leader of the First Battalion of Mountaineers, California Volunteers.

Whipple had earlier been the editor of one of the early Humboldt County newspapers, the *Northern Californian*. In its maiden issue of December 15, 1858, he had taken a clear stand on the Indian-white conflict. Whipple reviewed an eight-year history of alleged outrages by the Indians and then exhorted his readers to support drastic action:

> Now is just the time to rid Humboldt County of this pest—now while the volunteers are in the field, and the General commanding the Pacific Division has troops that may be sent in this direction. . . . If the [white] people who intend to live here, who have their interests here, will earnestly take hold of this matter, the last tawny rascal may be taken from the county before next spring. And if one dares to show his head here after being removed, send him speedily to the happy hunting grounds of his race.[263]

Four and a half years after publishing this incitement to murder, Whipple had now become commander of a military force capable of fulfilling his wishes. And so it happened. A tally of the Mountaineers' activity showed that in less than two months Whipple's troops "had killed at least twenty unidentified Indians without losing any soldiers."[264] The exact circumstances under which the Indians died are not clear, but on August 7, Whipple received a dispatch from headquarters that began:

> Sir: It is the desire of the general commanding the department that in all operations against the Indians in the District of Humboldt particular care must be taken that no indiscriminate murder of Indians is permitted.[265]

The "general commanding" was none other than George Wright,[266] who the previous year had issued the order to hang captured male Indians on the spot. Although Wright had initially failed to follow General Order N⁰ 100, it appears that he now desired the record to show that he was no longer endorsing his old policy.[267] If Wright had really wanted to restrain Whipple, however, he would not have given him two additional companies of Mountaineers, which troops were mustered into service about three weeks after Wright's August 7 dispatch.[268]

Among the other volunteer units that served in Humboldt County was Company D of the Second Regiment of Infantry. In 1863 and 1864 the company, under the command of Captain William E. Hull, patrolled in the Mad River, Mattole River, and Eel River drainages, among other locations. In April and May 1864 Hull reported that his company killed 33 Indians and captured 181, with another 102 surrendering of their own accord. Early in this lethal expedition, Hull sent 125 Indians to Camp Grant, "to be forwarded from there to the Humboldt Reservation."[269]

Meanwhile, the camp's namesake was making an ever-growing name for himself back East. In February 1864 Congress approved reviving the rank of lieutenant general, last held by George Washington, and bestowing it on Grant. By then the former lieutenant from Fort Humboldt was near the apex of his phoenix-like rise from the ashes of his forced retirement. The Senate was apprised of his accomplishments since returning to the army: "Grant had won seventeen battles, captured 100,000 prisoners, and taken 500 pieces of artillery."[270] As Lt. Hull was leading the attacks on Humboldt County's small groups of beleaguered Indians, Lt. Gen. Grant was fighting the huge battles of the Wilderness and Spotsylvania, which together claimed over 50,000 casualties.[271] With the nation focused on the titanic fight between the Union and the Confederacy, how easily was the fate of a few thousand distant Indians overlooked.

During this time the noted Indian-killer[272] Seth Kinman claimed he served with Lt. Hull's company, although his name does not appear on its muster rolls. Kinman contrasted the attitude of the long-absent regular army soldiers with that of the volunteers:

> Our Captain, William E. Hull, understood Indian fighting after the Humboldt pattern perfectly. The result was that his command slaughtered and captured any amount of them. At one time we took as many as 160 captives to Fort Humboldt, captured on the head waters of Eel River. Then again, the heart of the regular soldier was not in this kind of warfare. It was unnatural to him. He could and would protect the settlers in their towns and houses, but his transforming himself into a kind of wild cat or hyena and silently sneaking and creeping on to his enemies, was out of his calculations. With the settlers it was a different thing and a different motive. It was with them a matter of life and death. It was their only mode of warfare and was taught to them by the wily savages themselves.[273]

"Indian fighting after the Humboldt . . . pattern"—what Kinman was describing, and praising, echoed editor Whipple's and editor Wiley's calls for extermination or removal, as Hull's troops "slaughtered and captured" all the Indians they could find.

About two weeks after Hull set off on his April 1864 rampage along the various Humboldt County rivers, a parallel event occurred in Henning, Tennessee. There, on April 12, a Confederate raiding party led by Nathan Bedford Forrest attacked the Union-held Fort Pillow. The garrison, about half of whom were runaway slaves, at first refused to surrender. The Confederates, who outnumbered the Union troops about five to one, stormed the fort, and the Union troops fled down the bluff by the fort to the Mississippi River. Trapped there in a deadly crossfire, the Union troops then attempted to surrender, throwing down their weapons. The Confederates gave no quarter, however, and continued to kill the Union troops. Only about 65 black soldiers out of some 300 survived.[274] An official investigation after the war determined that "the Confederates were guilty of atrocities which included murdering most of the garrison." However, Forrest, who commanded the Confederate soldiers, was never prosecuted. After the war he became the first Imperial Wizard of the Ku Klux Klan.[275] Although the Confederates were condemned in the Northern press[276] for their actions at Fort Pillow, their killing of Union prisoners of war was being replicated in Humboldt County by the U. S. Army volunteers' treatment of the local Indians.

The same month as the Fort Pillow massacre in distant Tennessee, a new force of destruction was visiting itself upon the Humboldt County Indians. In February 1864 Whipple was replaced by West Point graduate and regular army officer Colonel Henry M. Black, who brought 250 fresh infantrymen with him. There were now about 1,100 soldiers operating in the Humboldt Military

Lt. Gen. Ulysses S. Grant at Cold Harbor, 1864 (LC, colorized by JR).

District.[277] Black soon reinstituted Lippitt's policy of two years earlier; a report from Fort Gaston in the Hoopa Valley indicated that "Col. Black has issued a special order that all Indian men taken in battle shall be hung [sic] at once; the women and children to be humanely treated."[278] Thus, nearly a year after the issuance of General Order N₀ 100, it was still being violated in the Indian conflict on the North Coast.

An instance of such violation occurred in March 1864, when two Indian leaders, Jack and Stone, were captured after a skirmish at the mouth of the Klamath River that left most of the other Indians dead. As reported in the *Daily Alta California*, "the chiefs were taken to Fort Gaston and executed."[279]

Although the years of killing and capturing the Humboldt Indians took an enormous toll, groups of tribesmen still resisted. In July 1864, despite all the efforts of the military, about 75 armed Hupa men were still at large in the Hoopa Valley. It was a tense situation, made all the more difficult by the appointment, in late May, of former *Humboldt Times* editor and extermination advocate Austin Wiley as California Indian Affairs superintendent. In his new position, Wiley soon recommended sending the Indians to Santa Catalina Island, but he was overruled by his superior. Then, to the surprise of virtually everyone (including his former self), Wiley successfully negotiated a treaty with the Indians in August that set aside the Hoopa Valley as a reservation.[280]

Wiley had succeeded in convincing the younger Indian leaders of his good intentions, and, true to his word, established a reservation that encompassed not only the entire Hoopa Valley but also mountainous areas to either side. It was "set aside for the sole use and benefit of the Hoopa [sic], South Fork, Redwood, and Grouse Creek Indians,"[281] which meant that although the Hupas could stay where they were, the Chilula (Whilkut) and Tsnungwe tribes would have to leave their homelands and move to the new reservation.

With the treaty came a lessening of the killing of the Indians. On July 19, 1864 Captain James Simpson and 21 men form Company E, First Battalion California Mountaineers, went out on patrol from Camp Grant. They traveled east to the Yolla Bolly Mountains, where by the end of the month they had captured 68 Indians.[282] Simpson indicated that "no Indians have been killed by this command, the object being to induce them to come in voluntarily. . . ."[283] The troops then moved to the Middle Fork Eel River. On September 16 the soldiers surrounded a large encampment of Indians near the mouth of the North Fork; the group had "slaughtered a considerable number of cattle, hogs, and sheep. . . ." In previous times the next step would have been for the soldiers to open fire and kill as many Indians as possible, but instead Simpson called on them to surrender, which, "after a few ineffectual attempts to escape," they did. When Simpson told the 88 prisoners that they would be taken to a reservation "they appeared well satisfied and willing to go." Simpson then proceeded to the Round Valley Reservation with his new captives and the others that he had previously acquired. He "arrived on September 24, and turned over to Austin Wiley . . . 161 Indians, taking receipt for same." Simpson and his soldiers then set out for Camp Grant, which they reached on September 30. The expedition had lasted over two months and their record remained perfect: not a single Indian killed.[284]

Finally, on November 23, 1864 came the instruction that should have been issued at the start of the conflict. Major General Irwin McDowell, commander of the army's Pacific Department, issued General Order No. 53, which in part stated:

> It has come to the notice of the major-general commanding that officers in this department have assumed to act in a summary manner in reference to Indians charged with crimes, and there are cases where they have even had Indians executed by the troops. This is against the law, is in no way to be justified, and will not be sanctioned. . . .
>
> Hereafter no officer or soldier will execute or aid in executing any Indian prisoners on any pretext whatever. . . .[285]

It came too late to have much effect. The conflict in Humboldt County was nearly finished, and the various companies of the First Battalion of Mountaineers were mustered out of service between April and June 1865.[286] Indian agent

Three Tragedies

Wiley had seen his wish come to pass—almost all the Humboldt County Indians were either confined on reservations or were dead. The Indians were victims of an activity for which no term existed at the time. Only decades later would the necessary word come into use—genocide.

The Civil War had ended in April, and Grant was hailed as the Union's greatest military hero. His popularity was such that in 1868 he was elected president. On December 6, 1869, Grant gave his first annual message to Congress. In it he said:

> Wars of extermination . . . are demoralizing and wicked. Our superiority should make us lenient toward the Indian. The wrongs inflicted upon him should be taken into account and the balance placed to his credit.[287]

But by then, the balance in Humboldt County was beyond calculation.[288]

The Mistaken Enemy
To wage, by force or guile, eternal war . . .
—Milton, Paradise Lost

Untimely deaths are always tragic, but when they are inflicted upon one set of victims by another set they are doubly so. Such was the case in 1859, when the abducted Chilula (Whilkut)[289] Indians tried to make their way home.

The journey would have never occurred had it not been for the deceitfulness of white militia leaders, yet only one white died as a result, and he innocent of any wrongdoing. All the other victims were Indians, and although they were largely in the right, they were guilty of two mistakes: they misplaced their trust, and they clung too long to their traditions. By the time the last blood was shed, the soldiers had gained far more than they hoped—many dead Indians, killed by each other, with no hand lifted by the whites.

Hundreds of people—white and Indian—found themselves involved in a relentless progression of events, but the course they followed would have never reached its destructive conclusion had it not been for one man—Joseph Porter Albee. If he had been less honorable, or more circumspect, the drama would have ended abruptly, or veered off in another direction, and it would not have cost him his life.

Albee, his wife Caltha,[290] and their several children arrived in Humboldt County in 1853. The following year they moved to a ranch on Redwood Creek.[291] Their property was about halfway between Union (Arcata) and the mines on the Klamath River. A trail into the Bald Hills and on to the Klamath ran through their land and offered an easy route for transporting the ranch's products.[292] The Indians were often resentful of such ranchers, for the white newcomers had taken over hunting and gathering areas that had provided much of the tribes' food. Joseph Albee, however, managed to develop a far different relationship with the local Chilulas, for he gained not only their friendship but their trust.[293]

But Albee, and a few others like him, were small islands of virtue in a sea of villainy. Many whites saw the Indians only as obstacles or objects, to either be removed or exploited. Indians were driven from their land and killed if they resisted, and sometimes killed anyway. Indian children were taken and sold as slaves. Young Indian women were taken by whites and forced to cohabit with them. The Indians were enraged by these wrongdoings. Fires of enmity smoldered and, increasingly, burst into flames.

In January 1858 an outraged white wrote the *Trinity Journal* on the Indians' behalf:

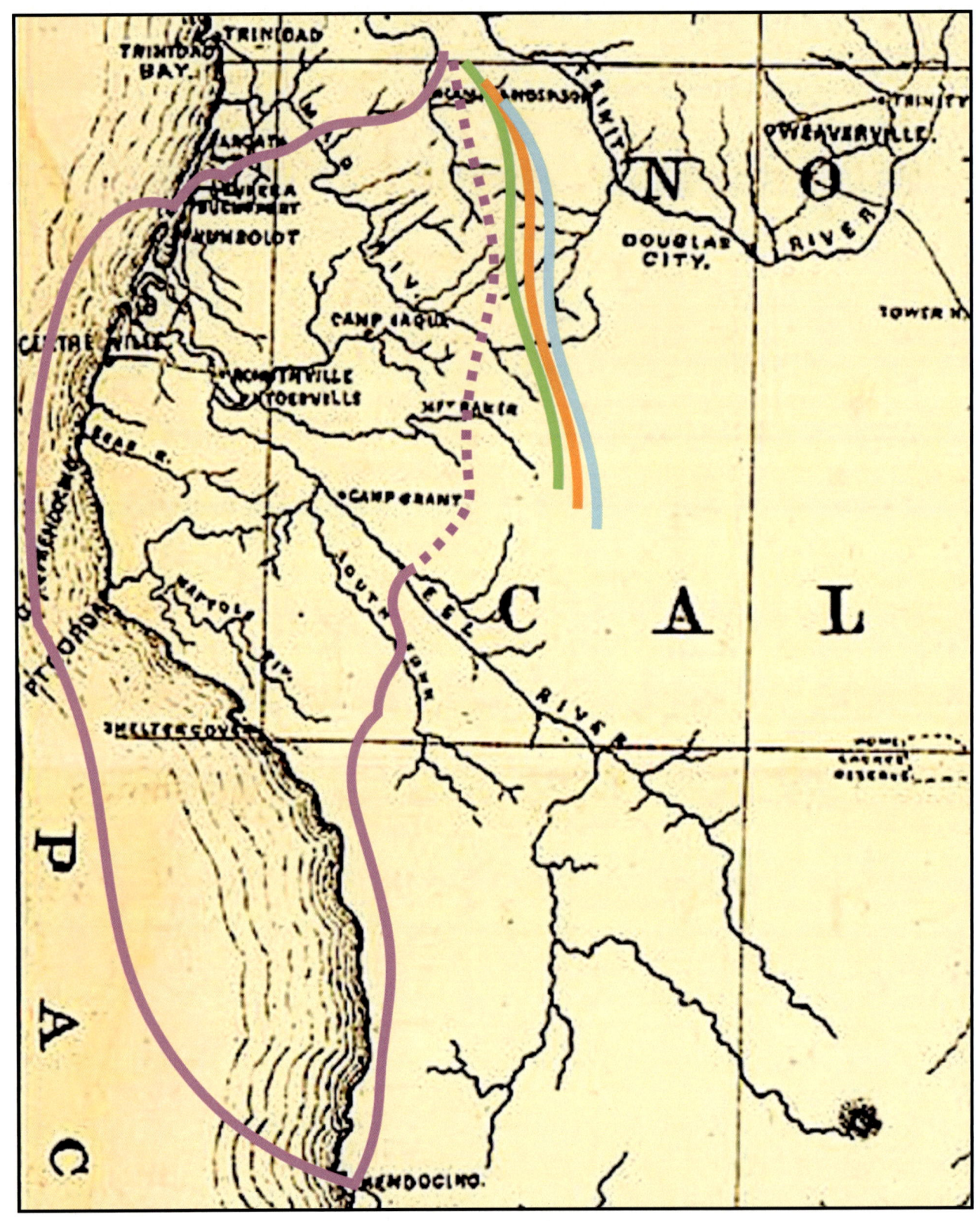

The Chilulas' trails of tears. Solid pink line: route of the Chilulas' forced removal to the Mendocino Reservation and subsequent escape to the Eel River. Dotted pink line: route of Chilula survivors back to Redwood Creek after the attacks by the Lassiks. Green, orange, and blue lines: routes Chilulas took when making their three attack on the Lassiks (base map by SMH, colorized by JR).

There may be no objection to white men living with squaws where it is done by consent of both parties. But this is not always the case. There are white men who, when they cannot obtain a squaw by fair means, will not hesitate to use foul. But little persuasion is too often used in the matter, and to drag off a squaw, and knock down her friends if they interfere, not uncommonly occurs; and very often I have known instances where these women were obliged to leave the [Indian] ranches and seek safety in flight, remaining in the mountains for days together, to avoid the violence of men who under the influence of liquor do not hesitate to do any deed. Every person who knows the character of our Indians knows that above all things they fear a drunken man. I have also known families to be driven from their homes in the dead of winter by crowds of drunken men, and in the absence of legal proof nothing could be done for their protection.[294]

That June, after three whites killed two Indians and wounded two others on the lower Eel River, two white men were shot and wounded by Indians north of Eureka. The *Humboldt Times* thought that the second attack was probably made in retaliation for the first. Looking for a larger cause and effect, the paper saw the white murderers as men who would "mar the beauty and destroy the harmony of our social fabric, and by causing ruptures with the Indians, jeopardize the lives of good and useful citizens. . . ."[295]

Two weeks later the *Times* reported another Indian attack; this one left one man wounded. Henry Allen and William E. Ross were leading a pack train over Grouse Mountain when Indians shot Ross from ambush. Having found no motive for this attack, unlike the earlier one, the *Times* asked, "will the citizens turn out and kill off a lot these Indians now, or shall they be left alone, to shoot down any man who may chance to pass on the trail?"[296]

If the *Times* sounded nervous, it had reason to be, for it was reporting portentous news. During all of the preceding year it had noted only one attack on a pack train by Indians, and this was when an *Indian* packer was shot, apparently for revenge.[297] And then almost half of 1858 had passed with no report of trouble on the trails. Suddenly, three whites were wounded in two attacks, and the *Times* was left to wonder if these were acts of war.

For war it could be. During the last eight years the local Indians had endured the abuses of the whites, suffering frequently, resisting occasionally, but nearly always trapped in situations where the whites held the upper hand. Now a different possibility presented itself—guerrilla warfare—where the mountain Indians, who lived between the coastal ports and the inland mines, could interrupt or halt the commerce that was essential to the whites. Pack trains, mail carriers, travelers in general—all were vulnerable when passing through isolated areas, obscure locations where the rugged topography offered countless opportunities for the deadly flash of an ambush and the befuddling obscurity of a quick escape. When, a day after the Grouse Mountain attack, Dr. Baldwin and A. W. Gould reached the site, they found that the Indians had left three musket balls in Ross's body but no sign of their tribe's identity.[298] The whites of Humboldt County were learning what Napoleonic troops had discovered when fighting what they called "guerrillas" in Spain a half-century earlier—the little enemy you cannot see, and cannot anticipate, is far more fearsome than a known force ten times its size.

The same day that the *Times* reported Ross's wounding, it also announced that on the Mad River "the Indians have made an outbreak, and . . . the trail to Humboldt Bay is not safe to travel."[299] The newspaper digested this information for three weeks and then announced the obvious: "It is perfect folly to expect that our mountain trails will ever be safe to travel, so long as Indians roam at large throughout the country."[300] Another account in the same issue described the perils of pursuing an unseen foe in its own territory. A group of vigilantes consisting of commander John Bell and 16 men located and attacked an Indian camp on Grouse Creek, near where Ross had been shot. They "killed quite a number of Indians" and proceeded to return to their own camp. Along the way they were ambushed by Indians and one of Bell's men "was shot dead at the first fire." Upon reaching their destination, Bell "found ten of his mules dead and missing, and his camp entirely broken up." He and his men retreated across the canyon of Redwood Creek to Pardee's Ranch. They arrived in disarray: "the whole party were completely worn-out with fatigue, and some of them barefoot. They will remain there until they receive assistance. . . ."[301] It could not be called a successful campaign.

On August 7 the *Times* told of more military difficulties. A contingent of whites from Trinity County, led by a Mr. Winslet, "fell in with a party of Indians near Three Creeks," on the divide west of Willow Creek. The whites first became aware of the Indians when Winslet was shot in the thigh. He nonetheless led a charge against the ambushers, but the Indians confounded the attackers by staying hidden in the brush. Two of the whites "stepped off a little way from the party," whereupon one them, Chauncey Miller, fell dead with a musket ball in his head. Once again the whites sought refuge at Pardee's Ranch, where Dr. Baldwin tended to Winslet's "severe, though not dangerous" wound. The *Times* noted that the ambushers "appear to have adopted the natural mode of Indian warfare, and by this method they have a great advantage over the whites."[302] Reviewing recent events, the *Times* tallied up the scorecard and found the whites the losers:

> For the past six weeks the Redwood [Creek] and Mad River Indians have shown evidences of their hostility in such a shape as to cause alarm for the result. Immediately after Ross was shot steps were taken to chastise the Indians, and they, anticipating what would follow, prepared themselves for the contest. So far, the parties who have been in pursuit of them have had the worst of every engagement. They have been compelled to trail them into deep canyons and ravines, and fight them in thick brush. Two good men have been killed, and two wounded, and nothing accomplished.[303]

Starting with the wounding of Ross in late June of 1858, Indians had made the Redwood Creek area a danger zone for whites, ambushing both packers and vigilante groups. Then, in mid-September, the conflict took a new turn. Paul Boynton, a rancher who lived along the Union to Trinity Trail[304] on Fickle Hill ridge some 10 miles east of Union, was shot and killed within about 200 yards of his house when going for his cows in the morning.[305] Now the conflict was coming closer to Humboldt Bay. Much closer. The *Times* loudened its call for action, demanding "that a company of men should be raised by our citizens, and sent out immediately in order to at least keep the Indians at bay till some plan for their removal or extermination be matured."[306] The same issue of the *Times* reported that Pardee's Ranch, long a

Three Tragedies 65

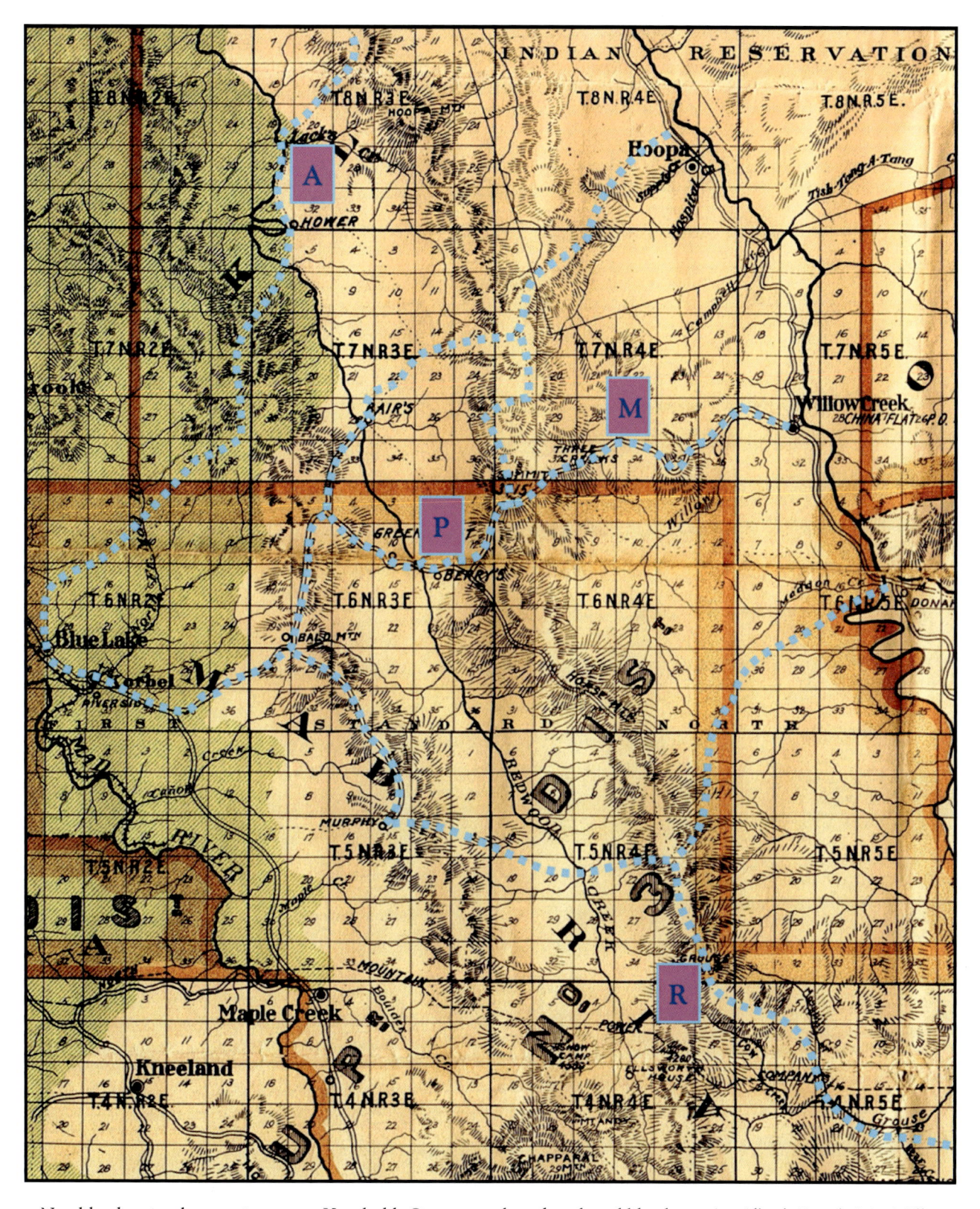

Notable places and events in eastern Humboldt County: pack trails = dotted blue lines; A = Albee's Ranch; M = Miller killed at Three Creeks; P = Pardee's Ranch; R = Ross wounded at Grouse Mountain (base map JNL).

place of refuge for whites, had been attacked and its residents forced to flee, while other Indians had killed a cow at Angel Ranch,[307] on the mountainside east of Blue Lake.

The citizens of Humboldt Bay responded immediately to the threat. A meeting held in Union resulted in the levying of a special tax to defray the expenses of dealing with the Indians, and the townspeople of Eureka endorsed a similar proposal, although they set their tax at only half that of Union's.[308] Both towns called for volunteers to provide four months' service.[309]

There is no record of how Joseph Albee reacted to the news of Boynton's death. Albee, who lived much closer to the center of Indian activity, stayed on his ranch and kept his family there also, apparently sensing no threat. He reportedly felt secure enough that he carried no firearms.[310]

Meanwhile, California's governor, John B. Weller, responded to citizen complaints about the Indian attacks. On September 5 Weller ordered his Adjutant General, W. C. Kibbe, north to ascertain conditions in the Humboldt-Trinity area. If Kibbe deemed it necessary to subdue the Indians, he was instructed "to organize a company of volunteer militia to suppress them."[311] Kibbe duly went to Weaverville forthwith, but

> . . . failing to find what he deemed to be reliable information in that vicinity, proceeded in company with an old and experienced mountaineer, J. G. Messic, to the country inhabited by the hostile tribes of Indians, in order to satisfy himself as to the number of savages, and if possible learn their future designs. These hostiles were from the Mad River and Redwood Creek Indian Tribes.[312]

The report Kibbe sent to Weller was startling. It claimed, with scant proof,

> . . . that the number of warriors belonging to these tribes were estimated at from 250 to 300 besides fifty braves from the Hoopa tribe. The hostile tribe was generally well armed with rifles, and there was proof that at one time at least forty shots were fired by a party of them from as many guns, killing two white men and wounding two others. The warfare they were waging did not seem to be entirely a predatory one. The Indians cared little for plunder, and were seeking to destroy men and animals, but would shoot a man or an Indian for his gun, being anxious to obtain arms. They also sent the friendly Indians with gold dust to the camps to purchase guns and ammunition for them, and frequently offered $150 for a rifle worth only $10.[313]

The white residents who provided Kibbe with this information were desirous of obtaining state aid. The Adjutant General apparently accepted these lurid accounts at face value, and he sought to give the locals what they wanted:

> General Kibbe under these circumstances was forced to the conclusion that it was the duty of the State Government to afford the frontier citizens the protection which justice and humanity demanded, and to enter at once upon this duty and if necessary to exterminate these savages.[314]

Spurred by Kibbe's forebodings, Governor Weller approved the enlistment of militiamen on September 28. General S. H. Dosh advertised for 80 volunteers on October 6, and presto! eight days later the Trinity Rangers, California's newest militia unit, enrolled 80 men. Its captain, coincidently, was none other than Kibbe's recent guide, I. G. Messic.[315]

Three Tragedies

The Trinity Rangers were organized in their namesake county at Big Bar, but by late October they had headed west towards the scene of recent action to establish a permanent camp above Redwood Creek near Pardee's Ranch, which was being garrisoned by federal troops under Captain Edmund Underwood.[316] The initial activity of the new unit met with mixed results. Messic's men managed to surprise an Indian camp "in the vicinity of Pardee's Ranch, near the new Trinity trail." They killed "four warriors" and two children. The latter, according to the *Times*, were shot "accidentally," but the paper did not explain how the young victims could have been mistaken for grown men. In addition, two women and two children were captured.[317] The Rangers were apparently so absorbed in killing men and children that they failed to adequately protect their home fortress, and that same week the *Times* reported that Pardee's ranch had been burned by Indians, its livestock and foodstuffs taken, and its oat crop "thrashed".[318]

Following the incidents near and at Pardee's Ranch, Messic's men spent almost a month during which, according to the *Times*, "that whole section of the country . . . [had] been thoroughly scoured and not an Indian could be found."[319] In point of fact the Trinity Rangers had actually been enjoying a sort of fun-filled, unofficial furlough, but that information had not been provided to the local news media.[320]

Finally, in mid-November Messic's troops bestirred themselves and attacked a band of Indians in the vicinity of Showers Pass, and, as near as the *Times* could determine, "killed some of them and took the remainder prisoner." One Ranger was wounded—but not by the Indians. Henry Allen was shot "by the accidental discharge of a gun in the hands of one of his comrades." The *Times*, perhaps impatient with such antics, grew grimmer in its attitude, indicating that

> We hope that Capt. Messic will succeed in totally breaking up or exterminating the skulking bands of savages . . . that have preyed upon the lives and property of our people for the last seven years.[321]

At the end of November the *Times* claimed that the Rangers' "expedition is progressing finely," and that in addition to the Indians killed there were some 30 to 40 prisoners. Adjutant General Kibbe had accompanied the expedition since its start; he noted that the country through which they had passed "will afford pasturage for from twenty to thirty thousand head of cattle" once the Indians were removed.[322]

In December Messic divided his company into three parties, ranging from Yager Creek northward past Boynton's place and eastward to Par-dee's burnt ranch.[323] Winter weather was the volunteers' friend, for it drove the Indians away from their hideouts in the vast high country and forced them to congregate in their low-lying winter villages, where they were easier to find and then attack. On January 1, 1859, the *Times* announced that Messic's troops had "captured seventeen ranches [villages], taking in all, eighty-four prisoners.[324]

On January 21 a detachment of Rangers was pursuing Indians near Albee's Ranch, when, once again, they were fired upon from ambush and one soldier severely wounded.[325] No mention was made of Albee and his family, nor was it noted that he had established his ranch in the vicinity of the Chilula village of Tondinnundin[326] and had apparently lived in peaceful proximity to the Indians for over four years.

The following week Messic, having detached most of the Rangers for expeditions on Redwood Creek and the Mad River, found himself with only 14 men. It was then that he learned of "suspicious movements" of the Whilkuts and Mawenoks, who

Site of Camp Iaqua, above North Yager Creek. From here soldiers could easily reach many Nongatl villages (JR).

until then had been considered friendly. Taking his reduced force he reconnoitered the area where the Indians were last seen, between Dow's Prairie and Liscom Hill. Messic heard dogs barking the next morning and deduced that the Indians were near at hand. Violating a basic maxim of warfare, he then divided his already small force into two even smaller parties of seven men each in an attempt to attack from two directions at once. The troops moved towards the yet-to-be-seen encampment. To Messic's surprise, he found not a small group of Whilkuts and Mawenoks but a full-scale village, with "fourteen large log houses" and an estimated 150 Indians. Undaunted, the Rangers charged. The *Times* reported that the "unerring aim of the volunteers' rifles" killed 15 Indians on the spot, while the troops also took 13 prisoners. Two of Messic's men were severely wounded, however, and he decided to break off the engagement in order to save them.[327]

The Rangers headed towards Dow's Prairie. Whilkut and Mawenok warriors followed them, firing from the bushes at various times. Late in the afternoon Ranger G. W. Werk was assuming a position at the rear of the line of prisoners when he was shot and severely wounded in the arm. Werk was unable to defend himself because he was carrying two rifles at the time and consequently could use neither. The next afternoon the bedraggled band reached Union.[328]

Three Tragedies

Having mulled over the most recent military debacle, the *Times* editorialized that "the prospects for a speedy termination of the Indian war . . . do not appear as flattering to us now as they did a month ago." The paper again summarized the Indians' effective tactics of stealth and surprise, without mentioning the growing evidence of the ineptitude of the Rangers. Although expressing "every confidence" in the fighting ability of volunteers, the *Times* also noted that the Rangers' capture of over 100 Indian women and children, who were currently en route for the Mendocino Reservation, "will also relieve the warriors from looking out for them and will scarcely have a tendency to make them less hostile towards us."[329]

Perhaps it was at this time that an idea began to form in Messic's, or perhaps Kibbe's, mind. It was one thing to march about as freshly minted soldiers, easily pursuing, killing, and capturing not just Indian men but also women and children. It was something else when the Indians proved to be the whites' match in combat, managing to wound, and even kill, a few of the soldiers. The disarray in which the troops had straggled to Pardee's Ranch and to Dow's Prairie after experiencing a few casualties, the lamentations that were voiced at their having received a few enemy bullets—such actions suggested a certain softness of both body and character, a lack of true martial spirit, and augured ill for the future success of the Rangers' campaign. Perhaps, as Messic made his way to the safety and succor of Union, hearing the groans of John Houk, shot through the hand and body, or those of Sam Overlander, wounded in both thighs, or those of G. W. Werk, his "arm smashed to splinters,"[330] perhaps it was then that Messic thought of an easier way to win the Rangers' war.

Whether from these or other causes, sometime during the dark early months of 1859 a new plan emerged. No accurate report was ever given by the *Times* of its implementation, only of its result. Anthony Jennings Bledsoe wrote extensively on the Indian-white conflict. If he knew the truth about the plan, he failed to tell it, writing instead of a

> . . . storm, on the mountains and in the valleys, [that] was the worst of the season, and had not been excelled in severity for several years preceding.
>
> The storm was a fortunate occurrence for the volunteers. The hostiles, unable to hunt on the mountains and afraid to go down to the streams, were actually starved into submission within four weeks.[331]

What happened, according to Bledsoe, was that the Indians, weakened by lack of food, either surrendered to the Rangers or were captured in their "camps or rancherias," too feeble to fight.[332]

What actually occurred was very different. It was left for rancher Jonathan Lyons, speaking nearly half a century later, to tell the true story.

Lyons was no ordinary white. He had taken a Hoopa woman, Amelia Misket, to be his wife, and unlike most of his contemporaries, had actually married her. He had sympathized with the Indians at Hoopa and had helped a Hupa woman flee to safety after she had killed a soldier who had tried to rape her. For his efforts Lyons was ordered off the reservation.[333]

Lyons had once worked for Joseph Albee, and together they had planted an orchard at Albee's Ranch.[334] In 1906[335] Pliny Goddard interviewed Lyons while preparing his study of the Chilula Indians. According to Goddard's notes, Lyons

> . . . told of a volunteer company organized by permission of the Governor . . . [which] spent a season on upper Redwood [Creek],

drinking and hunting. When fall came they had nothing to report and they had not killed anybody. They heard that Albers [Albee] was living at an Indian ranch [at the mouth of Lacks Creek] and the Indians were working for him. They [the volunteer company] came down. Albers wanted to know what they wanted. The commander said "Oh they only wanted to talk to them [the Indians], tell them to be quiet and they would not be troubled and to give them presents.["] Albers assisted in gathering the Indians in. They were surrounded and taken to Big River [Mendocino Reservation].[336]

It was in this way that Captain Messic, or perhaps Adjutant General Kibbe, deceived Joseph Albee, and in so doing caused him to deceive the Chilulas, with the result that a large group of Indians was captured. It was a perfect solution to the problem that the officers faced—how to defeat a dangerous and skillful enemy without endangering yourself or your troops. But within this deception lay the seeds of destruction, and within the fullness of time, it indeed bore fatal fruit.

The *Times* was ecstatic. Noting that Messic had collected 75 prisoners and Lieutenant Winslett 25 more, the paper announced, with the measured pomposity that is the prerogative of the self-righteous, that "it affords us pleasure to announce that the Indian war in our county may now safely be considered very nearly at an end."[337]

But the *Times*, so often wrong about the Indian-white conflict, was wrong yet again. The end was in sight only if seen through a telescope, for the conflict in Humboldt County still had more than four years to run, and many more lives would be needlessly lost before it was over. The whites, who had been on the North Coast for less than a decade, had obliterated a mostly harmonic set of Indian relationships that had been centuries in the making, and they had replaced it with a dirge of destruction that reached even the remotest confines of the county. It was soon to ring with

Mendocino Reservation, 1857 (BL).

a dissonance that pitted not Indian against white but Indian against Indian, as the Chilulas followed a trail of tears every bit as tragic as that of the Cherokees.

Goddard continued Lyons's story of the captured Chilulas after they were removed from Albee's ranch:

> After some delay, the captives were put on board a vessel and taken to Fort Bragg on the Mendocino County coast, where they were placed on a reservation. There they were indifferently cared for and insufficiently guarded. Although the Indians were 150 miles from their homes, from which they were separated by mountainous county absolutely unknown to them and inhabited by strange tribes whose customary reception of unknown people was hostile, they set out bravely toward the north, traveling by the sun and stars.[338]

The Chilulas crossed through the vast wilderness between the coast and the South Fork Eel. They passed over the great divide of Mail Ridge. They came down to the main Eel and forded it. By now they were more than halfway to their homeland, and perhaps their hopes rose as they crossed the largest river along their route.

But the Chilulas were in a dangerous place, for they had entered the territory of the Lassiks, a tribe that had often fought fiercely to protect its land. The Lassiks had endured raids by the Naiaitci, who came over from the Van Duzen to attack in summer, and by Wailakis, who came at them from up the Eel. On their lengthy annual trips the Lassiks had evaded other Indians, including Nongatls from the Blocksburg area. And then the whites, both ordinary citizens and soldiers, had come to kill and capture the Lassiks.[339]

At the mouth of Dobbyn Creek the Chilulas met the Indians who lived there. The newcomers asked for food by making signs.[340] The Lassiks responded by killing nearly all of them.[341]

The Chilulas, escaping from the whites, had miscalculated the Lassiks' response. The Lassiks, who should have been their allies against a common enemy, chose instead to follow the old ways, where any trespasser was to be smote unto death by a righteous people defending their homeland. But the Chilulas were making their trek as harbingers of a new time, where the customs created over centuries no longer applied. For custom was now being wrenched from these people with a fierceness and immediacy that defied understanding, but which demanded acceptance. The world the Chilulas and Lassiks had known was dying, and most of the Indians with it. The Lassiks, unable or unwilling to see beyond the strictures of the past, helped assure the desolation of the future.

Yet the twofold tragedy of Indians fighting against both whites and other Indians had yet to reach its climax. Survivors of the Lassiks' attack brought word of it back to Redwood Creek, where the remaining Chilulas learned of the massacre on the Eel.

Inflamed by the wrath of the unjustly persecuted, the Chilulas gathered allies and formed a war party sixty or seventy strong:

> All the Indians who used to live on upper Redwood went with the party. All the people who used to live below Iaqui [Iaqua] butte and at the Big Bend of the Mad river went also. They met on the ridge south of the head of Redwood creek and held the war dance. There were sixty men who had weapons. The dance line was so long that in two places a man stood in front of the line and danced. They shot with bows and arrows

and with white man's guns. The party was two days and two nights on the way. They came to the village of Taike . . . and fought with the Indians there. Many bodies were left lying there.[342]

The Chilulas then headed back to their home country. But,

> . . . while camped near the site of Blocksburg they saw smoke to the east near the base of Lassik Peaks. Scouts sent out reported a large summer camp. This was surrounded about daybreak and the people killed without mercy, neither women of children being spared. Some of the Lassik took refuge under a log, where they were killed and remained unburied for many years. The avengers are said to have made three trips to Lassik country before they were content.[343]

Apparently the Chilulas killed more than Lassiks in their three attacks. Van Duzen Pete, Goddard's Nongatl informant, indicated that the "Redwoods [Chilulas] killed lots of Pete's people at Buck Mt. On ridge east of Larrabee. Kill about 50."[344] Charlie, the Sinkene Indian from Salmon Creek, was probably referring to the Chilula attacks when he said that "Redwood Creek [Indians] came over and killed lots of Indians. Early days long time ago."[345]

And even then the Chilulas' need for vengeance was not assuaged. All the white ranchers on Redwood Creek but one had left and sought refuge in Arcata. Joseph Porter Albee had taken his family there, but, according to Lyons, he

Main Eel River near Fort Seward and Dobbyn Creek (JR).

Three Tragedies

Pilot Rock and Pilot Ridge, where the Chilulas and their allies held their war dance (JR).

. . . came back himself to look after his stock and ranch. The Indians were suspicious of him. He came to Hoopa and spent the night with [Jonathan] Lyons. Lyons told him to let his property go and get out of the country. He took a Hupa [man] back with him and sent him to see the Indians. He soon came back and advised Albers [sic] to get out at once. Said the Indians were very mad and would not talk. The [Hupa] Indian got hold of a bottle of whiskey and got dead drunk. Albers covered him up and in the morning he was gone. Albers went out the next morning to plow and cultivate in the orchard. The Indians killed him [and] he was found several days [there]after, the horse dragging the cultivator about the orchard.[346]

According to Dan Hill, one of Goddard's Chilula informants, it was his father, Tom, who "fired the shot" that killed Albee.[347]

And still the revenge slayings were not finished. Five years passed, five years of continued warfare between the Indians and the whites. Then, in 1864, the whites sought to make peace with the Chilulas, Hupas, and their allies. The Chilulas were willing to do so, but on one condition: "that the Hupa Indian who had summoned them to the council at Albers' [Albee's] house be given them." Accordingly, the Indian in question, Hostler Charlie,[348] "was sent with a message to Arcata and

The Chilulas' homeland on Redwood Creek (BLM).

was killed from ambush by a party of Chilula who were hidden in waiting."[349]

Thus, the Chilulas had killed everyone they could find who had contributed to their capture and subsequent massacre—everyone except the real culprits, who were Messic and his soldiers. The Chilulas, who had been victims of the Lassiks' insistence on following the old ways, had then done the very same thing. Two Indian tribes had nearly destroyed each other; two innocent participants in the tragedy had been killed, a Hupa Indian and a white man; and after all of this, the Chilulas had "peace." But by the terms of the treaty that eventually followed, the Chilulas had to give up their homeland and move onto the newly established reservation at Hoopa.[350] The last Chilula family to leave the Bald Hills and move to Hoopa was that of the man who shot Hostler Charlie—Tom Hill.[351]

Solitudinem faciunt pacem appellant—they create a desert and call it peace.

Chapter IV

Southern Humboldt Tribal Groups

If we want to learn about the history and geography of the southern Humboldt Indians, what better source of information than the Indians themselves? Although little has been published about these people, and some of that incorrect, the unpublished field notes of the southern Humboldt ethnographers are replete with fact-filled accounts by local Indians who were alive in 1850 or were born shortly thereafter. These statements provide eyewitness reports about tribal boundaries, the names and locations of geographical features and tribal groups, and important events in the lives of the members of these groups. This chapter relies heavily on these primary sources, most especially Goddard's numerous notebooks, but it also uses selections from the unpublished works of other ethnographers such as Merriam, Harrington, Hewes, and Murphey.[352] When necessary, the conclusions of researchers are included to fill in gaps in the primary record.

And what, in a broad sense, do these reports from the past tell us? Most clearly, that the local Indians did not think of themselves as being members of those large units that certain scholars have designated as the five or six southern Humboldt "tribes." Repeatedly, the Indians identified themselves by simply naming the place where they resided. Sometimes the location was fairly large, such as a section of a river valley or an entire creek drainage. In one case it was larger still, including all or part of three river canyons.[353] Other times it might be as small as a flat by the side of a stream. In providing this identity the Indians would give the name of the place they inhabited and then add the suffix "kai-ya" (or its phonetic equivalent), which means "people of."[354] It became apparent that this was a fundamental relationship in these Indians' lives—they saw themselves belonging to a group of people that were all connected to the same place. But many ethnographers insisted on collecting Indians from several tribal groups and placing them in the larger, more familiar units known as tribes. (See sidebar 1.)

The person most responsible for the persistent notion that the southern Humboldt Indians were divided into five large tribes was Alfred L. Kroeber. His 1925 *Handbook of the Indians of California* is still in print and still serves as the main source on the subject for general readers. But Kroeber continued to study the California Indians and much later in his career, in 1954, he wrote that what he called a "tribelet" was "the ultimate basic social and political unit of most California Indians." He estimated that the average population of a tribelet was "in the neighborhood of two hundred and fifty" and that "there were in California around *five or six hundred such groups.*" He indicated that the term "tribe," so freely used by him and other ethnographers, was applied to "larger clusterings" of Indians "*not because it is a really appropriate term but because we lack any better familiar word.*" [emphases added] However, he then searched for such a word and decided that "in comparable civilized European terms" it would be "a nationality."[355]

But Kroeber's 1954 paper was only publishedin 1962 in a somewhat obscure journal called the *University of California Archaeological Survey Reports*. And meanwhile, Goddard's field notes, which

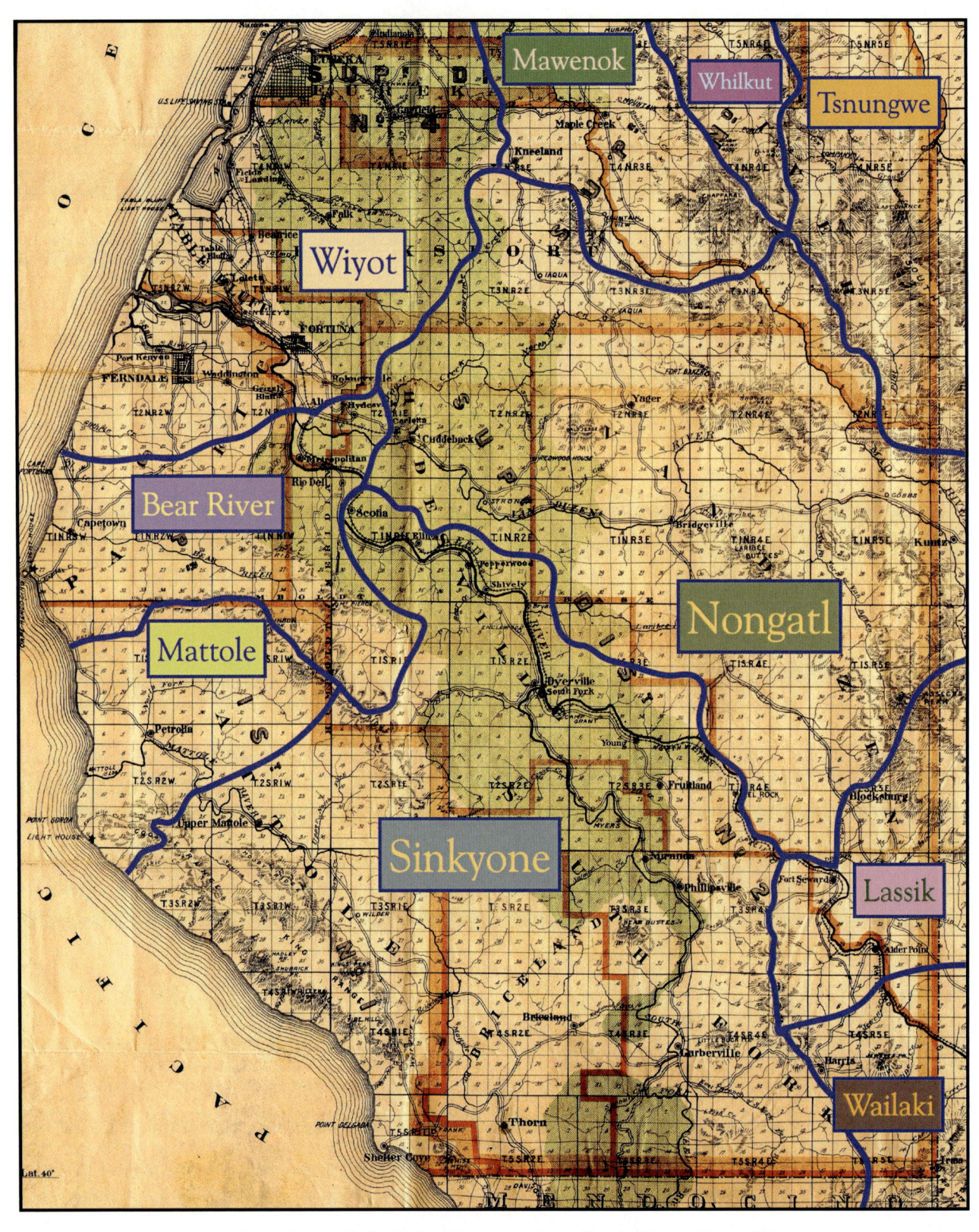

Southern Humboldt "tribes" and their northern Humboldt neighbors (JR).

1. Too Few Who Knew

As early as 1877, the public was told that there were a handful of southern Humboldt tribes. Stephen Powers named the "Mattoal," "Wai-lak-ki," "Lassik," and "Sai-az" as inhabiting that large but little-known area. The notion was refined and the nomenclature improved in Frederick Webb Hodge's two-volume *Handbook of American Indians*, issued in 1907 and 1910. There Pliny Goddard, in accounts of a half-page or less, described the Mattole, Lassik, Wailaki, and Sinkyone tribes (the last of which he called the "Sinkine" elsewhere in the handbooks). Missing were the Nongatls, for Goddard had yet to meet Van Duzen Pete and determine that tribe's separate identity. Then came Kroeber's *Handbook of the Indians of California* in 1925, which gave us five tribes: the Mattole, Wailaki, Lassik, Sinkyone, and—finally—the Nongatl. In 1958 Baumhoff bifurcated the Mattoles, separating out a sixth southern Humboldt tribe, the Bear Rivers. Pregnant with possibility, he also indicated that some of the six tribes could be subdivided into what he called "bands" or "tribal groups."

In 2011, linguist Victor Golla found that Baumhoff's perception of six southern Humboldt tribes had carried over into current thinking about what are called the California Athabascan languages.[356] Golla described a "Mattole-Bear River Language" spoken by those two tribes, and a set of closely related "Eel River Dialects" that "the ethnographic and linguistic literature usually assigns . . . to four major dialect divisions: Sinkyone, Nongatl, Lassik, and Wailaki." He noted that Sinkyone speakers were divided into "two well-defined groups."

It was a convenient concept—a large number of Indians, who were spread over a large area, could be reliably organized into a small number of units based on the language or dialect they spoke. It had the great virtue of organizing the ethnographic chaos of an undifferentiated mass of poorly understood Indians. But it also had a great fault—there was not enough data to support it.

The problem was the scarcity of information from the Indians who spoke the languages. Only a few speakers were ever interviewed, leaving large geographic areas entirely unrepresented. The most extreme example is that of the Nongatls, where just one member of the tribe, Van Duzen Pete, ever provided significant linguistical material.[357] Thus, in this case, information from a single speaker was applied to a collection of Indians comprising a score of tribal groups that occupied an area that ranged from Carlotta to Dinsmore,

28. GEOGRAPHIC OR PLACE NAMES

Main Eel River	Hah'-cho and Tah'-cho
Van Duzen River	Ken'-ne-kōk | Chin'-ne-kōk (Van Duzen mouth) | Kin'-ne-ke
South Fork Eel River	Sin-ke'-kōk (also by residents called Tah'-cho = the river)
Bull Creek	Lo-lahn'-kōk
Elk Creek	Sōl-te-kōk
Salmon Creek	Sah-nah'-kōk
East Branch So. Fk. Eel	Ken'-naw-loo'-gu-kuk (Kan'-no-lig'-ah-kōk)
Mattole River	Tah'-che
North Fork Mattole	Nahn-tsin'-tah-kōk
Taylor Peak	Nahn-tsin'-kah (high point standing up)
Canoe Creek	Nan-sin'-cho-ko
Redwood Creek (at Briceland)	Ahn'-chin-tah'-ko (tsin)
Bear River	Chahn'-kōk
Larrabee Creek	Slahn'-ko
Little Larrabee Creek	Sō'-kok
Bridgeville	Ahn-sin-tah-che-be'
Chalk Mt. (between Bridgeville & Larrabee Creek)	Nĕ-chin-tuk-kah (Name of the whole ridge) | Nă-chin-tă-kah | sā-til-bi' (Chalk Mt. itself)
Dyerville (place S. of main Eel & west of South Fork) (flat W & NW of town)	Chin-tah'-tah | Chin-tah'-te
Myers (open sloping flat never forested)	Ken'-tes-chō'-be
Miranda	Kahs-cho boo-ah'-me
'Phillipsville'	Ket'-tin-tel'-be
Bear Buttes (3 miles SW of Ket'-tin-tel-be)	Sā'-nan-tsin'-kah
Garberville (flat north of town, near new Concrete bridge)	Ko'-se-che
Briceland	To-cho'-be
Upper Mattole (Roscoe's place)	Kun-sah'-ke (Ken-suk'-kah)
Elk Ridge	Chi-chin'-kah
Rainbow Ridge	Tsă-bung'-ah / Tsa-bahng-um
Rainbow Peak	[74] Tsā-che'-be

Vocabulary sheet from C. Hart Merriam's interview with the Lolahnkok informant George Burtt (EDC).

and from Iaqua to beyond Blocksburg—the entire Van Duzen River drainage, almost all of the Larabee Creek drainage, and parts of the Mad River and Eel River watersheds. Moreover, Pete told Goddard that within these tribal groups there were at least five dialects—Nongatl, Se-nun-ka, Kit-tel, Kos-dun, and Dine-ke-ne-ox—and although Pete apparently understood all of them, he was a native speaker only of Nongatl.

Other areas are almost as poorly represented. Of the Indians who were alive at or near the time of white contact and were interviewed there was one Mattole, two Bear Rivers, two or three Lassiks, and an indeterminate number of Wailakis, likely no more than two or three. Only the Sinkyones had a somewhat larger group of interviewees—seven—but even so several Sinkyone areas, including the upper Mattole, main Eel, and Garberville-Redway are not covered. With such a small sampling of southern Humboldt speakers, it is impossible to determine that there was a clearly defined, comprehensive set of Indian languages or dialects and to map them precisely, let alone conclude that such linguistic units would each also constitute the socio-political unit commonly referred to as a "tribe." The standard view of southern Humboldt Indians and their languages is an easily collapsed house of cards, in which each card is a joker.

showed that triblets were indeed the basic unit of organization for southern Humboldt Indians, languished in the archives of the American Philosophical Society. The years passed, and the paradigm of the five or six southern Humboldt tribes grew more firmly entrenched with the passing of each decade. It has now reached the point where the term "tribe" has been used for so long in accounting for the southern Humboldt Indians that it cannot be easily discontinued here. Instead, this chapter will use for its subheadings the familiar names of the five tribes that Kroeber used in his *Handbook of the Indians of California*,[358] under each of which will appear the names and descriptions of the various tribal groups subsumed by the larger "tribe" unit. *Caveat lector.*[359]

A. Mattole Tribe

What Kroeber maps as the Mattole tribal lands, running from lower Yager Creek near Carlotta to the headwaters of the Mattole River,[360] are actually the territories of several separate tribes or tribal groups. The two northernmost such entities, the Bear River and the Mattole, are often unjustifiably conflated under the single name Mattole. To the south Kroeber expanded Mattole territory by erroneously including lands that belonged to Sinkyone tribal groups.

1. Bear River (Nekanni)

The Indians who occupied the Bear River canyon and adjacent areas to the north called themselves the Nekanni, but certain early ethnographers lumped them with the neighboring Mattole tribe and used the latter's name for both groups. Others referred to the Nekannis by the location where they dwelt, and thus that name, Bear River Indians, became an accepted term of usage.[361] The tribe occupied all of its namesake drainage, living in a string of villages that ran upstream on

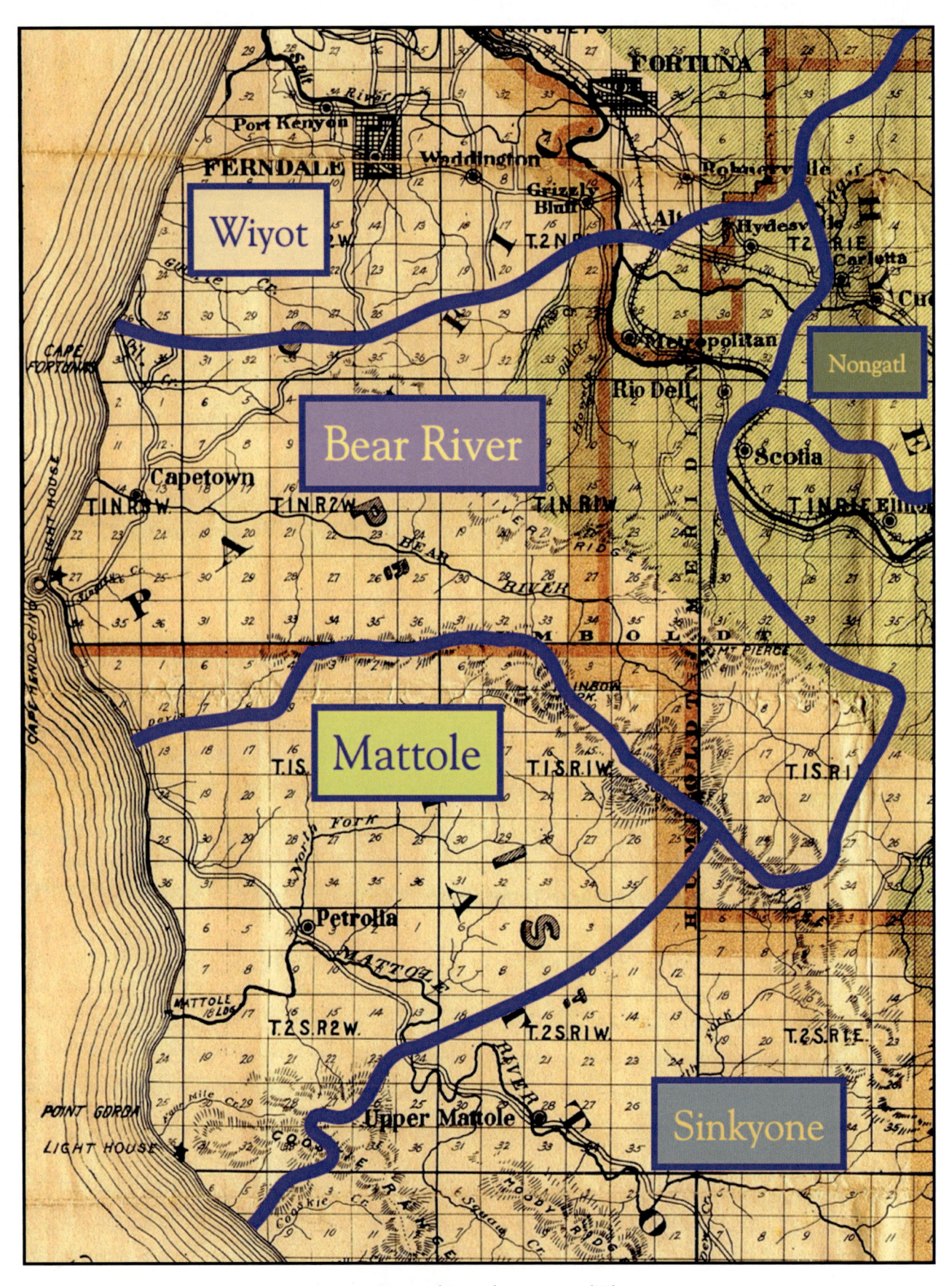

Bear River and Mattole territories (JR).

the north side of lower Bear River.[362] The easternmost of these, Mess-e-ah, was a "training place for shamans."[363] It was also the site of a victory dance "following success in war."[364] There was one additional village in the drainage, far to the east of the others, called Klaht-el-kos-tah.[365] It was near the headwaters of the river and was a "large town with Big Dance House."[366]

The Bear River tribe also claimed land beyond their namesake river's canyon. To the northwest, on the far side of Bear River Ridge, was a camp they called Ko-stah-che, at Oil Creek.[367] It lay on or near the Wiyot-Bear River boundary and may in fact have been part of a joint use area, since the Wiyots had a camp on the north side of the creek, which they called Datowok.[368] Some distance to the northeast, the Bear River Indians spilled over the top of Bear River Ridge into the valley below, occupying the area at and near the confluence of the Eel and Van Duzen rivers while also claiming land a short distance upstream on both. The boundary between the Bear River and Wiyot tribes ran eastward from the mouth of Oil Creek up onto Bear River Ridge. It probably left the ridgeline near Bunker Hill to run above the northern side of the Price Creek drainage, reaching the Eel at Weymouth Bluff. From there it crossed the Eel near Alton, ran northeast between Rohnerville and Hydesville, and continued to the vicinity of the confluence of Cooper Mill Creek and Yager Creek.[369]

The northwestern boundary, at Oil Creek, was where the first wagon road from Petrolia descended to the beach. Johnny Jackson, a Mattole Indian, said that when they reached the beach on their way to Centerville, they would build a fire and eat dinner before continuing north on what was called the Beach Road. He confirmed that the Oil Creek gulch was the boundary between the Wiyot and Bear River tribes.[370]

In addition to the villages in the Bear River drainage, the Nekannis also had a village at the mouth of the Van Duzen, the name of which has been lost, and a village called Inako in the vicinity of Hydesville.[371] Yager Creek served as a boundary between the Bear Rivers and a branch of the Nongatl tribe called the Tce-lin-dun, who occupied the land east of the creek.[372] On the Eel, there was a Bear River village in the Rio Dell area that the Wiyots called Tokemuk. According to the Wiyot elder Dandy Bill, "some of the people were Wiyot intermarried with Athabascans."[373] Across the river at the site of Scotia was a village the Wiyots called Tokenewolok. Dandy Bill indicated that this was the lowermost village on the Eel that was purely Athabascan.[374] George Burtt, a Lolahnkok Sinkyone from Bull Creek, gave the Athabascan name Kahs-cho Ken-tel-te to the Scotia site, and Merriam, who interviewed Burtt extensively, believed that location represented the northwesternmost extent of Sinkyone territory.[375]

At least two trails connected the Bear River canyon with their tribe's territory the Eel. One ran up over Monument Ridge to the future site of Rio Dell, located on what the whites called Eagle Prairie, while the other went over Bear River Ridge and down the Howe Creek canyon.[376] A third trail, which ran up the ridge west of Weymouth Bluff to the Bunker Hill area, probably continued southward to villages in the Bear River canyon.[377]

Near the mouth of Bear River was the village of Tcodallammi,[378] which the Mattoles called Bit-ci-bi. Joe Duncan, a Mattole Indian, indicated that "Eel river Indians [Wiyots] and Bear river stay there. Bear river Indians build there in winter. Eel river Indians came there to visit."[379]

To the south, the boundary between the Bear Rivers and the Mattoles was Davis Creek.[380] Ike Duncan, a Mattole, described a battle at the creek that involved several Indian tribes:

Prairies and conifers descend towards the Bear River canyon (JR).

Eel R[iver] Ind[ian]s[,] Humboldt Ind[ian]s & Mad Riv[er] & Trin[idad] Ind[ian]s all came together to war with the Mattole Ind[ian]s. So the Mat[toles] called on the Koosky Ind[ian]s & all as allies & they had a big battle at Davis C[ree]k & some fled into the ocean. At the end of the fight some women arrived with grub—in this war the Davis C[ree]k & Single[y] Flat Ind[ian]s all got killed off. Many Eel R[iver] got many killed[;] the coast Ind[ian]s here (Weaver's [Weaver Denman?] outfit) even had to pay whale.[381] The Mat[toles] were good warriors. My father's greatgrandfather was named t'ahsi' & was a big chief of the M[attoles].[382]

Bear River informant Nora Coonskin claimed that "the Bear River were more peaceful than other tribes . . . but they sometimes aided the Mattole in their disputes with the Sinkyone and Wiyot." She does mention "one serious war with the Wiyot" that may be the battle that Ike Duncan described. According to Nora,

> As the result of a personal grievance, a Davis Creek man killed a Wiyot. The latter [tribe] retaliated by stealthily entering Bear River territory, slaughtering the sleeping people, and throwing their bodies into Davis Creek. The survivors made war on the Wiyot and killed about twenty before a money settlement was arranged.[383]

In another instance, however, negotiations averted a battle. The setting was "at Lighthouse," which probably means a less-windy location south

Southern Humboldt Tribal Groups

of the Cape Mendocino Lighthouse, such as Singley Flat. As Nora Coonskin described it,

> They had a big camp; everybody came. In the morning each side sent out both men and women. They met in the center of the ground and crossed over between each other, then returned to their own sides. All had sharp sticks and arrows. Usually two women took the lead when they crossed over. As they passed each other, one side said: "We don't want trouble!" The other side replied, "We don't want trouble!." When they had crossed over and back, all sat upon the ground facing each other and the family of the murdered man had a big cry. Then the other side began to carry things over to pay them. When they carried over enough, they all stopped crying, and all were friends again. They visited and said, "Now we are friends." Then they ate, and had a big time. If they didn't give enough payment, they fought.[384]

It appears that most disputes, like the one near the lighthouse, were settled peacefully. The ethnographic record for most of southern Humboldt documents few instances of full-scale battles and almost no prolonged conflicts that could be called "wars."[385] The local Indians seemed intent on avoiding fighting by scrupulously honoring tribal boundaries, and there is no indication of the presence of any "combat cultures" as were prevalent in other parts of native America. (See sidebar 2.)

Bear River-Mattole boundary: riparian vegetation in the foreground marks the gulch that contains Davis Creek (JR).

2. A Peaceful Place

In 1858 a party of whites traveling along the Humboldt County coast came to a village "east of Cape Mendocino." Thereupon the female villagers fled, while the males used a heretofore unseen (or unheard of) tactic to confront the visitors—they began whistling. When the leader of whites departed, he indicated that the Indians

> . . . got up from their sitting posture, and filing in single file, whistled me back to camp. . . . During the night they posted themselves in the brush and continued the serenade; and when we broke camp in the morning, they accompanied us some 4 miles, giving us specimens of their skill in the art of whistling.[386]

Thus the Bear River Indians gently defended their homeland from intrusion. In other parts of the country such behavior was inconceivable. The standard image of American Indians has long been that of raiding parties of fierce fighters, mounted on horseback and covered in war paint, galloping around a circle of covered wagons defended by a few dozen fearful whites. Movies and comic books have intensified the impression, which, although often exaggerated and over-simplified, had a certain basis in truth.

Soldiers who were fortunate enough to fight the plains Indians and survive lauded the skill of their opponents. Colonel Richard I. Dodge, a veteran of 30 years of such combat, simply called them "the finest soldiers in the world." Even before the advent of wagon trains and army forts, "fighting was a cultural imperative" for the various tribes, "and men owed their place in society to their prowess as warriors."[387]

Training for plains Indian boys began at age five or six with endurance running and swimming, followed by bow and arrow practice starting at age seven. Adolescents of fourteen or fifteen joined their first raiding party, and "by age eighteen a young man was expected to have counted coup, stolen a horse, and taken a scalp." Gaining these "war honors" led to admission into a warrior society and were often a prerequisite to taking a wife. Young Cheyenne males "could not even court girls until they had demonstrated their courage in battle or on raids." A successful warrior who was still alive at age twenty-five might become a subchief and might "have two lodges (tipis) with a wife and children in each."[388]

It was a stark, spartan existence for the plains warriors, conditioned by the

> mobility and power brought by access to the horse and gun. Wide-ranging expanses of open land offered few barriers to raiding parties and meant that territorial claims often had to be enforced by armed might without the assistance of topographical barriers.
>
> But in northwestern California, where such barriers were everywhere present, a culture of caution and compensation developed. Children, instead of being trained in the arts of warfare, were taught to know the features and boundaries of their tribal group's territory and to honor the borders as a way of maintaining peace. And when someone was harmed by someone else, punishment was replaced by payment, so that the victim held the right to receive a settlement rather than the chance to claim vengeance.
>
> It does not strain the truth to claim that for most of the Indians of southern Humboldt, peace was the peoples' goal. And if that goal was not always attained, the aspiration to achieve it was almost always present, like a blanket offering warmth on even the coldest night. Like a soft voice saying, "life is for living, not for killing, so let us do what life wants."

Kitty Prince, one of Goddard's and Merriam's Bear River informants, 1921 (MCNAP, colorized by JR).

When Pliny Goddard visited Bear River in 1907, he found one member of the tribe still in residence, his home "a rude cabin." Known only as Peter, the man indicated that his people had been "nearly exterminated in conflicts with the white settlers about Humboldt Bay." Peter told Goddard that he had been sent to the Hoopa Valley Reservation, where he was "kicked by the [Indian] agent" and where his wife died by hanging.[389] It was unclear whether her death was a suicide or an execution.

In the early 1920s another ethnographer, C. Hart Merriam, found Bear Rivers living at the Rohnerville Rancheria, where Indians from several southern Humboldt tribes had come to make their homes.[390] When Gladys Ayer Nomland came to Bear River in about 1928 to research the tribe, there was nothing left to see, since she found that "all village sites have been plowed up by white settlers."[391] Both Goddard and Merriam relied heavily on Kitty Prince, who was born about 1840,[392] for their information, while Nomland's main source was Nora Coonskin, the niece of Goddard's informant Peter.[393]

2. Mattole

Much of the information about the territory of the Mattole Indians comes from Joe Duncan, who was probably born in the early 1840s.[394] In 1907 he traveled through his homeland with Pliny Goddard, revealing the locations of significant places. Although the Mattole-Bear River tribal boundary was Davis Creek, Duncan mentions places as far north as Set-co-be-nin-do-nin, a campsite north of the Cape Mendocino lighthouse, and indicates that Set-co-din was the Mattole tribe's name for the area around the lighthouse itself.[395]

Mattole territory ran down the coast from Davis Creek to the vicinity of the Mackey Ranch, which lay between Sea Lion Gulch and Cookie Creek.[396] From there, as best as can be determined, the boundary went north onto Johnny Jack Ridge, continuing on ridgelines to Cookie Mountain, then ran northwest on Prosper Ridge, and next turned northeast until it dropped to cross the Mattole at the northern end of Shenanigan Ridge.[397] Thence the boundary headed east and then northeast, probably following Everts Ridge, Van Schoaick Ridge, and Little Rainbow Ridge until it reached Rainbow Ridge somewhat north of South Rainbow Peak. It appears that the border then ran north along Rainbow Ridge, turned west at Rainbow Peak, and then generally headed west over Griffith Hill and Walker Ridge to reach the coast near the mouth of Davis Creek.[398]

In at least one instance, the Mattoles ceded a small part of their territory to Wiyot Indians from the Eel River. Ike Duncan, Joe's son, stated in an interview with Harold E. Driver that

> [A] prominent man from Eel R[iver] [a Wiyot] was criticized by a Mattole for not paying enough for tarweed seed. In anger he struck a Mattole man's wife. Dispute finally grew into war with Eel R[iver] Indians vs. Bear R[iver] and Mattole R[iver] Indians. Eel R[iver] suffered heaviest losses, so "big doctor" or chief of Mattole gave them tarweed field at Morgan's Pt., a few miles S of Bear R[iver]. Both sides exchanged women (for wives) as part of settlement.[399]

The Wiyot Indian Amos Riley gave what might be another version of the same incident:

> [A] certain Wiyot was visiting with Mattole Indians near Petrolia. An argument started and he kicked over food receptacles at a meal. They came to blows and [the] Wiyot was killed. War between Wiyot and Mattole followed.[400]

After whites arrived in the area, it took but a few years for the federal government to attempt to gain control over the Mattoles and other coastal tribes. Thus the Mendocino Indian Reservation was established by Superintendent T. J. Henley in 1856. A year later the agent in charge indicated that the reservation's northern boundary was at Bear River, in Humboldt County. This information was not well received by white residents in the Bear River-Mattole area. By late 1858 Superintendent Henley, his bureaucrat's ears burning from expressions of outrage, had drastically reduced the size of the reservation, so that it extended a mere 10 miles north of the Noyo River in Mendocino County. The following year the Indian Department, having "entertained charges of fraud and malfeasance made against Henley," removed him from office. His successor, J. Y. McDuffie, "easily

North Fork Mattole River, where Joe Duncan escaped from a white slaver (CEFP, colorized by JR).

adjusted" the trouble Henley had caused, and "in December, 1859, the last claim to lands in the Mattole Valley was given up by the government officials."[401]

The fate that befell the Mattoles was no different than that of other rural Humboldt tribes— time and again white vigilantes and militia attacked and otherwise mistreated the Indians with impunity, and with little public outcry about what they had done. Joe Duncan, who lived near the mouth of the Mattole River, told part of the story. (See sidebar 3.)

Duncan indicated that his grandfather was killed near the mouth of the Mattole "the day the whites cleaned them out."[402] He provided no other details about the massacre.

At an unknown date, but probably in the early 1860s, several Mattole Indians fled from the lower Mattole River to the vicinity of Fort Seward, having been "driven from the valley by the activities of the white citizens and soldiers."[403] They may, however, have also encountered hostility at their destination, which about that time was the site of a massacre of numerous Lassik Indians.[404]

Joe Duncan and his son Ike eventually obtained separate Indian allotments near the mouth of the Mattole.[405] This put them close to offshore locations where the Mattoles had traditionally hunted, such as Sea Lion Rock.[406] By the 1920s Joe, Ike, and about 20 other Indians, including some from the Wiyot tribe, held allotments in the lower Mattole vicinity.[407]

3. "I never sleep at night."

Joe Duncan was captured near the Goff place, southwest of Petrolia, by a man who wanted to "use him as a slave." He was kept overnight near Petrolia and then taken up the North Fork Mattole. Joe "jumped off the horse and ran all the way back to the mouth of the river," so that "they did not get him." But the next winter a man named Duncan did catch him and Joe "lived there [at Duncan's] some time." When he "was about grown" Joe left and started for the Smith River Reservation in Del Norte County "to see his people." Joe met up with some Hupa women near the Cape Mendocino Lighthouse and went to Hoopa with two of them. He lived there with a woman for three years at Medilden village. Then Joe "managed to get away and went to Smith River." He returned briefly to Hoopa but stayed only a short time.[408] These early experiences left Joe suffering from what today would be called post-traumatic stress. He told C. Hart Merriam that:

Joe Duncan, 1907: Goddard's main Mattole informant (DTC, colorized by JR).

> I never sleep at night. I saw first white men—10 or 12 years old. They hunt Indians, kill 'em off, only few left. Lots they kill, women, babies. So I get out of here; run to Eel River. Then they fight all over. White men too much fight. Nothing any peace. Nothing in the world.
>
> White man take Indians Smith River Reservation. Indians go. White man make 'em work; work for white people. Women, children, everybody, make 'em work. That's what white man did. Keep him down, Indian people. Three men boss; go round and make 'em work; make plow. If he go slow, kick him, hit him club; kill 'em right on road.
>
> Government all right. Government send grub, blankets, clothes. Agent sell on road. Government don't know. One Indian find out. We don't do this any more. Government take land, sell to citizens. They not pay us. We

> shortly see. Government after while say, "Send Indians home where born." They sent home. Government send them to Hoopa; herd 'em like sheep. Not enough grub. One eat full not enough for everybody. Starvation come; some die hungry. Then Government agent come, kill 6 or 7 cattle; not enough. Government send two men. More talk. Tell us go any place where want to, go any place where belong. We come back here. Everything quiet down.
>
> [Whites] shoot lots men, take women. No more Indian. Woman all gone. Many men burned. Woman once in while. Kill 'em off.
>
> They kill grandfather, grandmother, all—all killed. Indians no guns. White man take 'em out; tell 'em "You go this way in brush; then kill 'em. First settlers pretty bad. Hoopa fight for land; kill white man; chase in River and kill 'em.
>
> President Abe Lincoln going give back land. They kill him. That done; all settled; all gone.[409]

B. Sinkyone Tribe

Goddard, interviewing Indians in the 1900s, heard references to Sin-ki-kok, the South Fork Eel River; Sin-ke-ne, the name for his informant Briceland Charlie's tribal group; and Sinkyone, the neighboring Nongatl tribe's word for the "South Fork Indians."[410] Goddard used the latter word for the name of a collection of Indian groups whose territory extended from the lower South Fork Eel to the Usal area in northern Mendocino County. He brought the term into common usage when he provided a short statement about the Sinkyones for Hodge's 1910 *Handbook of American Indians North of Mexico, part 2*,[411] in which he claimed there was a southern section of the tribe called the Usal and a northern part known as the Lolanko.[412] Nothing in Goddard's field notes explains the reason for this bifurcation.

In all, Goddard interviewed five Indians that he considered Sinkyone: George Burtt from Bull Creek, Briceland Charlie from Salmon Creek, Sam Suder from the Miranda area, Sally Bell[413] from Shelter Cove, and Albert Smith from the East Branch South Fork Eel. Taken together, these five elders provided first-hand accounts about most, but not all, of Sinkyone territory. They also described and located numerous Sinkyone tribal groups. This information would have provided Goddard with ample material for a monograph on the Sinkyones, which he probably would have written if he had stayed longer in California.

But Goddard did not stay and did not write the monograph. So things stood until the early 1920s, when C. Hart Merriam interviewed the three Sinkyone informants of Goddard's that were still alive, along with Indians from neighboring groups. One of Merriam's goals was to create a complete geography of the local tribes, but he lacked enough information to fully accomplish this. Instead, he stretched tribal boundaries beyond what his evidence supported. Based on the three Sinkyones' responses, Merriam decided that each informant represented a large and distinct tribal entity. As Merriam saw it, George Burtt was from a Lolahnkok tribe on the lower South Fork Eel, Sally Bell belonged to

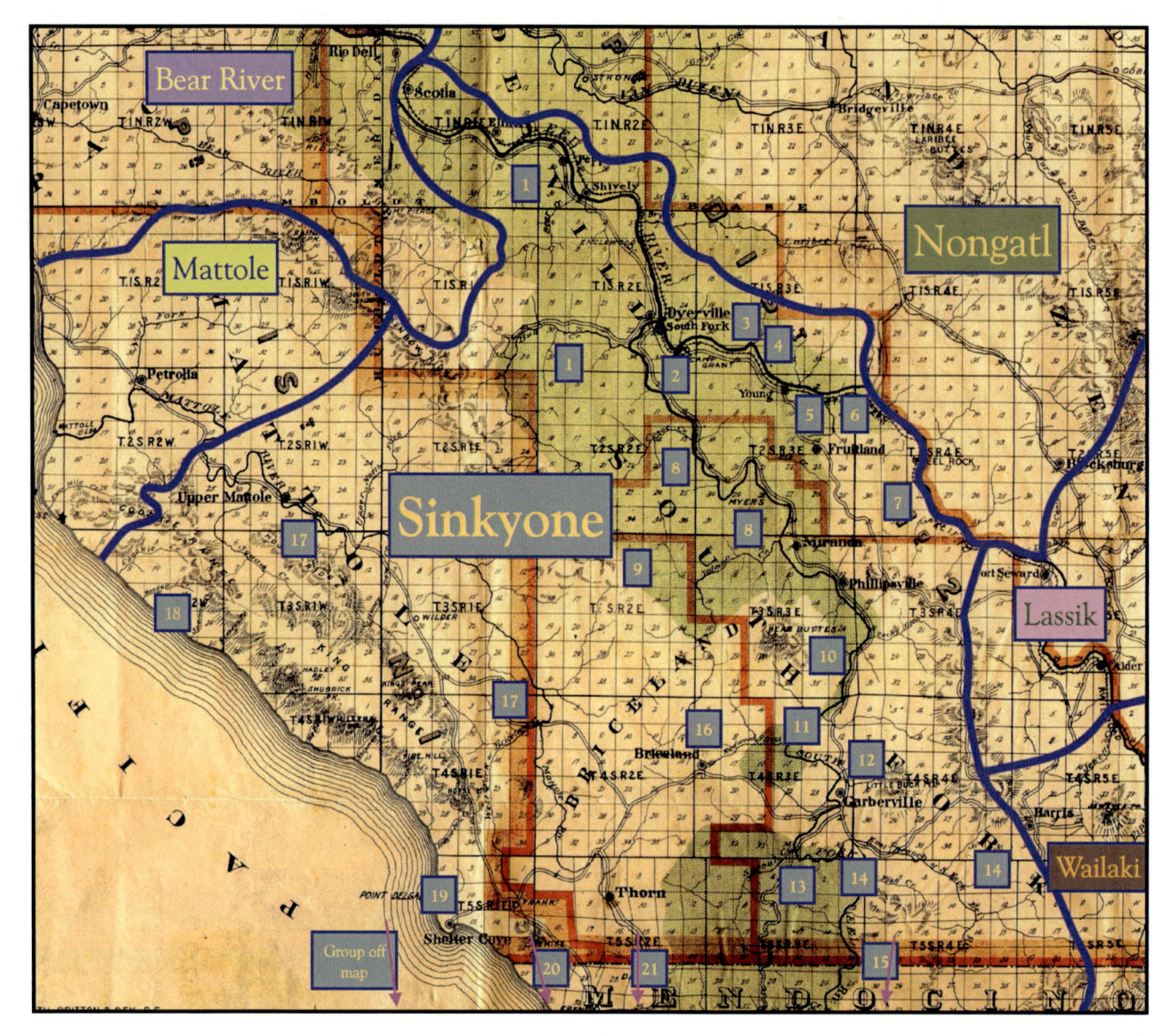

Sinkyone territory, showing approximate location of the 21 tribal groups mentioned in the text (JR).

a To-cho-be tribe that had occupied the Briceland area and was connected with "bands speaking the same dialect from west side South Fork Eel River (in Garberville region) to coast," and Albert Smith (from whom he collected little information) was from a To-kub-be group that inhabited the East Branch South Fork Eel area and which Merriam believed was affiliated with the Lassik Indians on the far side of Mail Ridge.[414] In this way Merriam completed his map of southwestern Humboldt, but he did so without the benefit of most of Goddard's material and asserted more than what was claimed by his own informants.

When Gladys Ayer Nomland published *Sinkyone Notes* in 1935 she did not mention Goddard's or Merriam's divisions of the tribe and instead mapped a single Sinkyone territory that ranged from north of Dyerville to Usal.[415] She included a considerable amount of cultural information, but, as indicated earlier, it was based on sources of questionable reliability. Then, in 1958, Martin Baumhoff's *California Athabascan Groups* included a section on the Sinkyones that divided the tribe into a northern, or "Lolangkok" [sic] unit, and a southern unit that he called the Shelter Cove Sinkyone.[416] Using Goddard's village

Southern Humboldt Tribal Groups

notecards as a sort of guide, Baumhoff chose for his division point the approximate boundary between two Sinkyone tribal groups, Briceland Charlie's Sinkenes and Sam Suder's people, the line of which crossed the South Fork near Fish Creek.[417]

So it was that over the course of half a century, four ethnographers each created a version of a Sinkyone tribe, but none of them—including Goddard himself—could, or would, make full use of the one resource that far outshone all the others, Goddard's field notes.

Now comes yet another chance to use the notebooks, and what follows is based largely on the information contained within them. In broad strokes, Goddard's notes support an expanded scope of Sinkyone territory by adding the following areas: 1) the main Eel River from Dyerville to the vicinity of High Rock; 2) the South Fork Eel drainage, on *both* sides of the river,[418] from its mouth southward to the boundary with the Kato tribe in northern Mendocino County, including the East Branch drainage and the Sproul Creek drainage; 3) the Mattole River drainage from about Conklin Creek south to the Mattole's headwaters; 4) coastal areas from about Cooskie Creek south to Spanish Flat. In addition, a closer look at Merriam's material further extends the Sinkyones' northern boundary, moving it all the way downriver to Scotia.

Based primarily on Goddard's information, supplemented by some of Merriam's material, we know the approximate boundaries of eighteen Sinkyone tribal groups and the names of sixteen

Northern Sinkyone country: Tah-cho, the main Eel River, as seen from Sa-cho-te, High Rock (JR).

of them. There are also three other areas within Sinkyone territory where the names and boundaries of the groups are uncertain. It thus appears likely that there were a minimum of twenty-one Sinkyone tribal groups.

1. Lolahnkok

Lolahnkok was both the name of the stream that is now called Bull Creek and of the tribal group that occupied the drainage.[419] The exact extent of Lolahnkok territory is uncertain, but melding and harmonizing information from Merriam and Goddard creates a plausible geography.[420]

Using statements from George Burtt, Merriam concluded that the Lolahnkoks' northern boundary was at the future site of Scotia. Their territory then ran upriver on the main Eel to the South Fork.[421] According to Merriam's working map, Lolahnkok land along this section of the main Eel included both of sides of the valley up to the ridgelines.[422]

There was a Lolahnkok village in the Scotia area called Kahs-cho ken-tel-te.[423] Across the river, at the future site of Rio Dell, was the Bear River tribe's community of Tokemuk,[424] which also included some Wiyot Indians who had intermarried with the landholders. Kahs-cho ken-tel-te, however, was fully Athabascan, and the Wiyot Indian Amos Riley remarked that the inhabitants were "nice people."[425] Upriver from Scotia, George Burtt provided place names for the flats where the towns of Pepperwood, Shively, Holmes, and Redcrest were later built.[426] Briceland Charlie named four other locations, ranging from below High Rock to the Dyerville area, that Goddard recorded.[427]

At the confluence of the main Eel and the South Fork, Charlie gave the place name Ltcin-ta-din,[428] while Burtt called the spot Chin-tah-tah.[429]

At this point, the Lolahnkoks' land on the main Eel ended, but it extended up the South Fork to a point about half a mile south of the mouth of Bull Creek.[430] It also included the entire drainage of Bull Creek.[431]

2. Nal-tcunk-kuk-ki-a (Nal-tcun-ka)
3. Ta-dut-tci-ki-a
4. Ki-lun-dun-ki-a (Tcil-lun-dun)
5. Kuc-tco-be-ki-a (Gac-tco-be)
6. Se-ta-dun-ki-a (Se-da-dun)

These five small Sinkyone tribal groups were located in close succession on the main Eel River, ranging from below Camp Grant to the vicinity of Cameron Creek. Briceland Charlie was the sole source of this information.[432] On the north side of the Eel it appears that the Sinkyone-Nongatl boundary was east of the Se-ta-dun-ki-a, probably just upriver from Cameron Creek, with the Nongatl tribe occupying the northeast side of the Eel for the next stretch upriver.[433]

7. Unnamed tribal group or groups on west side of Eel River upstream from Eel Rock

It is unclear which Indian tribe or group occupied the western side of the main Eel from the vicinity of Tanoak (later a railroad stop) upriver (southward) to the vicinity of Fort Seward. Goddard reported that the land on the eastern side of the river was inhabited by speakers of Se-nun-ka,[434] one of the dialects of the Nongatl tribe, but he does not name the tribal group. He gives no indication that the Nongatls claimed the land on the opposite side of the Eel. This suggests, but does not prove, that the river served as the boundary between two tribes—an unusual situation. The candidate tribe for the western side of the Eel is the Sinkyones, whose Se-ta-dun-ki-a tribal group

The heart of Lolahnkok country: Grasshopper Peak rises behind the canyon of Bull Creek (JR).

occupied the area immediately downstream. And thus it appears on this book's tribal territories map, albeit provisionally.

8. Sinkene

Most of the information about the Sinkenes was obtained from Briceland Charlie, himself a member of the group, who was "about 10 when [the] white men came."[435] He told Goddard that the "Redwood and Briceland people came over and killed his people." Then "his people went over and made even."[436]

Charlie described villages that Goddard indicates were Sinkene lying along the South Fork Eel from about a mile upriver from Bull Creek to a short distance above Butte Creek.[437] All or most of the Salmon Creek drainage also belonged to the Sinkenes, who had numerous villages along the lower sections of the creek.[438]

9. Chi-chin-kah ke-ah

George Burtt told Merriam that this "band" occupied Elk Ridge (Chi-chin-kah) and the area adjacent the headwaters of Bull Creek.[439] This may have meant the group spilled over into the upper Salmon Creek drainage east of the ridge. It would have been most unusual for a tribal group to occupy only a ridgeline area without having territory for lower-elevation winter village sites.

Harrington interviewed the Mattole Indian Johnny Jackson, who told him that:

> Southfork Jack was of the Elk Ridge lang[uage] & said that there was a lang[uage] division there, 2 dialects joining each other.[440]

It is unclear which dialects Jackson referred to. The tribal groups known to be nearby were the Lolahnkoks from Bull Creek, the Sinkenes

Sinkene Country: upper Salmon Creek drainage, 1908 (CEFP, colorized by JR).

from Salmon Creek, the To-cho-be ke-ahs from Briceland, and the "upper Mattole people" from the Honeydew-Ettersburg area. All four groups are considered part of the Sinkyone tribe.

10. Sam's people

Goddard apparently failed to obtain a name for this group, which he simply calls "Sam's people," a reference to his informant Sam Suder. Goddard indicates that the group's northern boundary was on the South Fork Eel upriver from Fish Creek.[441] The group's southernmost locale that Goddard specifically notes was in the vicinity of Dean Creek.[442]

Sam indicated that his people danced in a "large round conical house" called a ne-git. To the north, Charlie's people (Sinkene) and George's (Lolahnkok) did not have this structure but instead they "danced in [a] brush enclosure open above."[443] Suder died under unusual circumstances. (See sidebar 4.)

11. Unnamed tribal group or groups between Dean Creek and Bear Canyon

There is no known tribal group affiliation for the area along the South Fork Eel between Dean Creek and Bear Canyon. Albert Smith, Goddard's informant from the East Branch South Fork, named a village, Ltug-ga-no-bi, in the Redway area, but Goddard does not record the name of any group associated with it.[444] Since there are rugged stretches of the South Fork canyon both upstream

4. A History Book Closes

When ethnographers began visiting Humboldt County in the early 1900s they embarked on a race with time. They sought out Indian elders whose memories went back to the middle of the 19th century or earlier, people who could describe their tribe's culture before it had been disrupted by the violence unleashed upon it by the newly arrived whites. In many cases there were no members of a particular tribal group left. In other situations there were only a handful of elders available to interview. Sometimes, as was the case with Sam Suder,[445] there was only one.

Pliny Goddard interviewed Suder in 1903.[446] He learned that Sam's wife, Polly, was a Lolahnkok from Bull Creek.[447] Sam had spent time at the Smith River Reservation in Del Norte County and at the Hoopa Reservation in Humboldt County.[448] Sometime after 1898 he and Polly each obtained a 160-acre Indian Allotment on Blue Slide Creek about two miles northwest of Briceland. North of them in the creek drainage were the allotments of four Indians who were members of the Woodman family.[449]

Most of the information Sam provided Goddard concerned the names of various plants and animals. Although Sam indicated that "old people never used to go to ocean,"[450] he gave words for whale (te-tu-lan), clams (sa-ba-kyo), and mussels (ke-sai-kto).[451] Sam did not provide a word for beaver, which suggests they may not have inhabited his home territory; George Burtt, who lived on Bull Creek, told Merriam that Ba-chen-tel ("tail flat") was the Lolahnkok word for the animal.[452]

Sam also gave a few other words and some miscellaneous information, including names and locations of various important places.[453] And that was about it. The Sam notebook ends on page 13, indicating a much shorter interview than what Goddard usually conducted. Perhaps Sam was difficult to communicate with, or perhaps Goddard hoped to interview him again at a later date, but the chance to do so ended on January 15, 1908, when Sam died.[454]

His passing merited a headline in the *Humboldt Standard*: "Indian's Death Creates A Stir." The article stated that "it was learned that Indian Sam had been threatened with poisoning by one of his tribe, so an inquest was held." A jury of seven men, including the part-Indian[455] Truman Merrifield, concluded that Sam had "died of old age." It turned out there had been considerable excitement prior to Sam's death:

> On Sunday an Indian came running to the home of Alec Holman, saying that Indian Sam was dead and asking that a coffin be built, but an hour later he returned with the news that the dead man had returned to life. On Monday morning, however, he died in earnest. . . .[456]
>
> Readers who chuckled at the story might, on reflection, have wondered if the *Standard* would have given a similar death of a white person the same sort of sardonic treatment.
>
> Sam's death certificate, which recorded his last name as Solto, indicated that he was a "laborer," 60 years old, and had died from peritonitis.[457] If the age given for him is accurate, he would have been a youngster when the whites cut through his tribe's territory like a scythe—a mindless force, impersonal, bent only on cutting. When Goddard interviewed him, Sam was the last link to a people's past that otherwise would have escaped attention—that would have floated out onto the ocean of obscurity like debris upon the South Fork Eel, upon the immutable river of time.

and downstream from the flat at Redway, the resultant isolation of the area suggests that Ltug-ga-no-bi may have comprised most or all of the members of a distinct tribal group.

12. Ko-se-ke

There was a village in the vicinity of Garberville called Ko-se-ke, which appears to have also been the name of a tribal group. George Burtt told Merriam that the "Garberville tribe" was called the "Ko-se-ke."[458] When Burtt and Merriam drove up the South Fork in 1923 Merriam noted that "Ko-se-che" was an "area on both sides of the river" in the vicinity of Garberville.[459] Sam Suder gave Goddard "kosciki" as the name of a location "a short way below Garberville."[460] Charlie gave "ko se tci" as "Garberville"[461] and then spoke of "Garberville" as if it encompassed a tribal group: "Garberville Indians come," "Garberville they talk like us," "Garberville fellows," "Garberville Indians."[462] Sam, however, told Goddard that Sebiyedadun was "a village at Garberville," and elsewhere Charlie referred to "kos se tci" or "kos e tci" as a location "just below Garberville."[463] Goddard also records several other nearby locations of Indian activity.[464] Although it seems clear that a tribal group called the Ko-se-ke was centered in the Garberville area, the extent of its territory along the South Fork is uncertain.

13. Nas-lin-tci ke-ah

Nas-lin-kok was the name for Sproul Creek. There were two villages near the creek's mouth. Net-nah-la-ki was apparently somewhat north of the creek and Nas-lin-tci somewhat to the south.[465] Albert Smith, whose tribal group was located just upriver and included the East Branch South Fork Eel, told Goddard that "Nas lin tci is as far down as Albert's people came."[466] According to three of Merriam's interviewees this village gave

Briceland Charlie in Chi-chin-kah ke-ah country at a distinctive outcropping on Elk Ridge, 1908 (CEFP, colorized by JR).

its name to the Sproul Creek tribal group.[467] The extent of Nas-lin-tci ke-ah territory is not known, except that it went no farther up the South Fork than its namesake village. It probably included, at a minimum, the entire Sproul Creek drainage. Indians from the Cahto tribe, which occupied the uppermost section of the South Fork Eel, gave "Nahs-ling-che ke-ah-hahng" as their name for the "Garberville tribe" that occupied the "South F[or]k Eel to coast."[468]

14. To-kub-be ke-ah

Albert Smith was interviewed extensively by Goddard and very briefly by Merriam. He provided Goddard with detailed information about the territory of his tribal group. According to Albert, his people occupied the canyon of the South Fork Eel from above Sproul Creek[469] to the vicinity of the Joseph D. Smith Ranch,[470] which was located about two miles downriver from later-day Richardson Grove State Park. In addition, they claimed the entire East Branch (Ke-no-lug-ge-ke)[471] drainage, from the South Fork eastward to the top of Mail Ridge.[472]

In September 1907 Goddard interviewed Smith at his home near the South Fork Eel. Albert begins by giving Goddard several pages of vocabulary—"tis tca" is wind, "Ltuk ka" is black oak, etc. But then a word will set Smith off on a digres-

The South Fork Eel southwest of Garberville, 1929. The area on both sides of the Briceland Road bridge was probably Ko-se-ke territory. The Nas-lin-tci ke-ahs occupied the Sproul Creek drainage, which lies in the V-shaped canyon just above the center of the photograph (FM, colorized by JR).

sion that opens a door to the life of his people. He gives "nun" as the term for an Indian house and suddenly he is talking about how the To-kub-be ke-ahs built their dwellings. They "split redwood" using an "elkhorn wedge" and a "stone hammer." They dug a hole for the firepit and packed the dirt out. From the door they would "build out [a] kind of porch way out." And the "roof was made of split redwood."[473] For a moment the word list is forgotten as Albert creates an image from the long-ago past, an image of something that may never be seen again.

Goddard did not record Smith's name for his own tribal group, but Merriam learned from George Burtt and Sally Bell that at least some Indians on the East Branch were called the To-kub-be ke-ah,[474] from the name of one of their villages in the area. Goddard's informant Sam indicated that "To-kub-bi" was an "Indian town on ridge above Garberville,"[475] which could mean it was in the East Branch drainage. Smith died before Merriam collected much information from him, and in the absence of any tribal affiliation claimed directly by Smith, Merriam identified him as a member of the To-kub-be ke-ah group.[476]

In addition to listing strings of villages in the canyons of both the South Fork Eel and the East Branch, Smith described several summer camp sites.[477] He noted that that at Das-an-dun, on the ridgetop between the South Fork and main Eel drainages, there was a "big camp there, like picnic ground."[478] Albert's accounts that Goddard recorded are filled with information about himself and his tribe at the time of their greatest trouble. (See sidebar 5.)

5. South Fork Survivor

Albert Smith was probably born at Ke-no-lug-ga-tci-ye, a village part way up the East Branch South Fork Eel.[479] His father was killed by other Indians before Albert's birth.[480] This may have happened when Wailakis from the Blue Rock area in northern Mendocino County came down and fought with Albert's people: ". . . all day they shot this way some one way they chase south they chase north they there after a while they quit."[481]

Other difficulties came soon enough, for Albert's boyhood coincided with the arrival of the whites. Albert told of soldiers taking some of his people away and the remaining Indians being killed. One time, to avoid detection, he "was hid under a basket." Some of his people escaped to Red Mountain, which was "not their country," and then came back to the South Fork to Lug-gus-dun, upriver from Benbow. One day, John Wood and some other men were riding up a nearby hillside. Wood looked back, took aim, and shot and killed Albert's mother.[482] According to Albert, Jim Wood, John's brother, "kill women and men. Ross big tall man [also] kill our folks."[483]

Up near the Bell Springs Road, at a pond east of the head of Tom Long Creek called Bun-kut-tco-tcin-ne-dun, was the place where soldiers, according to Albert, "kill all my people."[484] Albert's two older brothers were killed there by the soldiers, "one on an open hillside," while the other's body was found two days later in the brush.[485]

Somehow Albert managed to survive the series of murders and massacres that claimed several members of his family. Eventually he spent half a winter at Hoopa. An Indian named Kneeland Jack was the "boss" there. He told Albert, "don't kill anybody [and] you may go home." He apparently did not do any killing and that summer came back to southern Humboldt.[486]

Eventually Albert married Sally Alford. She had previously been married to another Indian, name unknown, who was noted for singing elk and deer songs, probably in connection with hunting them.[487] For a time the Smiths lived in a cabin on the flat where the Benbow Lake State Recreation Area campground was later built.[488] It was probably while the Smiths were living there that Goddard made his September 1907 visit and interviewed Albert, perhaps also receiving a little information from Sally.[489] A photo from about that time shows the Smiths standing together, fishing in the South Fork.[490]

Albert and Sally would go to the Elk Ridge area during summers. This was a place where several other local Indians, including Jack and Jennie

Woodman, Hanson Woodman, and Sam and Polly Suder, had Indian Allotments.[491] The Smiths had their picture taken in nearby Briceland about 1907 by professional photographer Ray Jerome Baker.[492]

Sally Smith died at the home of her daughter near East's Ferry in west Fortuna in 1920. Her obituary made no mention of Albert.[493]

In both 1921 and 1922 C. Hart Merriam interviewed Albert "near Fortuna," which probably means Albert was living at the Rohnerville Indian Rancheria. Merriam determined that Albert "had lived with related tribes, especially the To-cho-be ke-ah of Briceland and the Lolahnkok of Bull Creek and South Fork River." On his second visit, Merriam found Albert "sick in bed and too feeble to give much information." In fact, Albert then passed away, causing Merriam to remark that "he died before I was half finished with him."[494]

Thus Albert's death was considered inopportune by Merriam, who recorded

Albert and Sally Smith, probably at Briceland, 1907 (CPH, colorized by JR).

barely more than a score of the Indian's words. But 15 years earlier, Goddard had filled page after page of his notebooks with Albert's accounts, which provided both a history and a geography of the To-kub-be ke-ahs. Albert, who had managed to survive a time when his family and almost all of his kinfolk had been killed, had lived long enough for his story to be heard—but just not by Merriam.

15. Unnamed tribal group or groups on South Fork Eel south of the To-kub-be ke-ahs

There is little information about the area along the South Fork upriver from To-kub-be ke-ah territory. No Indians were ever interviewed from this rugged, remote country. At Richardson Grove was the village of Kahs-cho-so-be, which probably belonged to an unknown Sinkyone tribal group. A few miles farther south, there likely was a village near the mouth of Indian Creek that also belonged to an unknown tribal group.[495] Then, a few more miles south, near the mouth of Red Mountain Creek, was the village of Lheeliingchowding, which probably belonged to either the Cahto tribe[496] or to a Wailaki tribal group called the Tsen-nah-ken-nes, which, according to Merriam's informant Wylakke Tip, ranged westward from the main Eel across the Bell Springs-Blue Rock ridge all the way to the South Fork. The area between the river and the coast probably belonged to the Tco-kun-ni-tci, the Sinkyone tribal group at Usal.[497]

16. To-cho-be ke-ah

Sally Bell provided Merriam with this name for the people of the Briceland region, where there was a village called To-cho-be.[498] Bell's mother's family was from Garberville,[499] and Bell herself was born at Shelter Cove.[500] (See sidebar 6.) It appears that To-cho-be was the village attacked by Pierce Asbill and his gang of white vigilantes at an undetermined date in the 1860s. The surviving Indians fled and were pursued for days, many of them finally being caught and killed near Island Mountain.[501]

The only site in the vicinity of Briceland specifically linked to Indian inhabitation was an

To-kub-be ke-ah territory southwest of Das-an-dun (JR).

6. Saving a Life

It was late one night in 1901 and all was not well at Four Corners, the tiny crossroads community near the head of the Mattole River, just over the line in Mendocino County. Fred Wolf was waiting to be born in the family's cabin, next to the saloon that Fred's dad owned. The Wolfs had called a doctor in Garberville, but he drove a horse and cart—a slow form of transportation—and hadn't arrived yet. The family asked Sally Bell, the old Indian woman who lived next door, to help.

And sure enough, Fred needed it. Seven decades later, he described what happened:

> . . . Sally delivered me. It was three o'clock in the morning, and I was a blue baby. Well, she mumbled something to old Tom [her husband] in Injun, and he took off. He come back, Dad said, with a bunch of roots about like that and she had a pot of water goin', she threw them roots in there and steeped it up, whatever it was. Dad said just as quick as I took it, I commenced to perk up.[502]

It was a close brush with death for little Fred, a situation that the Bells already knew something about. Sally had witnessed the massacre of several members of her family, including her baby sister, by whites at Needle Rock, a location on the coast several miles south of Four Corners.[503] Not far away Tom Bell and his brother, both young children, survived a massacre at Shelter Cove in 1861. They were found crying in the woods, were rescued, and were subsequently raised in Mendocino County by a man named Sam Bell.[504]

Sally Bell, at her home at Four Corners, 1923 (MCNAP, colorized by JR).

> If white vigilantes had succeed in their aims, neither Sally nor Tom Bell would have been alive 40 years later to save the life of Fred Wolf. And if Sally and Tom had held a hatred of the whites in their hearts, they would not have bestirred themselves to keep Fred Wolf from dying. But the Bells had been, as a phrase so aptly puts it, "tempered by the fires of negation,"[505] and that tempering had left them not despising life, but honoring it.

area northeast of town.[506] However, Goddard's informant Briceland Charlie stated that there "was rancheria all over Briceland." He added the all-too-frequent statement, "all dead now."[507]

17. Unnamed tribal group on the middle Mattole River

This group is referred to by Goddard simply as the "upper Mattole people." It occupied the Mattole River valley from about Indian Creek, some three-and-a-half miles southeast of Petrolia, southward to at least the Ettersburg area. Goddard received information about the group from Briceland Charlie, who lived in the neighboring drainage of Salmon Creek, which lay eastward on the far side of Elk Ridge. Goddard noted that "all these people on [upper] Mattole are probably Charlie's kind, not Mattole Indians."[508] Their southernmost known village, Lenillimi, was likely near their southern boundary.[509] Most accounts erroneously show this group's territory as belonging

"Upper Mattole people" territory near Honeydew (JR).

to the Mattole tribe, but Goddard's field notes clearly indicate that Mattole land ended east of Petrolia near Conklin Creek.[510]

18. Yi-na-ki (Kuskic)

The Yi-na-ki occupied the coast south of the Mattole tribe. Their name came from Yi-na-tci, an area later called Spanish Flat.[511] The group's northern boundary was on the north side of Cooskie Creek, which the Yi-na-kis called Kuskic, a name Goddard applies to the tribal group. Goddard, who received information about this group from Joe Duncan, used both names,[512] but at one point quoted Joe as saying "yin a ki the people [while] kus kic [is the] land's name."[513] Elsewhere Goddard records Joe as saying "yi na ki the people who owned from Kooskie south."[514] The Yi-na-kis' southern boundary reportedly was in the vicinity of Spanish Flat. Goddard also called them "Shelter Cove people,"[515] but this appears incorrect. Duncan told him that the Yi-na-kis had a "language like the Shelter Cove [people] who talk like the Briceland people not like Mattole [people]."[516] It appears from this that the Yi-na-kis were a Sinkyone tribal group, closely connected with the group south of them, the To-not-ken, who occupied the territory around Shelter Cove.[517]

Duncan described two massacres of the Yi-na-kis:

> . . . whites came down [to Spanish Flat]... after killing on Mattole and killed all but women. Messenger was sent to warn them and whites came almost as soon as him. 3 years after [later] killed woman, child everything at last to stop breeding because some were wild and stayed in hills.[518]

Duncan does not give dates for these events, but it is clear from his account that the attacks were genocidal in intent.

19. To-not-ken (Tan-a-dun ki-a, Tahng-i-ka-ah)

In 1853 members of the Coast Survey landed at what they named Shelter Cove. They encountered the local Indians, who had a village next to the cove. These people said that the cove was called To-not-ken, the same word as their name for themselves.[519] Fifty years later, Pliny E. Goddard interviewed Briceland Charlie, who told him that Shelter Cove was called Tan-a-un and the people from there were the Tan-a-dun ki-a.[520] A third name, Tahng-i-ka-ah, came from Sally Bell.[521] She also told of a massacre of the To-not-kens: "At Big Flat used to be lots of Indians. [I] saw [rifle?] shells after they were killed."[522]

20. Tcil-le-dun ki-a

Briceland Charlie told Goddard that the name for Needle Rock and "the whole place including Bear Harbor" was Tcil-le-dun. The people from the area accordingly called themselves the Tcil-le-dun ki-a.[523] Merriam disagreed, citing Sally Bell's claim that the Needle Rock Indians were part of the Tahng-i-ka-ah, the group that occupied Shelter Cove.[524] By the time Merriam interviewed Bell, however, she may have been the victim of a failing memory.[525] Tom Bell, who grew up in northern Mendocino County in Coast Yuki territory, indicated that the Coast Yukis sometimes traveled as far north as Needle Rock and at times even lived there.[526]

21. Tco-kun-ni-tci (Yo-tci, Yo-sawl)

Merriam claimed that this group extended northward from Usal Creek, which is located in northwestern Mendocino County.[527] He indicated that south of Usal was a tribe he called the Oh-ko-ton-til-lik-kah,[528] which is otherwise known as the Coast Yuki.[529] In 1923 Sally Bell told Merriam that the name for Usal was Chaw-ken-na-che,[530] but 16 years earlier she had told Goddard that the place was known as Yo-tci.[531] Goddard's informant Albert Smith gave Tco-kun-ni-tci as the name for Usal. Smith added that the Usal people "talk like Tom Bell. Talk different from here [South Fork Eel East Branch]."[532] Tom was married to Sally Bell.[533] By his own account he was a Coast Yuki,[534] but his obituary indicated that he survived a massacre at Shelter Cove when a small child,[535] raising the possibility that he was actually a member of one of the Sinkyone tribal groups. In any case, both Sinkyone and Coast Yuki dialects were spoken at Usal.[536] Merriam indicated that the Coast Yuki said that the Indians there were called Yo-sawl, who themselves pronounced the name that way.[537]

C. Wailaki Tribe

Probably no local tribe's name is more confusing than that of "Wailaki." Powers applied the term in 1877 to all the Indian groups who lived from Hayfork southward to the North Fork Eel and the main Eel.[538] Early-day whites in the area near where the boundaries of Humboldt, Trinity, and Mendocino counties met used "Wylackie" or some variant for virtually all of the local Indians.[539] Goddard made sure the name stuck, but applied it to a more select collection of Indians, when he published his "Habitat of the Wailaki" in 1923.[540] His grouping has generally prevailed to this day, describing three major divisions, all connected with the Eel River, within the Wailaki umbrella term.

Goddard, writing in 1923, stated that:

In the middle of the last century there were living along Eel river, in a distance easily traveled by horseback in a day, eighteen small political divisions of the Wailaki, each having a chief and a definite territory, which included hunting and fishing grounds and favorable places for winter villages. Of these winter villages there were approximately sixty-six, not counting rock shelters and places where only one or two houses were situated....

The population is hard to estimate. There certainly were no less than a thousand and possibly twice as many. This estimate would yield an average population of fifteen to thirty per village, and from sixty to a hundred or more per subtribe. At the time this region was visited in 1906, there was practically no one living in this desolated valley. It was being used as cattle range and supported few people.[541]

Merriam interviewed three Wailakis—Fred Major, Nancy Doby, and Wylakke Tip—who were members of a tribal group he called the Tsen-nah-ken-nes, which was located in the Blue Rock and Bell Springs area.[542] This placed the group in northern Mendocino County, and it appears that Merriam never received information from a Humboldt County Wailaki.

The photographer and ethnographer Edward S. Curtis described certain geographically related activities of the Wailakis. He indicated that:

As fish were an important part of their diet, the Wailaki built their permanent houses... at favorite fishing stations, and there passed the winter months of rain and high water. During the rest of the year they wandered far and wide over the hills, wherever the

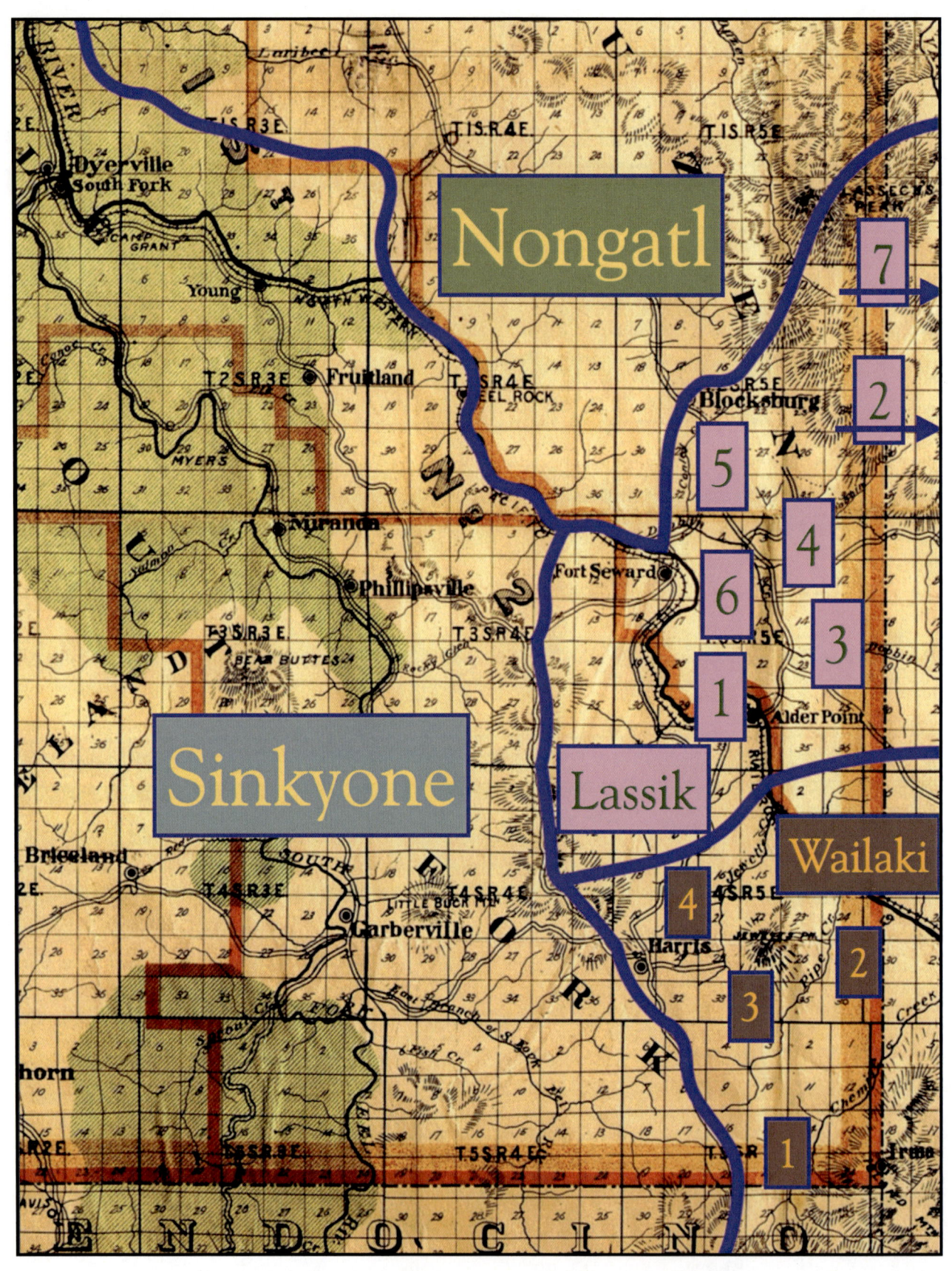

Wailaki and Lassik territories, showing the approximate locations of the four Wailaki and seven Lassik tribal groups (JNL, colorized by JR).

promise of game, roots, and seeds was most promising.[543]

Fishing started with the fall salmon run. The streams were still low, and the salmon were caught with dipnets and spears. When the rains came and rivers rose, it was time to catch steelhead in dipnets. Then, about April, came the spring salmon. In summer the Wailakis caught lampreys in nets "or by torchlight with a gaff-hook made by lashing deer bone to a stick." Both men and women fished for trout, wading in the stream and driving the fish into pools, where they were caught in nets.[544]

Then came the biggest change of the year:

> At the beginning of hot weather the Wailaki left their permanent villages and travelled from place to place among the mountains, camping in the open, gathering various roots and nuts, and hunting deer.... Five species [of acorns] were harvested and stored separately....
>
> Next to acorns pinole was of prime importance. It was prepared from a great many species of small seeds.... The principal plants yielding seeds for pinole are tarweed, sunflower, and the wild oat....
>
> Deer were very plentiful, and were taken by the combined use of snares, ambush, and beaters.... After the hunt women and children from the camps flocked out to help butcher and transport the meat and skins.[545]

Several species of birds were eaten by the Wailakis, including grouse, quail, robins, and yellowhammers, but "the greatest delicacy known was young swallows obtained in crevices along the river." The Wailakis burned fields and gathered

The dark mass of Jewett Rock broods over northern Wailaki country (JR).

the roasted grasshoppers that resulted, eating some on the spot but drying and pulverizing most of them for later use. They also roasted and ate yellow-jacket larvae.[546]

Merriam supplied information from Wylakke Tip:

> Each band had its own chief and its own hunting, fishing, acorn, and seed grounds. In winter the families of each band were scattered along the river in small rancherias, each consisting of from four to seven families, mostly blood relations, living together in two or three houses. Usually there were seven or eight people in each house.
>
> The winter houses were of split pine slabs, standing upright or sloping in at the top to form a conical house.[547]

Goddard indicated that the Wailakis had been a

> . . . tribe or group of many villages formerly on the main Eel r. and its N. fork. . . . Their houses were circular. They had no canoes, but crossed streams by weighing themselves down with stones while they waded. They lived by the river during the wet months of the year, when their chief occupation was fishing, done especially at favorable places by means of nets and spears. The summer and fall months were spent on the sides and tops of the ridges, where the women were able to gather the bulbs, seeds, and nuts, and the men could unite in deer drives and other methods of hunting.[548]

Both Goddard and Merriam identified numerous tribal units located in Wailaki territory. Only four of the northwesternmost groups claimed land in Humboldt County. Unlike most of the

Wylakke Tip in a pensive moment, 1922 (MCNAP, colorized by JR).

other tribal groups in his *Habitat of the Wailaki*, here Goddard does not map village locations and provides only a partial list of village names. The villages were likely either adjacent or fairly near the river, as was the case with the upriver Wailaki groups.

1. Kaikichekaiya (Ki-ke-che ke-ah-hang)

Goddard associated this group with "Chamiso" (Chamise) Creek, where the group "camped . . . in summer and at other times went there to hunt elk."⁵⁴⁹ The upper reaches of Chamise Creek lie in Humboldt County, about five miles east of the town of New Harris. Merriam gave three different names for this group, of which Ki-ke-che ke-ah-hang is the rendering closest to Goddard's.⁵⁵⁰

2. Dalsokaiya (Taht-so keah)

The name means "blue ground people." The group occupied the western side of the Eel River downstream (north) of the Kaikichekaiya. Goddard called them the Dalsokaiya and said "it is doubtful that they should be counted as Wailaki, but they were not Lassik and probably spoke the same dialect as the Wailaki."⁵⁵¹

Merriam referred to this group as the Taht-so keah and indicated that they were "on the west side of main Eel River north of Chemise Creek between Harris and Bell Springs." He stated that they "came down [the] Eel at Ning-ken-ne-chet, place now (1924) owned by Bob Glen. . . ."⁵⁵² The "Glenn Ranch House" was located about a half-mile west of Chemise Creek and about three miles southwest of the creek's confluence with the

Captain Jim provided Goddard with information about Wailaki groups on the main Eel River, 1901 (CEFP, colorized by JR).

Eel River.⁵⁵³ In 1949 the site of the Glenn Ranch House was mapped as the Marr Ranch.⁵⁵⁴

3. Setaltcitcokaiya

According to Goddard the Setaltcitcokaiyas were located "at or near Jewett rock, close to Harris." This vague statement suggests an unusual situation where the Setaltcitcokaiyas may have lived year round exclusively in the mountainous areas west of, but not near, the Eel River. Their name means "pestle red large people." They lived north of, and were friends with, the Dalsokaiyas.⁵⁵⁵ Merriam apparently did not locate and name this group, although it is possible they were his Tahs-ahng ke-ah-hahngs, described in the following section.

4. Kandankaiya (Tahs-ahng ke-ah-hahng)

This group, the "bow people," occupied Jewett Creek. Goddard had no information about their villages but stated that "they are represented only by mixed bloods living in the neighborhood of Harris. North of them in the bed of Eel river were the villages of the Lassik."⁵⁵⁶ Jim Wilburn, a Lassik Indian, said that these people were not his "folks."⁵⁵⁷ Merriam gives Tahs-ang ke-ah-hahng for the "tribe or band in the Harris region,"⁵⁵⁸ which probably refers to this group.

D. Lassik Tribe

The tribal name Lassik was derived from the whites' name for the most prominent leader of a certain group of southern Humboldt Indians.⁵⁵⁹ But the man known as "Chief Lassik" was actually named Sa-tah-bin-tah.⁵⁶⁰ He led one of seven groups that are subsumed within the so-called Lassik tribe.⁵⁶¹ Jim Willburn, Goddard's main Lassik informant, was a "small boy" when he saw Chief Lassik; he was a "big Indian" who sometimes camped on either the north or south fork of Dobbyn Creek.⁵⁶²

It appears that the western boundary of the Lassik tribe was what is now called Mail Ridge, which is the divide between the South Fork Eel and main Eel rivers.⁵⁶³ To the south, the Lassiks abutted the northwesternmost branch of the Wailaki tribe, the Kandankaiya, which occupied the Jewett Creek area. This southern boundary dropped from Mail Ridge to cross the main Eel between Alderpoint and Jewett Creek. It then continued eastward into Trinity County along a line that has not been specified.⁵⁶⁴ The eastern boundary of the Lassiks is vague, for they traveled all the way to the Yolla Bolly Mountains to gather salt but probably claimed territory only as far as South Fork Mountain.⁵⁶⁵ North of the Lassiks were the Nongatls, who occupied the headwaters of Larabee Creek in the vicinity of Blocksburg and also had a village at the mouth of Dobbyn Creek. The Lassiks inhabited the remainder the Dobbyn Creek drainage, the farthest point north being the headwaters of Conley Creek. From there eastward the exact Nongatl-Lassik boundary is unknown, although it probably went north over the Lassik peaks and along Swayback Ridge before dropping northwest to cross the Mad River south of Olsen Creek.⁵⁶⁶

1. Set-ten-bi-den ke-ya

This group derived its name from that of a rock on the Eel River near Alderpoint.⁵⁶⁷ Much of the information about the Set-ten-bi-den ke-ya comes from Lucy Young, who was born about 1852 at a large rancheria across the Eel from Alderpoint.⁵⁶⁸ She was described 90 later years by Kroeber as "simply a person of exceptionally superior mentality, which she manifests in every respect despite her advanced years."[569]

Young and another member of the tribe, Mary Major, told about the year-round activities of the Set-ten-bi-den ke-yas, which appears to apply to all the Lassik tribal groups: "About the time the acorns ripen," in the fall[570] the Indians returned to the Eel River country, where "every family builds a new permanent winter house." They gathered and stored "acorns, buckeyes, and some late grass seeds." They hunted "deer, elk and black bear," smoked the meat, and preserved the hides. Following the first big rain they caught the fall run of salmon, smoking and partially cooking it for later use. The months of December through February were the "critical period of the year" for the Set-ten-bi-den ke-yas, and once or twice each decade they experienced a lack of adequate food. In late February or early March came the spring salmon run, followed by that of the steelhead. Most of the fish were "caught in nets and basketry traps." The spring rains were usually heavy and this kept the Set-ten-bi-den ke-yas in their winter houses.[571]

When the rains subsided the Set-ten-bi-den ke-yas migrated:

> ... the Lassik scatter out into the hills east of the Eel River. The usual pattern is for each family to go by itself though several families

Lassik country, looking east from Mail Ridge. Kettenpom Peak, in Trinity County, appears to touch the clouds at upper center (JR).

may be together for weeks at a time. The men hunt deer and squirrels, the two most important game animals. Grouse, quail, black bear, elk, porcupine, etc., are also hunted.... The women gather clover, roots, seeds, berries, and hazelnuts. "People live high then." There are periodic get-togethers of the whole tribe at places where there is an extra large supply of food. One of these places is at Kettenchow, where camas root is gathered for a big feed. Another feast takes place on the Mad River, where summer salmon (steelhead?) provide the bulk of the food. A third celebration is held in the South Fork Mountains when the hazelnuts ripen. At these feasts, everyone sings, dances, plays games, or gambles. The Hayfork Wintun are the only outsiders invited in.[572]

Some of the young Lassik men and women made "a trip to the Yollabolly country... nearly every summer to obtain salt." It was "a dangerous undertaking because enemy tribes also . . . [got] their salt there." So the salt gatherers traveled only at night, built no fires, and left as soon as they could.[573] At the salt grounds,

> . . . the springs were very salty. Crusts of salt covered the ground, and frequently low-hanging shrubs were encrusted also and could be stripped quickly into the baskets.... If they were lucky their foray was successful and resulted in nearly a year's supply of salt.[574]

Then:

> Late in summer the homeward march begins. Instead of retracing their route, they usually swing over to the western edge of Lassik territory. In a general sense their route during the summer is a rough circle, some 200 miles in circumference, which is traveled in a counterclockwise direction.... The tribe may take a month to move a mile or two or cover ten to twenty miles in a day. Some places are visited one year and not the next. The two major factors involved are the abundance of food supply and the presence of enemy groups. The territory the Lassik claim as their own is in part also claimed by the Wailaki, Nongatl, Hayfork Wintun, Cottonwood Wintun, and the Naiaitci.[575]

When the Set-ten-bi-den ke-yas reached the Eel, their yearly cycle began again. Some Lassiks wintered elsewhere, either on the upper Mad River near today's Ruth Lake, or at Soldier Basin, a place in very remote country about six miles east of Zenia on the North Fork Eel.[576] The latter location became a camping area for military units during the 1860s. It was here in about 1864 that a Captain Davis, with a detachment from the 1st California Battalion of Mountaineers,

> . . . wiped out a settlement of Indians who had avoided the earlier roundups. Only a few Indians escaped. One of these, the famous Yellowjacket, was found dazed and wandering and was taken in by the French family from Zenia. . . . The only Indian spared in the infamous raid was a 17 year old Indian girl whom Captain Davis married and then settled down with on southern Long Ridge.[577]

Lucy Young was another young Indian woman who survived the massacres. Her story of her life describes the fate of her tribe. (See sidebar 7.)

Merriam had located Young at Zenia, a tiny ridgetop town northeast of Alderpoint, in June

7. The Lost Life of the Lassiks

First soldiers ever I see, my 'lil sister 'bout three feet high. Took us Fort Baker down Van Duzen River. Mother run away, twice. Last time tookted us to lower country. I run off, too, many times.[578]

And for a time, running became the life that Lucy Young led.[579] She told her story, some 80 years later, with the breathless immediacy of someone who would never forget being hunted:

It was in August. Soldier had all Inyan together. Gonta takum to Hoopa....
  Mother run away when we hit redwoods. Offus dark in redwoods. Can't see nothing....
  Two days we lay in hollow log. Hear soldier in camp, go li'l ways, listen. Go li'l further, listen....
  We see horse track. Hide again. Somebody whistle. We drop in fern. Just see soldier hat go by. We watchum long ways. When dark come, we go way down open ridge.
  Something rustle, I think dogs overtake us. We look back. Skunk family follow us—mother, five li'l ones....
  Get pretty close our own country. Bunch grass country. We make li'l hole, so we lay down to sleep. Mother never sleep. I never sleep. Li'l sister sleep. Too tired, li'l sister....
  We go round behind Lassik Peak on top of ridge. Rocky. I want hunt water. I starve for water. I hunt for water like in redwoods, see li'l ferns, drink water, carry to mother, rest awhile, then go on. Too hungry we feel. I want to go back on road, let soldiers catch us. Then we find sunflower, plenty. We gather head, seed dry 'nough to eat. We go down creek, catch crawfish. Mother can't eat hardtack, make it sick.[580]

Lucy and her mother and sister navigated their way through the mountains, visiting the Kettenshaw Valley, Soldier Creek, upper Mad River, and South Fork Mountain. They returned to Kettenshaw ("ketten" = camas) and found several Indian relatives. In the fall, they wanted to go back to their home country at Alderpoint, but some whites took them to Fort Seward instead. While they were there, Chief Lassik came in with a small group of other Indians. Then Lucy was taken by a white man to South Fork Mountain to care for the man's wife and baby. After a week Lucy ran away. She crossed a river (probably the Mad) and then, while in the forest, Lucy

... see hog got killed, laying there, neck and shoulder eaten up. Hog warm yet. When I put foot on it, something come up behind me. Grizzly bear growl at me. Wind blow from river. He smell me. I fall over back in tall ferns. I feel same as dead. Grizzly set there, his paw hang down. Head turn look every way. I keep eye on him. He give up listen, look, turn around, dig hole to sleep in. I keep still, just like a dead. Fainty, too, and weak.

That's time I run—when he dig deep. Water up to my waist. I run through. Get to Fort Seward before I look back.

At last I come home [Fort Seward, where Lucy's mother was]. Before I get there, I see big fire in lotsa down timber and tree-top. Same time awfully funny smell. I think: somebody get lotsa wood.

I go on to house. Everybody crying. Mother tell me: "All our men killed now." She say white men there, others come from Round Valley, Humboldt County too, kill our old uncle, Chief Lassik, and all our men.

Stood up about forty Inyan in a row with rope around neck. "What this for?" Chief Lassik askum. "To hang you, dirty dogs," white men tell it. "Hanging, that's dog's death," Chief Lassik say. "We done nothing, be hung for. Must we die, shoot us."

So they shoot. All our men. Then build fire with wood and brush Inyan men been cut for days, never knowing their own funeral fire they fix. Build big fire, burn all them bodies. That's funny smell I smell before I get to house. Make hair raise on back of my neck. Make sick stomach, too."[581]

Lucy Young and Yellowjacket at Zenia, 1922 (MCNAP, colorized by JR).

Southern Humboldt Tribal Groups

For a time after that Lucy was forced to be a slave, attached to the families of various whites. She finally escaped and lived on her own. A white man took her little sister away and Lucy never saw her again. Lucy went back to Fort Seward, got her mother, and took her to Hayfork. They stayed together until Lucy's mother died.[582] In about 1870 Lucy went to live with Abraham Rodgers, a white man, in Blocksburg. They had four children together. Lucy left Rodgers about 1902, moved to the Van Duzen River and stayed with another white man, Arthur Rutlidge, for five years. Then she left him and moved to remote Soldier Basin, where two elderly Lassik women lived. In 1910 Sam Young, who was half white, one-quarter Lassik, and one-quarter Hayfork Wintun, came to live with Lucy, who cared for the elderly women until they had both died.[583] Lucy and Sam also spent time near Zenia, where a daughter of Lucy's named Katie had a 1,200-acre ranch with her white husband William W. Clark.[584] Then, in 1927, Lucy and Sam left, moving to Round Valley and buying a small farm. They were married shortly afterwards.[585]

Lassik land in Zenia: Part of the Katie and William Clark ranch is shown in the middle right of the photo. It included the pond on the hillslope. Zenia is just off-camera to the lower left (JR).

Lucy gave accounts to various ethnographers, providing some of them with substantial information. Among the southern Humboldt Indians she was the only female to be extensively interviewed.[586] In June 1922 C. Hart Merriam took a "hard trip" to Zenia, where he located two Lassik Indians, John French, or "Yellowjacket," and Lucy Young. Merriam learned that Lucy's name for her branch of the Lassik tribe was Set-ten-bi-den ke-ah, and that Yellowjacket belonged to a "subtribe" that lived to the east called the "Che-teg-ge-kah."[587]

In 1938 Frank Essene arranged for Sam Young, Lucy's husband, to interview her as part of the final Culture Element Distribution survey, a series of studies initiated by Kroeber at U. C. Berkeley.[588] Essene used additional information to create several short narratives about the Lassiks and about Young herself.[589] He indicated that Young had been born near Alderpoint, as had her father, and that her mother had come from Soldier Basin, in Trinity County. Essene described Lucy as "possessing a remarkable memory, a great ability for graphic description, and absolute honesty and first-hand knowledge of aboriginal customs. . . ."[590]

The following year Young was interviewed on the Round Valley Indian Reservation by Edith Van Allen Murphey. The results were a detailed account of the Lassik tribe and considerable autobiographical information.[591] It was the only time Young was allowed to tell her full story. At the end of Murphey's interview with her, Young summarizes the history of her people and of her own life:

> White people want our land, want destroy us. Break and burn all our basket, break our pounding rock. Destroy our ropes. No snares, no deerskin, flint knife, nothing. . . .
>
> All long, long ago. My white man die. My children all die but one. Flu take restum. Oldest girl die few years ago, left girl, she married now, got li'l girl, come see me sometimes. All I got left, my descendants.
>
> 'But twenty-five years ago I marry Sam. Marry him by preacher. Sam, he's good man. Hayfork Inyan. Talk li'l bit different to us people, but can understand it. We get old age pension. Buy li'l place here in Round Valley, keep our horses, keep cow, keep chickens, dogs, cats too. We live good.
>
> I hear people tell 'bout what Inyan do early days to white man. Nobody ever tell it what white man do to Inyan. That's reason I tell it. That's history. That's truth. I seen it myself.[592]

1922. She and her husband, Sam Young, were living there near the ranch of Lucy's daughter, Kate Clark, and her white husband, William W. Clark. Merriam had driven to this remote mountain spot especially to interview Young, but he also had "the great good luck to find here an old full blood man called Jack French or Yellowjacket . . . who lives . . . in the upper Mad River country not accessible by road and whom I particularly wanted to find."[593]

Merriam determined that Yellowjacket belonged to a heretofore unrecognized tribe called the Che-teg-ge-kah, that was located in southwestern Trinity County and northern Mendocino County. North of them was Young's Set-ten-bi-den ke-ya, and Yellowjacket knew enough of Young's language that he provided Merriam with some additional vocabulary.[594] Merriam also learned that Yellowjacket "had endured more than one man's share of trouble and suffering." As proof, he related an account by a rural storekeeper of an affray involving Yellowjacket and an unnamed Indian:

> He shot Yellowjacket fair in the middle of the brisket. If the ammunition had been good for anything, it would have finished him, but as it was, the bullet just stuck. He [Yellowjacket] came running in to me and opened up his shirt and showed me where he had been hit, and said he wanted a drink. I told him that what he wanted was to have the bullet picked out. I pried at it with my old jack knife but it didn't come, so I then got a fellow with a pair of sheep shears and together we fixed him. He never made a face or gave a grunt, but after we were through, he said he still needed a drink, and I gave him one."[595]

South Fork Dobbyn Creek drainage, Tai-tci-kuk kai-ya territory, 1922 (MCNAP, colorized by JR).

Upper Conley Creek, southeast of Blocksburg. Tec-ti-kuk kai-ya territory (JR).

2. Le-lin-dun kai-ya

Jim Wilburn, Goddard's Lassik informant, indicated that Le-lin-dun kai-ya was the name of the "Soldier Basin people."[596] Based on Essene's information, Lucy Young's mother was a Le-lin-dun kai-ya, as were likely the two elderly women that Lucy cared for at Soldier Basin.

3. Tai-tci-kuk kai-ya

Wilburn said that these were "the people on big Dobbin [sic],"[597] by which was meant South Fork Dobbyn Creek.[598]

4. Se-ta-kuk kai-ya

According to Wilburn, these were the "Little Dobbin people."[599] The village of Kon-the-tci-dun was located on the North Fork Dobbyn Creek, which Goddard referred to as "little Dobbin."[600]

5. Tec-ti-kuk kai-ya

Wilburn called this group the "Conley Creek people."[601] Conley Creek meets Dobbyn Creek about a mile and a half from the latter's mouth. It heads about a half-mile east of Blocksburg.

Southern Humboldt Tribal Groups

6. Ta kai-ya

Wilburn designates this group as "the people on main Eel River."[602] Goddard mapped two villages that probably belonged to the Ta kai-ya on the east side of the Eel across from the southern end of the Fort Seward flat.[603]

7. Yen kai-ya

This group is known only by a reference made to them by Van Duzen Pete, who indicated that they were the Indians south of his Nongatl people on the upper Van Duzen River, their territory starting at a point south of Olsen Creek and running southward from there.[604]

E. Nongatl Tribe

Ethnographers have used the term Nongatl as if it described a single tribe, one whose expansive territory included the entire Larabee Creek drainage, part of the Mad River drainage, a small portion of the Eel River drainage, and much of the Van Duzen River drainage.[605] In actuality there were numerous, relatively small tribal groups occupying these various areas, and unraveling their exact names and locations requires a detailed examination of Goddard's unpublished field notes. Even then, the picture is incomplete and not fully focused.

Through his work with Van Duzen Pete, Goddard collected more information about the Nongatls than any other so-called "tribe" that he researched.[606] Despite this, Goddard was unable to provide a fully coherent account of the interrelationship between Nongatl tribal groups and the dialects they each spoke, nor was he completely clear about either the names of all the groups or their dialects.[607] The endnotes for this section deal with these issues in detail, but here is a brief summary of what Goddard's field notes reveal about the Nongatls:

First, there was a large collection of tribal groups that Goddard called the Nongatl tribe, but nowhere in his notebooks does he record Pete referring to a specific tribe by that name. Instead, it seems that Goddard conjoined all of the groups that Pete described under the name of the dialect that Pete himself spoke, which was "Nongal" or Nongatl.

Second, Goddard recorded information about 20 distinct tribal groups that Pete mentions, usually using the suffix "kai-ah" or one of its variants to indicate that these are each "the people of" a particular place. In two cases, Goddard recorded names that lack the "kai-ah" suffix. One of the two is Pete's own group. In this case Goddard uses the name of the dialect that Pete spoke, "nongal," as if it were the name of Pete's group.

Third, with one exception, Goddard recorded the names of the dialect that each tribal group spoke. The groups are organized by dialect in the descriptive section that follows.

Se-nun-ka

Goddard's village note cards describe villages that he lists as "Senunka"[608] but which his field notes indicate belonged to distinctly named tribal groups. Indians spoke the Se-nun-ka dialect on both upper and lower Larabee Creek and also on the Eel River in the vicinity of Coleman, Mill, and Dobbyn creeks. Goddard states that "the most northerly village of the senunka on Laribee creek . . . [was] 200 yds. north of Curless's house."[609] This location is about two miles downstream on Larabee Creek from its confluence with Boulder Flat Creek.[610]

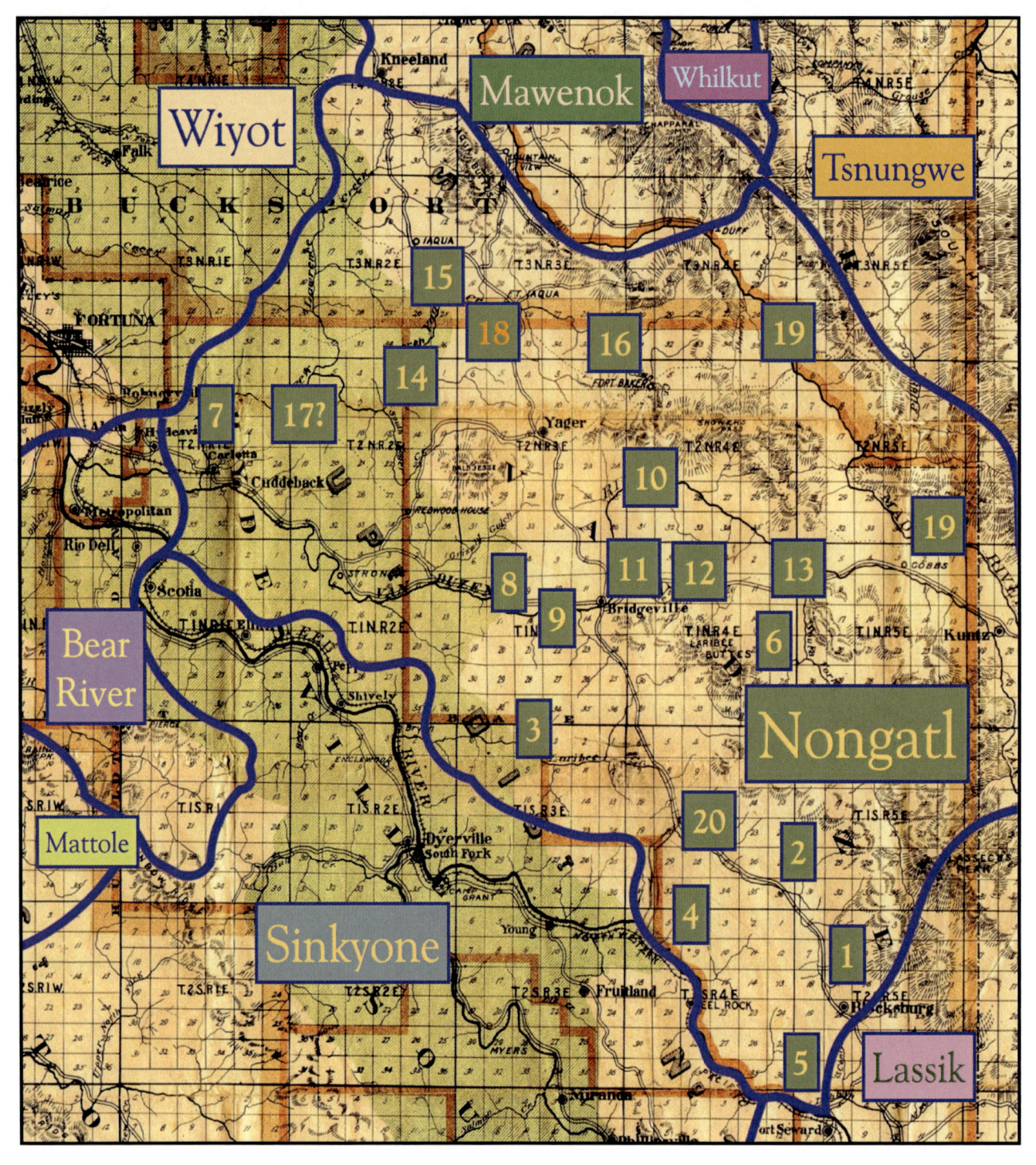

Map of Nongatl territory, showing the approximate locations of 20 tribal groups. Group 18, the Tcil-lun-din-kai-ya, recieves an orange numeral because it shared a dialect with Indians from a seperate tribe, the Mawenoks (JR).

The southernmost Se-nun-ka speaking village that Goddard lists on Larabee Creek was in the vicinity of Thurman Creek,[611] although the dialect was almost certainly spoken in unnamed villages all the way to Blocksburg.[612] Se-nun-ka dialect usage extended west from Larabee Creek through mountainous terrain to reach the Eel. Along the river this territory began about three-quarters of a mile west of Coleman Creek and extended up the Eel to the mouth of Dobbyn Creek.[613]

1. Ye-lin-din kai-ya

Pete told Goddard that "Ye-lin-dun-yi-na-kun . . . is Larrabee [sic] Creek."[614] He stated that the Ye-lin-din kai-ya were "taken to reservation at . . . Crescent City. All die there."[615] Goddard does not map any of the group's villages nor does he locate their exact territory. It is likely, however, that the Ye-lin-din kai-ya occupied the uppermost section of Larabee Creek, from south of Boulder Flat Creek to its headwaters near Blocksburg. The Ye-lin-din kai-ya are probably the group that the Lassik Indian woman, Lucy Young, called the Kus-katundun, whose "village was situated near the present town of Blocksburg."[616] Young on another occasion noted that the Blocksburg region Indians, the "Kos-kah-tun-deng ka-ah," were "now extinct,"[617] which corresponds with Pete's information about the Ye-lin-din kai-yas.

2. Bus-ta-dun ki-ya

Bus-ta-dun-kot was the Nongatl name for Boulder Flat Creek, which enters Larabee Creek about four miles north of Blocksburg.[618] Near here Larabee Creek, which has been flowing north, makes a wide bend to the west and three subsidiary creeks—Hayfield, Boulder Flat, and Thurman—join it on the outside of the bend. Goddard mentions the Bus-ta-dun ki-ya without specifying the boundaries for their territory, but he describes four areas of activity in the vicinity of Bus-ta-dun-kot[619] and directly associates the Bus-ta-dun ki-ya with the creek.[620] Pete indicates that several of his uncles (his mother's brothers) were from this area.[621]

3. Ne-tcin-dun-kut kai-ya

The Ne-tcin-dun-kuts claimed land along the lower section of Larabee Creek and in the prairie and oak woodland area on the south-facing hillslope of Oak Ridge in the Chalk Mountains. According to Pete, "lots" of members of the group "were taken to Crescent City [the Smith River Reservation] died there." Ne-tcin-dun-kut territory ended about two miles above the mouth of the creek[622] and the Sinkyone tribal group called the Lolahnkoks reportedly controlled the short section of Larabee Creek below that.[623] Nick Richard, the only significant Nongatl informant other than Pete, indicated that the Van Duzen people "owned Larabee Creek," but that "some different people, not V[an] Duzen, owned Pepperwood and Skelly,"[624] the latter being the name of the post office at the mouth of Larabee Creek.[625]

4. Unnamed group or groups on Eel River from near Coleman Creek to near Mill Creek

Goddard lists several habitation areas on the main Eel River, ranging from west of Coleman Creek to north of Mill Creek, all of which he calls Se-nun-ka. He does not, however, provide the name of the tribal group or groups that lived there.[626]

5. Di-yic-kut ki-ya

Goddard's notes on this group are difficult to decipher, but it appears that the Di-yic-kut ki-ya occupied a section of the Eel River at the mouth of Dobbyn Creek, making them the southernmost Nongatl tribal group and the southernmost Se-nun-ka dialect speakers. They bordered the Lassik tribal groups to the south and east.[627]

6. Kos-dun ki-ya

Kos-dun was the Nongatls' name for what is now called Larabee Valley. Pete apparently lacked direct

Se-nun-ka was spoken on the eastern side of the Eel in the vicinity of the later town of Eel Rock. This view from near the townsite looks toward Great Butte, beyond which is Larabee Creek (JR).

knowledge of the area, indicating that he had been told the name by another Nongatl known only as "Nick Richard's father."[628] A main area of activity was along lower Butte Creek.[629] According to Pete there were 25 people, including four old men, from Kos-dun who "used to stay there all winter"[630] despite sometimes having snow. Pete indicated that Tony, a Kos-dun, "talk se nunk."[631] He also stated that "kos dun is a dialect" of Se-nun-ka.[632]

Kit-tel

Kit-tel was a Nongatl dialect named for one of the groups that spoke it, the Kit-tel ki-ya.[633] The dialect was widespread. It was used on a long stretch of the Van Duzen, from the boundary with the Bear River tribe at the mouth of Yager Creek[634] eastward to Low Gap, the divide between the Van Duzen and Mad River drainages.[635] It was also the dialect used by most of the Indians in the extensive Yager Creek drainage.[636]

7. Tce-lin-dun [ki-ya]

The area at the mouth of Yager Creek was the homeland of this tribal group.[637] West of them were the Bear River Indians, who had a village named Inako in the vicinity of Hydesville.[638] The exact boundary between the two tribes is unknown; it was probably either Yager Creek itself or the eastern edge of the tableland just west of the creek valley.

8. Kon-tel-dun ki-ya

Kon-tel-dun ki-ya territory lay along the Van Duzen just downriver from Pepperwood Falls.[639] Pete said that the "boss" of this group was an old man called Be-te-wil-kas.[640] According to Pete, "people from all around came to get fish" above the village of Kon-tel-dun.[641] There were "lots of Indians didn't come back from reservation"[642] that were Kon-tel-dun ki-yas.

9. Kik-ki-ye kai-ya (No-le-dun kai-ya)

There were two names for this group. The first was derived from one of their villages, Kik-ki-ye. The group's eastern boundary was on the Van Duzen at Goat Rock (Kus-tci-to). According to Pete the huge rock "slid from mountain south of it into the river making a waterfall which used to stop salmon." The waterfall was called No-le-dun, which provided the group's alternate name, No-le-dun kai-ya. The absence of salmon above Goat Rock probably accounts for the group's lack of interest in inhabiting the area upriver from the waterfall, hence the boundary at that point.[643] According to Pete, the village of Kik-ki-ye "had a large population" with 30 houses, an extraordinary number compared with other villages in southern Humboldt. Nearby was Fish Creek (Ban-ni-kut), which lived up to its name by having "lots of salmon," so that the "Kik ki ye always fish there."[644] Speaking of Goat Rock, Pete revealed that "coyote put it there. . . . [He] split [it] off with wedge."[645]

Kit-tel ki-ya country: conifers, oak woodlands, and prairies blanket the slopes that descend to the middle section of the Van Duzen River (JR).

10. Kit-tel ki-ya

The Kit-tel ki-ya were located on the middle Van Duzen downstream from Hogback Ridge, which was the boundary with the Na-ai-tci tribal group.[646] Their western boundary was "below Bridgeville,"[647] at Goat Rock, beyond which were the Kik-ki-ye ki-ya.[648]

Van Duzen Pete lived in Kit-tel ki-ya territory. His Indian allotment was on the river at Ellington Gulch (formerly called Phelan Creek) a short distance downstream from Fort Baker.[649] Pete indicated that his "old man" sometimes lived winters at a camp in the vicinity.[650]

Susie Burtt, the wife of the Lolahnkok Indian George Burtt, was a Kit-tel ki-ya who had lived several miles below Fort Baker on the Van Duzen River.[651]

11. Co-kot-ki ki-ya

Co-kot-ki ki-ya territory was located near the confluence of Little Larabee Creek and the Van Duzen River, about a mile northeast of Bridgeville. There were two Co-kot-ki ki-ya villages.[652] According to Pete, his fellow Nongatl informant, Nick Richard, was from this group.[653] (See sidebar 8.)[654]

Kit-tel ki-ya country: on Van Duzen near Fort Baker, 1906 (CEFP, colorized by JR).

12. Se-tco-kin-ne-dun kai-ya

The Se-tco-kin-ne-dun kai-ya were situated east of the Co-kot-ki ki-ya on or near Little Larabee Creek, perhaps a mile west of McClellan Rock. Pete said that there "used to be lots" of Indians in this tribal group.[655]

13. Na-ai-tci ki-ya

Shrouded in mystery are the Na-ai-tci ki-ya. They may or may not be part of the Nongatl collection of tribal groups, but they are listed here because Van Duzen Pete included them in his account of Nongatl Indians of the area, never indicating that they were a separate tribe.

Pete reported that there were "lots" of Na-ai-tci ki-yas on both the "Big" Van Duzen and the Little Van Duzen. Goddard learned from Pete that the Na-ai-tci ki-yas occupied the area from Hogback Ridge, on the Van Duzen just above Fort Baker, up to the forks of the river, and then up the South Fork, or Little Van Duzen.[656] It is not clear how far they extended up the Little Van Duzen, but no farther than the edge of Larabee Valley, beyond which was the domain of the Kos-dun ki-ya. Pete reported that Na-ai-tci ki-ya territory also extended east on the main Van Duzen to Low Gap.[657]

---

8. In the Nick of Time

Besides Van Duzen Pete, the only other Nongatl informant who provided detailed information about the tribe was Nick Richard, who didn't give Nongatl names for the various tribal groups, but instead referred to them by geographical area. Richard indicated that the "Van Duzen people" owned down to Carlotta, all of Yager Creek, and Larabee Creek. Eastward they claimed land all the way to the Low Gap divide, between the Van Duzen and Mad rivers. The "Iaqua people" owned Showers Pass. "Some different people, not V[an] Duzen, owned Pepperwood and Skelly [Larabee]."[658] There "used to be about 60-70 people around Bridgeville" with more than 100 "out towards Larabee Valley."[659] Downriver on the Van Duzen near where Joel Whitmore later had his ranch there were about 200 Indians.[660] According to Richard there was "one chief at each place in old days."[661] The Van Duzen Indians were friendly with the Wiyots and camped on the Eel River near Pepperwood to be with them. They[662] "visited upstream Eel up to this side of Dyerville. . . ." Richard added that the "Dyerville people spoke like the Van Duzen people,"[663] a statement that conflicts with the information that both Goddard and Merriam collected.

Like other southern Humboldt tribes the Nongatls traveled with the seasons. According to Richard:

> Some winter[s] had to move down so they won't get stuck in snow. In summer, went up in hills—camped on Van Duzen for fish in winter—in summer way out in hills for deer, wild wheat (seeds—sunflower and tarweed also). Some people stayed on river all year round. Sometimes had to build new house every winter or perhaps once in 2-3 years.[664]
>
> Unlike some of the northern Humboldt tribes, the Nongatls held no regularly scheduled dances. When they decided to have one, they would build a set of walls with no roof and hold the dance there. There was a dance location in the vicinity of Bridgeville.[665]
>
> Richard said that the Nongatls "never used canoes on Van Duzen… [except] once when [the] bridge washed away at Bridgeville," which occurred almost 30 years after white arrival. He added that the "river was too swift for boats."[666] Although many Nongatls lived near the river, "fishing was much less practiced than deer and elk hunting."[667] Some years there were poor fish runs and "once or twice had starvation—couldn't catch nothing, couldn't kill deer…."[668] Some of the older people ate turtles, but not Nick. He kept one turtle on a string as a pet and then gave it away.[669]

Accounts from other early day Indians about the Na-ai-tci ki-yas are less detailed and quite different. The Lassik Indian Lucy Young claimed, perhaps erroneously, that the Na-ai-tci ki-yas "roamed over most of Trinity County." She added, in contradiction to Van Duzen Pete, that "the Naiaitci had no permanent villages; that they lived in the hills mostly; that they numbered fifty to sixty individuals; that they lived by raiding and thievery, primarily…." Young also claimed that the Na-ai-tci ki-ya spoke Athabascan,[670] while the Lolahnkok Indian George Burtt said they "talk like Hay Fork people,"[671] which would have made their language Wintu.[672] Young provided a detailed description of a deadly conflict between the Lassik tribe and the Na-ai-tci ki-yas. (See sidebar 9.)

14. Bus-tco-bi ki-ya

Pete indicated that this group was located on the middle and north forks of Yager Creek upstream from their confluence. Goddard noted that two of the villages "speak tcit tel ki ya [kit-tel ki-ya] dialect."[673] The Bus-tco-bi ki-ya villages were all situated above the deep gorges carved by both forks of the creek. One village had the tongue-twisting name of kon-tco-we-tci-kin-ne-dun.[674]

15. Yi-dan-din-nun-dun ki-ya

Goddard specified that this group occupied North Fork Yager Creek in the area near its confluences with Lone Star Creek and Digger Creek, approximately one mile southwest of the junction of the

9. The Lassiks and the Na-ai-tci ki-yas

Near the end of one summer sometime in the late 1840s, some Lassik Indians were camped at the later townsite of Zenia. A group of nine young women, with one young man as a guard, went about a mile west to Mud Creek to gather hazelnuts. Back near the main camp, one of the boys heard shouts coming from the direction of the creek. He ran to tell the others. The young men were all out hunting, but the older men cautiously went to investigate. They found six of the young women and the young man dead and the other two women wounded.

Na-ai-tci ki-ya country: the hillside north of the forks of the Van Duzen, 1907 (CEFP, colorized by JR).

The survivors identified the attackers as Na-ai-tci ki-ya. But, as Lucy Young put it, "Even if there had been no direct evidence, everyone would have assumed the Naiaitci were the culprits." Without the young men to help, the Lassiks formed no war party. The seven corpses were placed in a pit and cremated. Their remains were taken back to camp and buried. According to Young, "this was the worst massacre suffered by the Lassik prior to the coming of the whites."[675]

A couple of years later the Lassiks went into Na-ai-tci ki-ya territory. The Na-ai-tci ki-ya wanted to pay for the killings but the Lassiks wanted revenge. One day the Lassiks caught a Na-ai-tci and scalped him; "the people danced all night long with the scalp." The scalp was later sold to other Lassiks and then sold again to the Wintus. As Young put it, "a Naiaitchi scalp was particularly prized because everyone hated the Naiaitchi."

North Yager Creek drainage: Bus-a-kot kai-ya territory at far right (JR).

Southern Humboldt Tribal Groups

Kneeland-Bridgeville Road and the northern end of Showers Pass Road.[676] The Hunter Ranch is included this area. One member of the Hunter family reportedly "surprised some Indians... on this creek drying eels in the early days."[677]

16. Bus-a-kot kai-ya

Goddard's notes and village notecards indicate that the Bus-a-kot kai-ya were mostly located in the vicinity of Indian Creek and Freese Creek, both tributaries of upper North Yager Creek. Goddard noted that the elevation of some of the Bus-a-kot kai-ya villages exceeded 2,000 feet, thus subjecting the villagers to cold winter temperatures and snow.[678]

17. Kun-teh-bi kay-ya

"Yager creek people," no specific area given, but Pete indicated they were "all gone."[679]

Dine-ke-ne-ox

While on the North Fork of Yager Creek in the territory of the Yi-dan-din-nun-dun ki-ya, Goddard noted that the "Tcil-lun-din [are] above our camp and at this flat [and they] talk like dine ke ne ox."[680] Elsewhere Goddard, in listing certain dialects, writes: "Dine ke ne ox Kneelands, Iaqua, Big Bend etc."[681] These locations are linked to a related Athabaskan-speaking tribe called the Mawenoks, who inhabited the lower part of the middle section of the Mad River. The Tcil-lun-din kai-ya's territory abutted Mawenok land in the Iaqua-Lone Star area, so the linguistical connection is understandable. In fact, a break in the ridgeline at the Lone Star Ranch provides a relatively easy travel route between Big Bend, on the Mad River, and Iaqua, on the North Fork Yager Creek. This is the only instance of Pete reporting a dialect transcending the boundaries of Nongatl territory.

18. Tcil-lun-din kai-ya

Pete connected this group specifically with Iaqua Creek,[682] but Goddard noted locations belonging to the Tcil-lun-din kai-ya about a mile to the west, in the vicinity of Lone Star Creek.[683]

Nongatl

When traveling with Goddard on the upper Mad River, Pete indicated a place near Deer Creek where "the people this far north were Nongatl."[684] Elsewhere Pete told Goddard that "Nongatl name of Indians here [Van Duzen River] and on upper Mad River. Pete said his father was that kind."[685]

19. Nongatl

Goddard, in working with Van Duzen Pete, struggled to get a clear sense of the term "nongal" (Nongatl). Goddard ended up using the word as an umbrella term to cover numerous groups of Indians in the Van Duzen, Eel, Mad, and Larabee Creek drainages, but he also used it as the name for the dialect that Pete spoke. It was only when Goddard and Pete went all the way east to the Mad River that Goddard's notes indicate that "nongal" was not only a dialect, but that the word also was the name for a distinct tribal group—apparently the only one that spoke "nongal" as their native dialect.

When on the upper Mad River with Goddard in 1907, Pete pointed out numerous village sites. Their journey took them upriver on the Mad all the way into western Trinity County. Pete stated that he had visited the area as a little boy and he

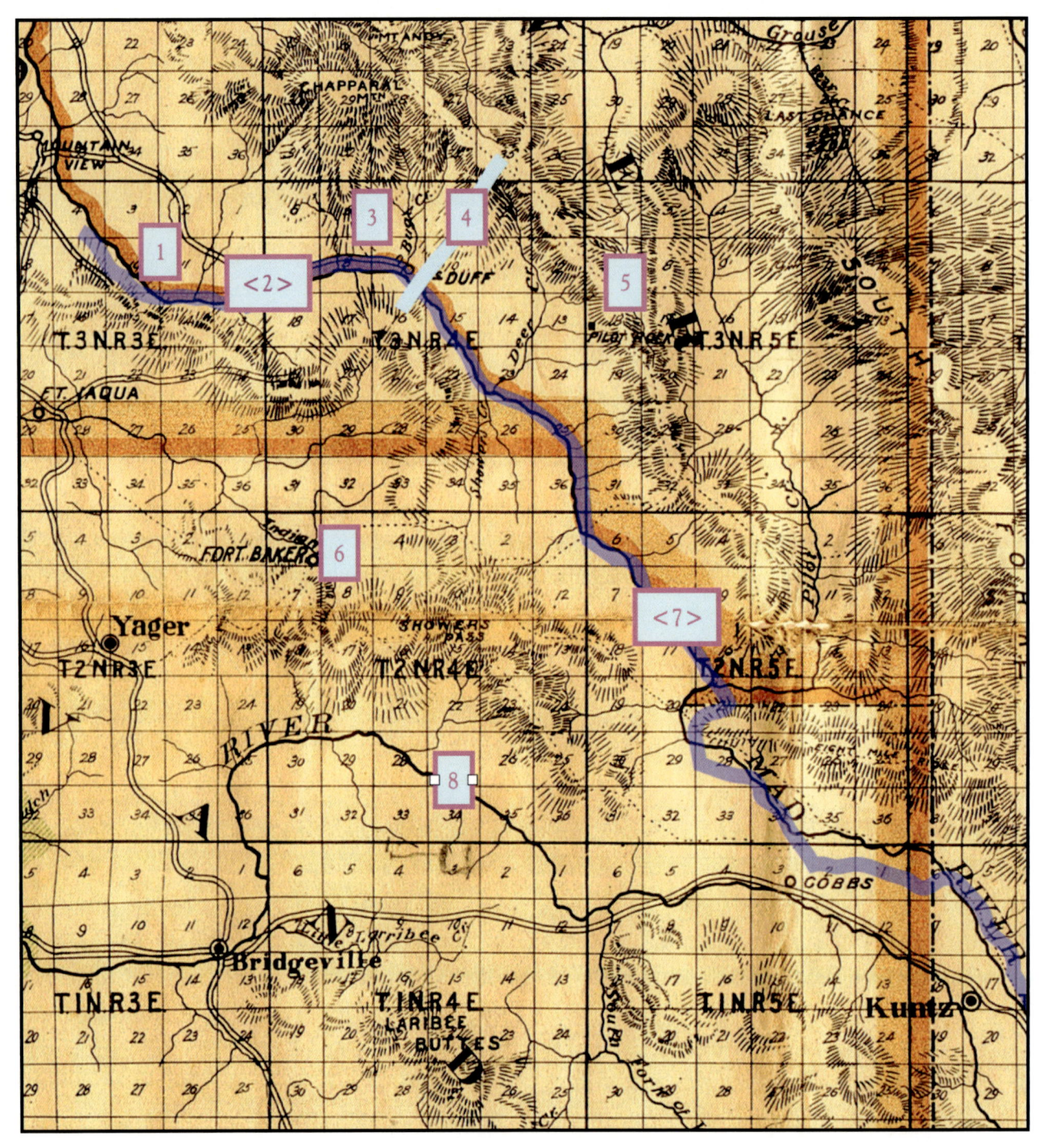

Pete and Goddard go down the Mad River: purple line marks most of their trip from Lamb Creek, on the upper Mad River (off map, lower right) to beyond Big Bend (upper left). 1. Big Bend, birthplace of Van Duzen Pete's wife, Minnie. 2. Mawenok territory (both sides of river). 3. Bug Creek, site of Mawenok massacre that killed Molly Brock's family. 4. Light blue line: approximate Mawenok-Nongatl boundary. 5. Pilot Rock and Pilot Ridge, site of Chilula war dance prior to attacking Lassiks. 6. The location for Fort Baker is in error. It was actually at location 8. 7. Nongatl tribal group territory (both sides of river). 8. Site of Fort Baker, on north side of Van Duzen just upriver from Pete's home (JNL base map).

A gathering of Indians near Blocksburg about 1903, a half-century after the Humboldt Indian genocide. They most likely are either Nongatl or Lassik, or perhaps both (HCHS, colorized by JR).

thought that the southernmost Nongatl village was in the vicinity of Olsen Creek, about two miles south of where today's Highway 36 crosses the Trinity County line. Pete indicated that the Indians farther upriver were called the Yen kai-ya, which was probably the Nongatl name for the northernmost tribal group of the Lassiks.[686]

Pete and Goddard then proceeded down the Mad River, locating numerous village sites. At a point near Deer Creek, Pete claimed that "the people this far north were nongal."[687] Pete said that "for salmon they had to go to Big Bend,"[688] a location farther down the Mad River in the territory of the Mawenok tribe.[689] Earlier, when collecting information on the Van Duzen River,

Pete told Goddard "nongal not on this river only on Mad river."[690] On another occasion Pete said that his sister, who was George Burtt's wife's cousin, was half Tcit-tel kai-ya "and talks it good. Other half is non gal 'like me.'"[691]

The men continued down the Mad River to the vicinity of the former swinging bridge at the end of Jack Shaw Road. Pete indicated that he had stayed winters at Un-tcin-ta-tci-ki, a village apparently on the nearby Ahlgren and Park Ranch.[692] Near there Pete also located a village that his "wife used to stay in when a little girl."[693] His wife, called Minnie Peet by the whites, was born at Big Bend, according to her obituary.[694] She was a member of the Mawenok tribe.[695]

Goddard's description of this journey on the Mad River strongly suggests that this area was Pete's homeland. But nowhere in Goddard's account is there a definite statement about what Pete's people were called. Pete indicates that "nongal . . . was on Mad River." It is clear that he means "nongal was *spoken* on Mad River," but whether he also meant that "nongal . . . was *the name of the people* on Mad River" is uncertain. Nowhere does Goddard provide the term that would have confirmed this: "nongal kai-ya."

Goddard makes no references to any other tribal group that spoke the Nongatl dialect.

Group without a Specific Dialect Affiliation

20. Tcin-nun-un ki-ya

This group was associated with the upper Larabee Creek area north of the Curless (later Payton) Ranch, which was located on the county wagon road about six miles northwest of Blocksburg.[696] Its territory was just north of where the Se-nun-ka dialect was spoken. To the north the closest other known dialect was Kit-tel, which was spoken along the Van Duzen.

Sources

American Philosophical Society
    2020 American Council of Learned Societies Committee on Native American Languages, American Philosophical Society [ACLS Collection]: Detailed Inventory. Web page. Electronic document, https://search.amphilsoc.org/collections/view?docId=ead/Mss.497.3.B63c-ead.xml accessed on January 4, 2020.

anthromuseum.ucdavis.edu
    2021a Clinton Hart Merriam 1855-1942 American Naturalist and Ethnographer. Web page. Electronic document, http://anthromuseum.ucdavis.edu/c-hart-merriam-biography.html accessed on June 12, 2021.

Arms, L. R.
    N.d. A Short History of the US Army Noncommissioned Officer. Webpage. Electronic document, https://www.ncohistory.com/files/NCO_History.pdf accessed on December 21, 2021.

Asbill, Frank
    1953 The Last of the West. Manuscript photocopy: Humboldt State University Library, Arcata.

Atherton, Gertrude
    1945 Golden Gate Country. New York: Duell, Sloan & Pearce.

avalon.law.yale.edu
    2016 General Orders No. 100: The Lieber Code. Web page. Electronic document, http://avalon.law.yale.edu/19th_century/lieber.asp#sec3 accessed on August 28, 2016.

Baldy, Cutcha Risling
    2021 NAS 05: Native American Literature. Web page. Electronic document, https://www.cutcharislingbaldy.com/uploads/2/8/7/3/2873888/example_syllabus_1_native_american_literature_and_social_justice__2___1_.pdf accessed on July 18, 2021.

Baumgardner, Frank H.
    2006 Killing for Land in Early California. New York: Algora Publishing.

Baumhoff, Martin
    1958 California Athabascan Groups. *Anthropological Records* 16 no. 5.
    1963 Ecological Determinants of Aboriginal California Populations. Berkeley: University of California Press.
    1978 Environmental Background. *In* Handbook of North American Indians, vol. 8: California. Robert F. Heizer, ed. Pp. 16-24. Washington: Smithsonian Institution.

Bancroft Library
    1997 A. L. Kroeber Papers, 1869-1972. Bancroft Library, University of California, Berkeley.
    2020 Guide to A. L. Kroeber Papers. Web page. Electronic document, https://oac.cdlib.org/findaid/ark:/13030/tf3d5n99tn/entire_text/ accessed on January 2, 2020.

Bear River Band
    2021 Wiyot/Mattole History. Web page. Electronic document, http://www.brb-nsn.gov/our-story/wiyot-mattole-history/ accessed on June 28, 2021.

Belcher Abstract & Title Co.
    1921-1922 Atlas of Humboldt County, California. Eureka: Belcher Abstract & Title Co.

BlackPast.org
    2016 Fort Pillow Massacre (1864). Web page. Electronic document, http://www.blackpast.org/aah/fort-pillow-massacre-1864 accessed on September 3, 2016.

Bledsoe, A. J.
    1885 Indian Wars of the Northwest. San Francisco: Bacon & Co.

BLM
    2018b Patent records for Township 2 South, Range 2 West, Humboldt Meridian. Web page. Electronic document, https://glorecords.blm.gov/results/default.aspx?searchCriteria=type=patent|st=CA|cty=023|twp_nr=2|twp_dir=S|rng_nr=2|rng_dir=W|m=15|sp=true|sw=true|s-adv=false#resultsTabIndex=0&page=6&sortField=11&sortDir=0 accessed on August 13, 2018.
    Patent record for Charlie Briceland, for property in Section 33, T2S, R2E, Humboldt Meridian. Web page. Electronic document, https://glorecords.blm.gov/details/patent/default.aspx?accession=0658-424&docClass=MV&sid=mss0dzab.rk5 accessed on March 4, 2021.

Bowcutt, Frederica
    2015 The Tanoak Tree. Seattle: University of Washington Press.

britannica.com
    2021 Athabascan language family. Web page. Electronic document, https://www.britannica.com/topic/Athabaskan-language-family accessed on August 16, 2021.

Brown, Theron, and Chris Baldo
    2010 Ernest "Max" McKee, Jr.: A Rebel in the Redwoods. *Highline* 28 no. 2, August 2010.

Cahto Dictionary
    2024 Lheeliingchowding. Web page. Electronic document, https://www.webonary.org/cahto/ga0619ab6-024b-4e81-95c8-86223d6d-6be8/ accessed on June 23, 2024.

Carranco, Lynwood, and Estel Beard
    1981 Genocide and Vendetta: The Round Valley Wars of Northern California. Norman, OK: University of Oklahoma Press.

Chernow, Ron
    2017 Grant. New York: Penguin Press.

Cook, Margarite Drucella
    1997 The Southern Humboldt Papers. 16 volumes. Photocopy: Humboldt County Library, Eureka.

Cook, Margarite, and Diane Hawk
    2001 A Glance Back: Northern Mendocino County History. Piercy, CA: Hawk Mountaintop Publishing.

Cook, S. F.
    2021 The Aboriginal Population of the North Coast of California. Electronic document. EBook, https://www.gutenberg.org/ebooks/33812 accessed on August 29, 2021.

Coy, Owen C.
    1982 [1929] The Humboldt Bay Region: 1850-1875. Eureka, CA: Humboldt County Historical Society

Cozzens, Peter
    2016a The Earth Is Weeping: The Epic Story of the Indian Wars for the American West. New York: Alfred A. Knopf.
    2016b Ulysses S. Grant Launched an Illegal War Against the Plains Indians, Then Lied About It. Web page. Electronic Document, http://www.smithsonianmag.com/history/ulysses-grant-launched-illegal-war-plains-indians-180960787/ accessed on November 12, 2016.

Crismon, Max
    N.d.a Interview with Jerry Rohde.

Curtis, Edward S.
    1970[1924]b The North American Indian, Vol. 14. New York: Johnson Reprint Corporation.

Daily Alta California
    1864a The Klamath Indian War: Capture and Execution of Two Indian Chiefs. *Daily Alta California*, April 19, 1864:1.

Denny, Edward
    1911 Denny's Official Map of the County of Humboldt California. San Francisco: Edward Denny & Co.

Dixon, Roland B.
    1930 Pliny Earle Goddard (1869-1928). *Proceedings of the American Academy of Arts and Sciences* 34 no. 12:526-528.

Driver, Harold E.
    1939 Culture Element Distributions: X: *Northwestern California. Anthropological Records* 1 no. 6.

Edeline, Denis P.
    1978 At the Banks of the Eel. N.p.

Egan, Timothy
    2012 Short Nights of the Shadow Catcher. Boston: Houghton Mifflin Harcourt.

Eggenberger, David
    1985 An Encyclopedia of Battles. New York: Dover Publications, Inc.

Elliott, Wallace W.
    1881 History of Humboldt County, California. San Francisco: Wallace W. Elliott & Co.

Elsasser, Albert B.
    1978 Mattole, Nongatl, Sinkyone, Lassik, and Wailaki. In Handbook of North American Indians, vol. 8: California. Robert F. Heizer, ed. Pp. 190-204. Washington: Smithsonian Institution.

Encyclopædia Britannica
    2016a Nathan Bedford Forrest. Web page. Electronic document, https://www.britannica.com/biography/Nathan-Bedford-Forrest accessed on October 10, 2016.

Encyclopedia.com
    2015a Kroeber, Alfred L. Web page. Electronic document, http://www.encyclopedia.com/doc/1G2-3045000665.html accessed on June 8, 2015.

Essene, Frank
    1942 Cultural Elements Distributions: XXI: Round Valley. *Anthropological Records* 8 no. 1.

Ethnological Documents
    2002 Ethnological Documents Collection of the Department and Museum of Anthropology, University of California, Berkeley, 1875-1958. Berkeley: Bancroft Library. Microfilm: Humboldt State University Library, Arcata.

Felt, T. D.
    1869 Another Indian Depredation—Heroic Conduct of Mrs. Bowman. *Humboldt Times*, April 3, 1869.

Garner, James G.
    1965 General Order 100 Revisited. *Military Law Review* 27:1-48.

Gibbs, George
    2016 George Gibbs' Journal of Redick McKee's Expedition Through Northwestern California in 1851. Web page. Electronic document, http://klamathbucketbrigade.org/Gibbs_1851JournalMcKeeExpedition040406.htm accessed on August 12, 2016.

Gifford, Edward H.
    1965 The Coast Yuki. *Sacramento Anthropology Society*, Paper 2.

Glaze, Robert L.
    2021 Albert Sidney Johnston. Web page. Electronic document, https://www.britannica.com/biography/Albert-Sidney-Johnston accessed on October 27, 2021.

Goddard, Pliny E.
    1903a #1 Sinkyone Notebook. In Selected Notebooks of Pliny Earle Goddard Relating to Humboldt County Tribes. Jerry Rohde, ed. PDF file archived at the Cultural Resources Facility, Humboldt State University, Arcata, CA.
    1906a Redwood Creek & Mad River Note book. In Selected Notebooks of Pliny Earle Goddard Relating to Humboldt County Tribes. Jerry Rohde, ed. PDF file archived at the Cultural Resources Facility, Humboldt State University, Arcata, CA.
    1906b Lassik 1906 Names of Places Names of Plants. [Lassik notebook #2]. Original at Special Collections Division, University of Washington Libraries.
    1907a Mattole Notebook #1, P. E. Goddard, October 1907. In Selected Notebooks of Pliny Earle Goddard Relating to Humboldt County Tribes. Jerry Rohde, ed. PDF file archived at the Cultural Resources Facility, Humboldt State University, Arcata, CA.
    1907b Places V[an] Duzen to Mad River Pete [Notebook] #21. In Selected Notebooks of Pliny Earle Goddard Relating to Humboldt County Tribes. Jerry Rohde, ed. PDF file archived at the Cultural Resources Facility, Humboldt State University, Arcata, CA.
    1907c [Untitled] Sinkyone Notebook II Albert Smith and George Burt [sic]. In Selected Notebooks of Pliny Earle Goddard

Relating to Humboldt County Tribes. Jerry Rohde, ed. PDF file archived at the Cultural Resources Facility, Humboldt State University, Arcata, CA.

1907d Untitled Sinkyone Notebook 1 Albert Smith and Sallie [Sally] Bell Interviews. *In* Selected Notebooks of Pliny Earle Goddard Relating to Humboldt County Tribes. Jerry Rohde, ed. PDF file archived at the Cultural Resources Facility, Humboldt State University, Arcata, CA.

1907e 1 Nongatl Peter Van Duzen 1907 [Notebook]. *In* Selected Notebooks of Pliny Earle Goddard Relating to Humboldt County Tribes. Jerry Rohde, ed. PDF file archived at the Cultural Resources Facility, Humboldt State University, Arcata, CA.

1907f Mattole [Notebook] #2. *In* Selected Notebooks of Pliny Earle Goddard Relating to Humboldt County Tribes. Jerry Rohde, ed. PDF file archived at the Cultural Resources Facility, Humboldt State University, Arcata, CA.

1908a Yager 1908 Village Sites copied on cards [Notebook]. *In* Selected Notebooks of Pliny Earle Goddard Relating to Humboldt County Tribes. Jerry Rohde, ed. PDF file archived at the Cultural Resources Facility, Humboldt State University, Arcata, CA.

1908b Sinkyone Notebook IV, July 1908. *In* Selected Notebooks of Pliny Earle Goddard Relating to Humboldt County Tribes. Jerry Rohde, ed. PDF file archived at the Cultural Resources Facility, Humboldt State University, Arcata, CA.

1908c Duzen Mrs. Pete (~ and Mad River) June 15, 1908. PDF file archived at the Cultural Resources Facility, Humboldt State University, Arcata, CA.

1908d Nongatl Van Duzen Pete [Notebook] 18[.] June 17, 1908. *In* Selected Notebooks of Pliny Earle Goddard Relating to Humboldt County Tribes. Jerry Rohde, ed. PDF file archived at the Cultural Resources Facility, Humboldt State University, Arcata, CA.

1908e Peter V. D. June 20 1908 Nongatl [Notebook] 19. *In* Selected Notebooks of Pliny Earle Goddard Relating to Humboldt County Tribes. Jerry Rohde, ed. PDF file archived at the Cultural Resources Facility, Humboldt State University, Arcata, CA.

1908f [Untitled Sinkyone Notebook Charlie Interview July 1908] *In* Selected Notebooks of Pliny Earle Goddard Relating to Humboldt County Tribes. Jerry Rohde, ed. PDF file archived at the Cultural Resources Facility, Humboldt State University, Arcata, CA.

1913a Wayside Shrines in Northwestern California. *American Anthropologist* 15 no. 4:702-703.

1914a Notes on the Chilula Indians of Northwestern California. *University of California Publications in American Archaeology and Ethnology* 10 no. 6:265-288.

1914b Chilula Texts. *University of California Publications in American Archaeology and Ethnology* 10 no. 7:289-379.

1919a Letter from P. E. Goddard to Dr. C. Hart Merriam dated February 25, 1919. Copy in author's possession.

1922a [Untitled Notebook Bear River and some Wailaki, August to September 1922.] *In* Selected Notebooks of Pliny Earle Goddard Relating to Humboldt County Tribes. Jerry Rohde, ed. PDF file archived at the Cultural Resources Facility, Humboldt State University, Arcata, CA.

1923 The Habitat of the Wailaki. *American Archaeology and Ethnology* 20. University of California Press.

1929 The Bear River Dialect of Athapascan. *University of California Publications in American Archaeology and Ethnology* 24 no. 5.

N.d.a Van Duzen [Notebook] #20. *In* Selected Notebooks of Pliny Earle Goddard Relating to Humboldt County Tribes. Jerry Rohde, ed. PDF file archived at the Cultural Resources Facility, Humboldt State University, Arcata, CA.

N.d.b V[an] D[uzen] Songs [Notebook] #23. *In* Selected Notebooks of Pliny Earle Goddard Relating to Humboldt County Tribes. Jerry Rohde, ed. PDF file archived at the Cultural Resources Facility, Humboldt State University, Arcata, CA.

N.d.d #2 Sinkyone [Notebook]. *In* Selected Notebooks of Pliny Earle Goddard Relating to Humboldt County Tribes. Jerry Rohde, ed. PDF file archived at the Cultural Resources Facility, Humboldt State University, Arcata, CA.

N.d.e. Lassik Misc. [Lassik notebook #1]. Original at Special Collections Division, University of Washington Libraries.

N.d.f. Bald Hills [Notebook]. *In* Selected Notebooks of Pliny Earle Goddard Relating to Humboldt County Tribes. Jerry Rohde, ed. PDF file archived at the Cultural Resources Facility, Humboldt State University, Arcata, CA.

Goetzmann, William H., and Kay Sloan
1982 Looking Far North: The Harriman Expedition to Alaska, 1899. Princeton, NJ: Princeton University Press.

Golla, Victor
2009 Meaning of the term "no-le." Personal communication with author, 2009.
2011 California Indian Languages. Berkeley: University of California Press.
2015a Personal communication with author regarding Goddard notebook #22, April 30, 2015.
2015b Personal communication with author regarding certain Athabascan language terms, July 10, 2015.

Golla, Victor, and Sean O'Neill, eds.
2001 The Collected Works of Edward Sapir. Vol. 14: Northwest California Linguistics. Berlin: Mouton de Gruyter.

Gomez, Melissa
2021 UC Berkeley removes Kroeber Hall name, citing namesake's 'immoral' work with Native Americans. Web page. Electronic document, https://www.latimes.com/california/story/2021-01-27/uc-berkeley-kroeber-hall accessed on February 2, 2021.

Harrington, James Peabody
    1983 The Papers of John P. Harrington in the Smithsonian Institution 1907 - 1957. Microfilm: Humboldt State University Library, Arcata.

Heizer, Robert F.
    1993 The Destruction of California Indians. Lincoln NB: University of Nebraska Press

Heizer, Robert F. and Alan J. Almquist
    1971 The Other Californians. Berkeley: University of California Press.

Hewes, Gordon W.
    1940 Notes, Book III. Photocopy of hand-written notebook in author's possession.

History Vault
    2016 Nathan Bedford Forrest. Web page. Electronic document, http://www.history.com/topics/american-civil-war/nathan-bedford-forrest accessed on October 10, 2016.

Hodge, Frederick W., ed.
    1907a Handbook of American Indians North of Mexico, Part 1. Washington: Government Printing Office.
    1910a Handbook of American Indians North of Mexico, Part 2. Washington: Government Printing Office.

Humboldt Historian
    1987a U. S. Grant—the West Coast Years. *Humboldt Historian*, November-December 1987:11-13.

Humboldt Standard
    1908a Indian's Death Creates A Stir. *Humboldt Standard*, January 17, 1908.
    1920a Well Known Indian Woman, 90 Years of Age, Died Mon. *Humboldt Standard*, January 29, 1920.

Humboldt Times
    1854a Mattole River and Valley. *Humboldt Times*, September 23, 1854:2.
    1855c Indian Hostilities—Three Men Killed. *Humboldt Times*, January 20, 1855:2.
    1857a A Digger Shot by Diggers. *Humboldt Times*, September 26, 1857:2.
    1858a Serious Indian Troubles—Removal or Extermination. *Humboldt Times*, September 18, 1858:2.
    1858b Indian Excitement.—Two White Men Wounded.—Two Indians Killed. *Humboldt Times*, June 12, 1858:2.
    1858c More Indian Outrages.—Man Shot Down in the Trail. *Humboldt Times*, June 26, 1858:2.
    1858d Mad River Indians. *Humboldt Times*, June 26, 1856:2.
    1858e Our Indians. *Humboldt Times*, July 17, 1858:2.
    1858f Fight with the Indians.—One White Man Killed.—Ten Mules Scattered and Missing. *Humboldt Times*, July 17, 1858:2.
    1858g Fight with Indians.—One Man Killed and One Wounded. *Humboldt Times*, August 7, 1858:2.
    1858h What's to be Done? *Humboldt Times*, August 7, 1858:2.
    1858i Horrible Murder by Indians. *Humboldt Times*, September 18, 1858:2.
    1858j Serious Indian Trouble.—Removal or Extermination. *Humboldt Times*, September 18, 1858:2.
    1858k Indian Troubles. *Humboldt Times*, September 18, 1858:2.
    1858l Action of the Citizens of Union. *Humboldt Times*, September 18, 1858:2.
    1858m Gone to Work Right. *Humboldt Times*, September 18, 1858:2.
    1858n No Authority. *Humboldt Times*, September 25, 1858:2.
    1858p Movement of Troops. *Humboldt Times*, October 23, 1858.
    1858q Fight with the Indians. *Humboldt Times*, October 30, 1858:2.
    1858r Ranch Burned by Indians. *Humboldt Times*, October 30, 1858:2.
    1858s Indian Matters. *Humboldt Times*, November 20, 1858:2.
    1858t The Volunteer Expedition in this County. *Humboldt Times*, November 27, 1858:2.
    1858u Volunteers. *Humboldt Times*, December 4, 1858:2.
    1859a The Murdered Men. *Humboldt Times*, December 24, 1859:2.
    1859b From the Volunteers. *Humboldt Times*, January 1, 1859:2.
    1859c Another Volunteer Wounded. *Humboldt Times*, January 29, 1859:2.
    1859d Fight with Indians.—Three Men Severely Wounded. *Humboldt Times*, January 29, 1859:2.
    1859e Our Indian War. *Humboldt Times*, January 29, 1859:2.
    1859f Indian War. *Humboldt Times*, March 12, 1859:2.
    1859g Send Them Out. *Humboldt Times*, April 23, 1859:2.
    1859h More Trouble with Indians. *Humboldt Times*, May 14, 1859:2.
    1859i Another Volunteer Company. *Humboldt Times*, May 28, 1859:2.
    1859j One of the Redwood Indians . . . . *Humboldt Times*, June 4, 1859:2.
    1861a Battle with Indians! Charley Huestis Killed! *Humboldt Times*, November 23, 1861:3.
    1862c Court-Martial. *Humboldt Times*, July 26, 1862:3.
    1864a Our Indian War. *Humboldt Times*, April 2, 1861:3.
    1864b Our Indian Affairs. *Humboldt Times*, August 27, 1864:2.
    1864c Indian Reservation Notice. *Humboldt Times*, August 27, 1864:2.
    1930a Anthropologist Conducts Indian Research Work. *Humboldt Times*, August 16, 1930:7.
    1939a Death of Thomas Bell Brings To Light Strange Early Day Story. *Humboldt Times*, May 14, 1939:12.

Hunt, Aurora
    2004 The Army of The Pacific. Mechanicsburg PA: Stackpole Books.

Hunt, L. C.
    1982 Report on six-month's old Fort Humboldt. *Humboldt Historian*, May-June 1982:12.

Sources

Impr. (pseud.)
    1858 Indian Women.—Their Treatment. *Trinity Weekly Journal*, January 9, 1858:2.

Jacobs, Melville
    1956 Statement regarding receipt of Goddard's notebooks. Original at the University of Washington Libraries, Special Collections Division.

Johnson, Lauren M.
    2021 UC Berkeley removes the name on a school building over an anthropologist's controversial past. Web Page. Electronic document, https://www.cnn.com/2021/01/27/us/uc-berkeley-removes-kroeber-from-anthropology-building-trnd/index.html accessed on June 28, 2021.

Jones, Alice Goen, ed.
    1981a Trinity County Historic Sites. Weaverville, CA: Trinity County Historical Society.

Kinman, Seth
    2010 Seth Kinman's Manuscript and Scrapbook. Ferndale, CA: Ferndale Museum.

Kircher, John C. and Gordon Morrison
    1993 Ecology of Western Forests. Boston: Houghton Mifflin Company.

Kroeber, A. L.
    1919 Notes and Queries: Sinkyone Tales. *Journal of American Folk-Lore*, April-June 1919.
    1925 Handbook of the Indians of California. Washington: Government Printing Office.
    1929a Pliny Earle Goddard. *American Anthropologist*, New Series, 31 no. 1:1-8.
    1997 Papers, 1869-1972. Microfilm available at the Humboldt State University Library, Arcata.
    2021a The Nature of Land-Holding Groups in Aboriginal California. Web page. Electronic document, https://digitalassets.lib.berkeley.edu/anthpubs/ucb/proof/pdfs/ucas056-003.pdf accessed on February 2, 2021.

Kroeber, A. L. and Robert Spott
    1942 Yurok Narratives. *University of California Publications in American Archaeology and Ethnology* 35 no. 9:143-256. University of California Press, Berkeley and Los Angeles.

Larson, William E. et al.
    2011 Archaeology of the Smith Creek Watershed, Humboldt County, California. Archaeological Research Center, Department of Anthropology, California State University, Sacramento.

Legier, Jules
    1958 Mattole Indians: 1854 to the Present. Photocopy of paper for History 198 class, on file under "History—Settlement Period 1850-75 Indian Wars" in the Humboldt County Collection, Humboldt State University Library, Arcata, CA.

Lentell, J. N.
    1898 Official Map of Humboldt County California. N. p.

Lewis, Al, et. al.
    1991 Interview by Jerry Rohde with Al Lewis, Ed Lewis, and Blanche Lewis Tompkins, July 29, 1991.

Lewis, Oscar, ed.
    1966 The Quest for Qual-A-Wa-Loo. Oakland, CA: Holmes Book Company.

Long, Clarence D.
    1960 Wages and Earnings in the United States 1860-1890. Princeton, NJ: Princeton University Press.

Li, Fang-Kuei
    1930 Mattole: An Athabascan Language. Chicago: University of Chicago Press.

Link, Adrianna, et al.
    2021 Indigenous Languages and the Promise of Archives. N. p.: University of Nebraska Press and the American Philosophical Society.

Loud, Llewellyn L.
    1918 Ethnogeography and Archaeology of the Wiyot Territory. *University of California Publications in American Archaeology and Ethnology* 14 no. 3.

Madley, Benjamin
    2016a An American Genocide: The United States and the California Indian Catastrophe, 1846-1873. New Haven: Yale University Press.

Makepeace, Anne
    2002 Edward S. Curtis: Coming to Light. Washington DC: National Geographic Society.

Margolin, Malcolm
    1981 The Way We Lived. Berkeley: Heyday Books.

Mattina, Nancy
    2019 Uncommon Anthropologist: Gladys Reichard and Western Native American Culture. Norman Oklahoma: University of Oklahoma Press.

McLean, Louise
    1917 Discovery of Humboldt Bay. *Overland Monthly* 70 no. 2.

Merriam, C. Hart
    1918a The Acorn, a Possibly Neglected Source of Food. *National Geographic Magazine* 34 no. 2 (August 1918):129-137.
    1921a California Journal 1921, vol. 1. Photocopy at the Cultural Resources Facility, Humboldt State University, Arcata.
    1922a California Journal 1922, vol. 1. Photocopy at the Cultural Resources Facility, Humboldt State University, Arcata.
    1923a California Journal 1923, vol. 1. Photocopy at the Cultural Resources Facility, Humboldt State University, Arcata.
    1923b Application of the Athapaskan Term Nung-kahhl. *American Anthropologist* 25:276-277.
    1966 Ethnographic Notes on California Indian Tribes. Berkeley: *University of California Archaeological Research Center* 68, part 1.
    1976 Ethnogeographic and Ethnosynonymic Date from Northern California Tribes. *Contributions to Native California Ethnology from the C. Hart Merriam Collection* 1.
    1993 C. Hart Merriam Papers Relating to Work with California Indians, 1850-1974. Berkeley: University of California Library Photographic Service, 1993.

Merriam, C. Hart, and Zenaida Merriam Talbot
    1974 Boundary Descriptions of California Indian Stocks and Tribes. Berkeley: Archaeological Research Facility, Department of Anthropology.

Mills, Ellen L., ed.
   1985 The Papers of John Peabody Harrington in the Smithsonian Institution: 1907 – 1957, Volume 2. White Plains, New York: Kraus International Publications.

Milota, Marilyn Keach
   1993a Humboldt County California Abstracts of Death Records 1873-1925, vol. I. Photocopy available at the Humboldt Room, Humboldt County Library, Eureka.
   1993b Humboldt County California Abstracts of Death Records 1873-1925, vol. II. Photocopy available at the Humboldt Room, Humboldt County Library, Eureka.
   2001a Humboldt County California Abstracts of Death Records 1926-1935. Photocopy available at the Humboldt Room, Humboldt County Library, Eureka.
   2003a Humboldt County California Abstracts of Death Records 1936-1947. Photocopy available at the Humboldt Room, Humboldt County Library, Eureka.

Merriam
   1922a California Journal I, 1922. Copy available at the Cultural Resources Facility, Cal Poly Humboldt, Arcata.

Monroe, Thomas H.
   1962 Notes on the Albee Family. Transcription of a speech given to the Humboldt County Historical Society, on file in the Biography collection at the Humboldt County Historical Society, Eureka, CA.

Moungovan, Mrs. T. O.
   1964a Shelter Cove Scalping. *Mendocino County Historical Society Newsletter* 3 no. 1:7-8.

Murphey, Edith V. A.
   1941 Out of the Past: A True Indian Story. *California Historical Society Quarterly* 20 no. 4):349-364.

Nelson, Byron Jr.
   1988 Our Home Forever: The Hupa Indians of Northern California. Salt Lake City: Howe Brothers.

New York Times
   1864a The Fort Pillow Massacre. *New York Times*, May 3, 1864.

Nomland, Gladys Ayer
   1931a A Bear River Shaman's Curative Dance. *American Anthropologist*, New Series, January-March, 1931:38-41
   1935 Sinkyone Notes. *University of California Publications in American Archaeology and Ethnology* 36 no. 2.
   1938 Bear River Ethnography. *Anthropological Records* 2 no. 2.

Nomland, Gladys Ayer, and A. L. Kroeber
   1936 Wiyot Towns. *University of California Publications in American Archaeology and Ethnology* 35 no. 5.

Northern Californian
   1858a Indian Affairs. *Northern Californian*, December 15, 1858:2.
   1860a Hydesville Volunteers. *Northern Californian*, February 8, 1860:3.

Orton, Richard H.
   1890 Records of California Men in the War of Rebellion, 1861 To 1867. Sacramento: State Printing Office.

Osgood, Wilfred H.
   1944 Biographical Memoir of Clinton Hart Merriam 1855-1942. Web page. Electronic document, http://nau.edu/uploadedFiles/Centers-Institutes/Merriam-Powell/_Forms/cmerriam_Osgood_bio_NAS.pdf accessed on July 6, 2015.

Palmer, T. S.
   1954 In Memoriam: Clinton Hart Merriam. *The Auk* 71 no. 2.

PBS
   2015a Harriman Expedition Retraced: The 1899 Expedition. Web page. Electronic document, http://www.pbs.org/harriman/1899/1899.html accessed on July 6, 2015.
   2015b Harriman Expedition Retraced: C. Hart Merriam 1855-1942. Web page. Electronic document, http://www.pbs.org/harriman/1899/1899_part/participantmerriam.html accessed on July 6, 2015.

Powers, Alfred
   1949 Redwood Country. New York: Duell, Sloan & Pierce.

Powers, Stephen
   1872a The Northern California Indians, No.1. *Overland Monthly* 8 no. 4.
   1872b Afoot and Alone; A Walk from Sea to Sea by the Southern Route. Hartford, CT: Columbian Book Company.
   1976[1877] Tribes of California. Berkeley: University of California Press.

Raphael, Ray
   1992 An Everyday History of Somewhere. Redway, CA: Real Books.

Raphael, Ray, and Freeman House
   2011 Two Peoples, One Place. Revised edition. Eureka: Humboldt County Historical Society.

Robinson, W. W.
   1948 Land in California. Berkeley: University of California Press.

Rohde, Jerry
   2001a Benbow SRA Campground Cultural Resources Investigation: Historical Review. Copy in author's possession.
   2008a The Sonoma Gang. Web page. Electronic document http://www.northcoastjournal.com/humboldt/the-sonoma-gang/Content?oid=2127928 accessed on October 22, 2013. Also available in: North Coast Journal, September 11, 2008:14-15, 17-19.
   2010a Genocide & Extortion. Web page. Electronic document http://www.northcoastjournal.com/news/2010/02/25/genocide-and-extortion-indian-island/ accessed on October 29, 2011. Also available, without endnotes, in: North Coast Journal, February 25, 2010:10-17.
   2014a Both Sides of the Bluff. Eureka: MountianHome Books.
   2016a An American Genocide. Web page. Electronic document, https://www.northcoastjournal.com/humboldt/an-american-genocide/Content?oid=4116592 accessed on February 28, 2021.

Rohde, Jerry, and Gisela Rohde
   1992 Humboldt Redwoods State Park: The Complete Guide. Eureka, CA: Miles & Miles.

Sources

Roscoe, James
    1985a The days of Chief Lassik and his people were sadly numbered. *Humboldt Historian*, March-April 1985.
    1985b An Ethnohistory of the Mattole. Photocopy of an Humboldt State University paper in possession of author.

Sacramento Daily Union
    1863a Alleged Kidnapping in Mendocino. *Sacramento Daily Union*, March 26, 1863:2.

Sam, Mrs. Jane
    1921a Revised statement regarding Indian Island Massacre, date March 27/21. Photocopy available, as part of the "Wiyot History Papers," in the Special Collections, Humboldt State University Library, Arcata.
    [1921?]a Statement regarding L. K. Wood and Gregg Party. Photocopy available, as part of the "Wiyot History Papers," in the Special Collections, Humboldt State University Library, Arcata.
    [1921?]b Statement regarding Indian Island Massacre. Photocopy available, as part of the "Wiyot History Papers," in the Special Collections, Humboldt State University Library, Arcata.
    [1921?]c Taken to Reservation. Photocopy available, as part of the "Wiyot History Papers," in the Special Collections, Humboldt State University Library, Arcata.
    [1921?]d Revised statement regarding L. K. Wood and Gregg Party. Photocopy available, as part of the "Wiyot History Papers," in the Special Collections, Humboldt State University Library, Arcata.
    [1921?]e Taken to Reservation [revised version]. Photocopy available, as part of the "Wiyot History Papers," in the Special Collections, Humboldt State University Library, Arcata.

Scott, Jeremiah, Jr.
    1997a Curless Family Leaves a Legacy. *Humboldt Historian*, Fall 1997:22-26.

Seidner, Carrie
    1939a Letter to "Friend" [Lucy Allard], dated July 24, 1939. Photocopy available, as part of the "Wiyot History Papers," in the Special Collections, Humboldt State University Library, Arcata.

Smith, Eric Krabbe
    1990 Lucy Young or T'tcetsa: Indian/White Relations in Northwest California, 1846-1944. Master thesis, University of California Santa Cruz.

Smith, Jean Edward
    2001 Grant. New York: Simon and Schuster.

Spartacus Educational
    2016 Fort Pillow Massacre. Web page. Electronic document, http://spartacus-educational.com/USACWpillow.htm accessed on September 3, 2016.

Strobridge, William F.
    1994 Regulars in the Redwoods: the U. S. Army in Northern California, 1852-1861. Spokane, WA: Arthur H. Clark Co.

Stuart, John D., and John O. Sawyer
    2001 Trees and Shrubs of California. Berkeley: University of California Press.

Subcommittee of the Committee on Indian Affairs: House of Representatives
    1926 Hearing . . . on H. R. 8036 and H. R. 9497. Washington DC: Government Printing Office.

Surveyor General's Office
    1858b [Map of] Township Nº IV North Range Nº II East, Humboldt Meridian. San Francisco: Surveyor General's Office.
    1876d [Map of] Township Nº 2 North, Range Nº 2 East, Humboldt Meridian. San Francisco: Surveyor General's Office.

Swanlund-Baker
    2018a Photo of Albert and Sallie Smith at Briceland Store. Web page. Electronic document, http://library.humboldt.edu/humco/holdings/photodetail.php?S=Albert%20smith&CS=All%20Collections&RS=ALL%20Regions&PS=Any%20Photographer&ST=ALL%20words&SW=&C=6&R=1 accessed on January 8, 2019.
    2018b Photo of Albert and Sallie Smith at Briceland. Web page. Electronic document, http://library.humboldt.edu/humco/holdings/photodetail.php?R=0&S=Albert%20smith&CS=All%20Collections&RS=ALL%20Regions&PS=Any%20Photographer&ST=ALL%20words&SW=&C=6 accessed on January 8, 2019.

Thoresen, Timothy H. H.
    1975 Paying the Piper and Calling the Tune: The Beginnings of Academic Anthropology in California. *Journal of the History of Behavioral Sciences* 11 no. 3, July 1975.

Trinity Weekly Journal
    1858a Organization of Indian Fighters. *Trinity Weekly Journal*, October 16, 1858:2.

United States Bureau of the Census
    1900a Federal Census, Indian Population, Humboldt County, California, South Fork Township.
    1910a Federal Census, Indian Population, Mendocino County, California, Round Valley Township, Round Valley Indian Reservation.

United States Department of Agriculture
    1920a Trinity National Forest, California: 1920 [map]. Washington DC: United States Department of Agriculture, Forest Service. [A version of this map, catalogued at the Bancroft Library as G4362.T7E1 1920; .U5; Case XD, contains annotations and hand colorings done by C. Hart Merriam to show the names of Indian tribes and their boundaries in the Humboldt-Mendocino-Trinity area.]
    2015a Clinton Hart Merriam. Web page. Electronic document, http://www.aphis.usda.gov/wps/portal/aphis/ourfocus/wildlifedamage/sa_programs/sa_nwrc/sa_history/ct_clinton_hart_merriam/!ut/p/a0/04_Sj9CPykssy0xPLMnMz0vMAfGjzOK9_D2MDJ0MjZdzd3V2dDDz93HwCzL-29jAwMTfQLsh0VAXWczqE!/
    2015b Tanoak. Web page. Electronic document, http://plants.usda.gov/plantguide/pdf/cs_lide3.pdf accessed on June 4, 2015.

United States Department of the Interior, Geological Survey
    1949a Alderpoint, California. Quadrangle.
    1955a Kettenpom, California. Quadrangle.

United States Department of Interior, Office of Indian Affairs
    1929 Enrollment Application for George Burt [sic].

United States House of Representatives, Subcommittee of the Committee on Indian Affairs
    1926 Indian Tribes of California. Washington: Government Printing Office.

United States War Department
    1897a The War of the Rebellion: A Compilation of the Official Records of the Union and Confederate Armies; Series 1 - Volume 50 (Part I). Washington DC: Government Printing Office.
    1897b The War of the Rebellion: A Compilation of the Official Records of the Union and Confederate Armies; Series 1 - Volume 50 (Part II). Washington DC: Government Printing Office.

Van Kirk, Susie
    N.d.a. Merrifield Family. Copy in author's possession.

Waltmann, Henry G.
    1971 Circumstantial Reformer: President Grant & the Indian Problem. *Arizona and the West* 13(4):323-342.

Waterman, Thomas Talbot
    1920 Yurok Geography. *University of California Publications in American Archaeology and Ethnology* 16 no. 5:177-314.

White, Ronald C.
    2016 American Ulysses: A Life of Ulysses S. Grant. New York: Random House.

Wikipedia
    2015b Pliny Earle Goddard. Web page. Electronic document, http://en.wikipedia.org/wiki/Pliny_Earle_Goddard accessed on June 1, 2015.
    2105c Clinton Hart Merriam. Web page. Electronic document, https://en.wikipedia.org/wiki/Clinton_Hart_Merriam accessed on July 4, 2015.
    2016c Fort Humboldt State Historic Park. Web page. Electronic document, https://en.wikipedia.org/wiki/Fort_Humboldt_State_Historic_Park accessed on August 25, 2016.
    2016d Albert Sidney Johnson. Web page. Electronic document, https://en.wikipedia.org/wiki/Albert_Sidney_Johnston accessed on August 25, 2016.
    2016e Lieber Code. Web page. Electronic document, https://en.wikipedia.org/wiki/Lieber_Code accessed on August 28, 2016.
    2016f Department of the Pacific. Web page. Electronic document, https://en.wikipedia.org/wiki/Department_of_the_Pacific accessed on August 30, 2016.
    2016g Battle of Fort Pillow. Web page. Electronic document, https://en.wikipedia.org/wiki/Battle_of_Fort_Pillow accessed on September 3, 2016.
    2021a Lakota people. Web page. Electronic document, https://en.wikipedia.org/wiki/Lakota_people accessed on February 14, 2021.
    2021b George Hearst. Web page. Electronic document, https://en.wikipedia.org/wiki/George_Hearst accessed on June 12, 2021.
    2021c Franz Boas. Web page. Electronic document, https://en.wikipedia.org/wiki/Franz_Boas accessed on July 18, 2021.
    2021d Stephen Powers. Web page. Electronic document, https://en.wikipedia.org/wiki/Stephen_Powers accessed on July 18, 2021.
    2021e Phoebe Hearst. Web page. Electronic document, https://en.wikipedia.org/wiki/Phoebe_Hearst accessed on August 8, 2021.

Williams, Jean Rose
    1977a Along the old New River Trail. *Arcata Union*, July 7, 1977:17.

Work Projects Administration
    1940a The National Guard of California 1849-1880, Part 1. Sacramento.
    1940b The National Guard of California 1849-1880, Part 2. Sacramento.

Yue-Hashimoto, Anne
    2000 Professor Li Fang-kuei: a Personal Memoir. *Asia Notes* 4 no. 1:5-6.

Endnotes

1. Goddard 1903a:1.
2. United States Department of Interior, Office of Indian Affairs 1929:2; Ethnological Documents 2002:12(4)206.
3. Driver 1939:308. Driver indicates that Burtt was born about 1855. Burtt's headstone at the Sunrise Cemetery near Fortuna gives the year as 1859, while his death certificate put the year as "about" 1850 (Milota 1993a:76). The description of the migration of Burtt's parents is a modest dramatization of the limited information available about the event.
4. Goddard 1903a:1.
5. Goddard 1903a:1-21.
6. Goddard 1903a:21-38.
7. Kroeber 1929a:2; Thoresen 1975:266.
8. Wikipedia 2021e; Golla 2011:40.
9. Golla 2011:300 note 60.
10. Golla 2011:40.
11. Roland B. Dixon was "Kroeber's closest professional colleague during his early years in California." He received a Ph.D. from Harvard in 1900 and subsequently taught there (Golla 2011:38-39). Dixon's research was not universally held in high repute. In 1927 two persons contacted John Peabody Harrington regarding their negative appraisals of Dixon's work with the Chimariko tribe of western Trinity County. On September 16 Viola Dailey wrote Harrington that the linguist Edward Sapir had been "correcting Dixon's work which didn't seem to take much longer than it did Dixon to write it" (Harrington 1983). Three days later Sapir himself wrote Harrington that he "was not satisfied with Dixon's record" (Golla and O'Neill 2001:1090).
12. anthromuseum.ucdavis.edu 2021a.
13. Nomland mistook her informant, Molly Brock, for a Nongatl, but Brock was actually from the tribe just to the north, the Mawenoks (Merriam 1976:125-125; Humboldt Times 1930a:7.
14. Nomland 1938:91.
15. Nomland 1938:91.
16. Milota 2001a.
17. Nomland 1938:92.
18. Goddard 1929a:292.
19. Nomland 1938:91.
20. Although Nomland lacked access to Goddard's field notes, she made use of his Bear River Dialect of Athabascan (Goddard 1929), in fact determining that Peter had spoken the Mattole language to Goddard, who had believed it to be Bear River (Nomland 1938:92). Goddard's notebooks for his interviews with Peter have not been located.
21. Nomland 1935:149.
22. Margolin 1981.
23. Baldy 2021.
24. Goddard 1907d:27, 39.
25. Nomland 1935:149.
26. Goddard 1903a:69. According to one account, in 1862 "Woodman became one of the few Round Valley Euro-Americans ever prosecuted for kidnapping Indians. Both he and his partner were found guilty in court and received a ludicrously low fine of $100. The case was closed when Woodman paid the fine. Both men were released from custody without serving any time in prison" (Baumgardner 2006:33). The following year Woodman was again taken to court on a charge of kidnapping Indian children, but this time he was exonerated (Sacramento Daily Union 1863a:2).
27. Goodard n.d.e.:83.
28. Goddard 1903a:2.
29. Baumhoff 1958:iii, 157-158.
30. Baumhoff 1958:180.
31. Baumhoff 1958:158.
32. In addition to the notebooks Goddard left at Berkeley, there were four notebooks dealing with the Lassik tribe that he took east with him. These notebooks were part of his "professional library" which was "dispersed to Goddard's "colleagues and admirers" by anthropologist Gladys Reichard, who was living with Goddard when he died suddenly in 1928 (Mattina 2019:74-76). The Lassik notebooks were sent to an anthropologist who did work the Indians of the Pacific northwest. Copies were eventually obtained by local repositories, including CRF.
33. Bancroft Library 1997:vii.
34. American Philosophical Society 2020.
35. Wikipedia 2021c.
36. Baumhoff 1958:iii.
37. Bancroft Library 2020.
38. Kroeber 1997:(127)433.
39. Kroeber 1925:142-154.
40. Kroeber 1925:v.
41. In 2021 Kroeber Hall, at UC Berkeley, was stripped of it name in response to "powerful letters from Native American student groups" (Gomez 2021) and other complaints about Kroeber's attitude and actions towards the "savages" whose "careers" he refused to chronicle. A UC Berkeley Building Name Review Committee had solicited comments from the Berkeley campus community and found that 85% of the respondents favored the removal (Johnson 2021).
42. Baumhoff 1958.
43. Goddard 1903a:66.
44. Goddard 1907b:72.
45. Goddard n.d.a.
46. Goddard 1907a:136.
47. Denny 1911.
48. Baumhoff 1958:197, 199.
49. When I requested access to the notecards in about 2014 the Bancroft Library, after three days of searching, could not locate them.
50. Ethnological Documents:12(4)81-128, 196-206).
51. Baumhoff 1958:196-197.
52. Goddard 1908b:59.
53. Subcommittee of the Committee on Indian Affairs House of Representatives 1926:52. Compare Merriam's heartfelt statement with that of Gertrude Atherton, California novelist and haughty historian: ". . . those Indians of Old California . . . with the exception of a very few tribes . . . were lazy, sullen, subhuman—and hideous" (Atherton 1945:4-5).

54. Powers 1872a.
55. Powers 1872b.
56. Powers 1872a:325.
57. Kroeber 1929a:1-2.
58. Kroeber 1929a:2.
59. Golla 2011:40.
60. Wikipedia 2015b.
61. Golla 2011:40.
62. Golla 2011:40.
63. Kroeber 1929a:5.
64. Ethnological Documents 2002:12(1):10.
65. Ethnological Documents 2002:12(5)62-64.
66. In the summer of 1922 Goddard briefly returned to Humboldt and Mendocino counties and conducted interviews that later led to monographs on the Bear River and Wailaki tribes (Goddard 1922a, 1923, 1929).
67. Goddard had also published significant material on the Hupa and Chilula tribes, but not on any of the others.
68. The Cultural Resources Facility (CRF) at Humboldt State University and I obtained copies of these notebooks. Pertinent sections of the notebooks were transcribed by upper division anthropology students, whose work I then edited. The Lassik notebooks, obtained later, have not been transcribed or edited, but, along with the other Goddard notebooks, have provided information for this book. As a research associate at CRF, I joined my colleagues there in determining that the Goddard notebooks contained sensitive cultural information, and that their use would therefore be restricted; only scholarly researchers, agency officials, and members of relevant Indian tribes are allowed access.
69. One source gives the year as 1883 (United States Department of Agriculture 2015a), another as 1885 (Osgood 1944:5).
70. United States Department of Agriculture 2015a.
71. Palmer 1954:130.
72. Wikipedia 2015c.
73. Osgood 1944:8.
74. Wikipedia 2015c.
75. Wikipedia 2015c.
76. Goetzman and Sloan 1982:208-209.
77. PBS 2015a.
78. PBS 2015b.
79. PBS 2015b.
80. Osgood 1944:22.
81. Golla 2011:43.
82. Merriam 1993:(129)25.
83. Merriam 1966:39-40.
84. Goddard 1908e:104.
85. Goddard 1908d:92.
86. Wikipedia 2021d.
87. Powers 1877:107-124.
88. Kroeber 1925:IX.
89. Golla 2011:45-47.
90. Williams 1977a:17.
91. The latter was the son of Joe Duncan, who had supplied significant information to Goddard and Merriam.
92. Harrington 1983.
93. Hewes 1940:32-52.
94. Curtis 1970b. Although Curtis is listed as sole author of the series, it is clear that Myers did substantial work on most of the volumes (Egan 2012:248, 272; Makepeace 2002:151).
95. Curtis 1970b:167.
96. Merriam 1993:(31)19.
97. Murphey 1941.
98. Essene 1942:84, 89-92.
99. Essene 1942:30, 32.
100. Elsasser 1978:190.
101. Baumhoff 1963:173-175.
102. "Hence these tears."
103. A wonderful visual aid to the southern Humboldt topography is the 14-foot-tall J. N. Lentell relief map of the county that covers part of a wall at the Clarke Museum in Eureka.
104. A compelling account of the tanoak tree is in Bowcutt 2015. For the importance of acorns as a food, see also Merriam 1918a and Baumhoff 1963.
105. Many field guides provide relevant information about local tree species. One of the most helpful is Stuart and Sawyer 2001.
106. Lewis 1991; Crismon n.d.a.
107. A very helpful account of the plants and animals of the area is Kircher and Morrison 1993. Brief accounts of the geology, plants, and wildlife of the South Fork Eel area are found in Rohde and Rohde 1992.
108. Goddard 1908b:104-106. Nomland describes the circular house as being used by the Sinkyone and a wedge-shaped lean-to used not only by them but also by the Mattole and Bear River Indians (Nomland 1935:157). The unprecedented visit by the northern Humboldt Indians is a dramatization.
109. Waterman 1993:208-209; Goddard 1908b:99-100.
110. Goddard 1907b:72.
111. Nomland 1938:106.
112. Nomland 1935:157.
113. Goddard 1908b:98-99,105-111.
114. Kroeber 1925a:145-146.
115. Baumhoff 1978:16-17.
116. Baumhoff 1963:161.
117. Curtis 1970:22.
118. Nomland 1935:154.
119. Nomland 1938:112.
120. Hewes 1940:34-37.
121. Essene 1942:84.
122. Nomland 1938:110; 1935:152.
123. Nomland 1935:152.
124. Goddard 1903a:67-68.
125. Curtis 1970:24.
126. Nomland 1938:111.
127. Nomland 1935:157.
128. Driver 1939:330.
129. Nomland 1935:154.
130. Nomland 1938:112.
131. Goddard 1907f:18-19.
132. Nomland 1938:109.
133. Baumhoff lists the preferences of 12 northwestern California tribes. None are from southern Humboldt and the only proximate tribe is the Hupas.
134. Baumhoff 1963:163.
135. Nomland 1935:154-155.
136. Bowcutt 2015:25.
137. Bowcutt 2015:29; Brown and Baldo 2010:5.
138. Merriam 1918:129-130.
139. Nomland 1938:110.
140. Noland 1935:155; 1938:110.
141. Nomland 1935:153.
142. Nomland 1938:110.

Endnotes

143. Essene 1942:84.
144. Nomland 1935:159.
145. Cook 2021:89-108.
146. Certainly this author at least.
147. The names and locations of these groups are given in chapter 4.
148. Baumhoff 1958. The actual total is probably much higher, chiefly because Baumhoff lacked the detailed information available in Goddard's field notes.
149. Goddard 1907b:29.
150. Goddard 1907b:19-21, 29-31.
151. Goddard 1907b:31-35.
152. Golla 2009.
153. The boulder that had helped form the no-le was perhaps a victim of the San Francisco Earthquake, which had occurred just a year earlier.
154. The author conducted a site inspection of the area on September 30, 2009.
155. Goddard 1907b:35-40.
156. Larson, et al. 2011.
157. Goddard 1923:95.
158. Goddard 1923:95.
159. He was also called Little Charlie or just Charlie. His land patent gives his name as Charlie Briceland (BLM 2021a).
160. Goddard 1903a:39.
161. Powers 1976: 109-110.
162. Kroeber 1925:145. It is unclear what his source was.
163. Kroeber 1925:145-146. It is unclear what his source was.
164. Nomland 1935:165-166.
165. Nomland 1935:166; Goddard 1903a:49.
166. Curtis 1970:27.
167. United States House of Representatives 1927:57.
168. General accounts of these events are found in Coy 1982:44, Lewis 1966:159, and Raphael and House 2011:73.
169. General accounts of these events are found in Coy 1982:44-70, Lewis 1966:159-170, and Raphael and House 2011:73-98.
170. Rohde 2008a.
171. Raphael and House 2011:109-125, 155-188; Madley 2016; Goddard 1907e:5; Sam 1921?c., 1921?e; Rohde 2008a, 2010a, 2016a.
172. Raphael and House 2011:187-188.
173. Elliott 1881:135-136.
174. Robinson 1948:17-18.
175. Belcher Abstract & Title Co. 1921-1922:1-4, 13.
176. Bear River Band 2021.
177. Elsasser 1978:195.
178. This area is mentioned by Briceland Charlie: "Water raised one time. All [the people] went up on Grasshopper ridge to north of Charlies place. They turned to stones that stick off there now in a row. Water didn't come that far" (Goddard 1903a:49).
179. Asbill 1953:ii-iv, xvii. In the late 1940s Frank Asbill wrote a lengthy account about the exploits of his father, Pierce Asbill, and other "mountain men" who roamed through the wilds of southeastern Humboldt, southwestern Trinity, and northern Mendocino counties in the 1850s and 1860s. Frank based his manuscript on the conversations among these men that he heard at the Asbill house when he was a youth. In 1953 the manuscript was annotated by Rowland Choate, a Humboldt State College student, for a History 288A class. In 1975 the manuscript was published as The Last of the West, with Frank Asbill and Argle Shawley listed as co-authors. Asbill had died in 1949 (Asbill 1953:iv). If the massacre was in retaliation for the Indians' attack on the Sproul brothers, it probably occurred in 1861 (United States War Department 1897a:8.)
180. Frank Asbill said that the Sproul brothers were "cut to pieces with elk-bone knives," implying they had been killed when they actually had been severely wounded. He also indicated that "the same merciless treatment would have been given to Mrs. Boman [sic] had her husband not come when he did" (Asbill 1953:111). Mrs. Bowman, however, had been shot at, not cut with knives, and she could not have been rescued by her husband as he was dead at the time of the attack (Felt 1869). The incident took place near McCann in March 1869 (Felt 1869).
181. United States War Department 1897a:8; Turner and Turner 2010:222.
182. Merriam 1993:(1)46.
183. Asbill 1953:109-110.
184. Asbill 1953:110-111.
185. Goddard 1923:95. Goddard, who researched the ethnogeography of the area extensively, states: "The term Wailaki . . . may be applied to those Indians of the Athapascan stock who occupied the valley of the North Fork and the valley of the main Eel river below (northward) from Round valley, Mendocino county, to Kikawaka [sic] creek in Humboldt county."
186. Asbill 1953:111.
187. Asbill 1953:113.
188. The inn was located just south of Richardson Grove State Park. Its buildings still stand.
189. Asbill 1953:116.
190. Asbill 1953:118.
191. Asbill spells the last name "Naphus," but it is usually rendered "Neaphus" (Jones 1981:346).
192. Asbill 1953:122-123.
193. Asbill 1953:112-117. Asbill's account of the last stages of the pursuit wanders and becomes disjointed. I have attempted to place the events he describes in their proper sequence.
194. Asbill 1953:118.
195. Carranco and Baird 1981:192-193.
196. Smith 2001:520. Smith erroneously claims that Grant was referring to the Indians of California, but Grant's statement was made while he was at Fort Vancouver in Washington Territory (White 2016:115).
197. Hunt 1982:12.
198. Hunt 1982:12.
199. Strobridge 1994:52.
200. Humboldt Historian 1987a:13.
201. Smith 2001:84-87.
202. Humboldt Historian 1987a:13.
203. Powers 1949:84.
204. Smith 2001:84-87.
205. Three sources that describe Grant's dismal days at Fort Humboldt are: Smith 2001:84-88; Chernow 2017:82-87; and White 2016:118-121.
206. Humboldt Historian 1987a:13:White 2016:120.
207. Strobridge 1992:53.
208. Strobridge 1992:60.
209. Strobridge 1992:61-62.
210. Strobridge 1992:63-65.
211. Rohde 2014:218.

212. Heizer 1993:47-52.
213. Rohde 2014:219.
214. This band of Indians was led by a man nicknamed "Red Cap, so called from a greasy-looking woollen head-piece, with which some miner had presented him, and which ordinarily constituted his sole dress, was a short, thickset individual, with a droll countenance, reminding one of the most authentic likenesses of Santa Claus. He is a man of considerable influence, friendly to the whites, and enjoying a high character for honesty" (Gibbs 2016:51).
215. Madley 2016a:236.
216. The number of troops under Judah's command is given as either 25 (Bledsoe 1885:165), 26 (Humboldt Times 1855c:2), or 30 (Madley 2016:237). The size of the detachment may have varied over time, but in any case, the number was small.
217. Madley 2016a:225, 234-237; Bledsoe 1885:163-176. Bledsoe's account is often tinged by his bias against the Indians but some of his reporting, such as that pertaining to Captain Judah, appears to approach truthfulness.
218. Bledsoe 1885:170. Bledsoe claims that another regular army officer was involved in the conflict as "several rancherias or tribes had surrendered to Capt. U. S. Grant" (Bledsoe 1885:168). This feat, had it actually occurred, would have been miraculous, since at the time of the surrender the recently resigned Grant was a civilian farmer in Missouri (Smith 2001:90).
219. Madley 2016:237.
220. Heizer and Almquist 1971:26.
221. Humboldt Times 1858a:2.
222. Coy 1982:147.
223. Works Project Administration 1940a:239-242.
224. Long 1960: 94. The figures for the skilled workers are based on a 60-hour work week.
225. The pay for a U. S. Army private in 1861 was $13 per month (Arms 2016:20).
226. Madley 2016:290.
227. Bledsoe 1885:310-312.
228. Rohde 2010a.
229. Northern Californian 1860a:3. Although the Northern Californian refers to the unit as the Hydesville Volunteers, official records list it as the Humboldt Volunteers, Second Brigade (militarymuseum.org 2016a).
230. Madley 2016:282; Heizer 1993:156.
231. Rohde 2010a.
232. Rohde 2010a.
233. Wikipedia 2016c.
234. Wikipedia 2016d.
235. United States War Department 1897a:458.
236. Madley 2016:292-293.
237. Madley 2016:292-293.
238. United States War Department 1897a:20-21.
239. United States War Department 1897a:19.
240. Hunt 2004:19.
241. Hunt 2004:19.
242. Hunt 2004:24.
243. Hunt 2004:26.
244. Madley 2016:300.
245. Works Project Administration 1940b:343-344.
246. United States War Department 1897a:907. The author of this March 1862 account was Col. Francis J. Lippitt, the new commander at Fort Humboldt.
247. Humboldt Times 1861a:3.
248. United States War Department 1897a:463-464.
249. Smith 2001:102.
250. Glaze 2021; Wikipedia 2016d
251. Work Projects Administration 1940b:344.
252. United States War Department 1897a:2-3.
253. United States War Department 1897a:916.
254. United States War Department 1897a:803-804.
255. At the time, the word "rancheria" usually referred to a small Indian settlement.
256. United States War Department 1897a:803.
257. United States War Department 1897a:55.
258. United States War Department 1897a:992.
259. United States War Department 1897a:994.
260. Wikipedia 2016e.
261. avalon.law.yale.edu
262. There is some question as to whether General Order 100 was meant to apply to Indians. The document focuses on what it calls a "Hostile Army," which was comprised of soldiers who wear uniforms and are essentially similar to members of the U. S. Army. It is unclear how Indian combatants were to be regarded (Garner 1965:18). As noted later in this article, however, General McDowell's General Order 53 of November 1864 clearly stated that executing Indians was against the law, which indicates that General Order 100 was finally being applied to Indian combatants.
263. Northern Californian 1858a:2.
264. Madley 2016:318.
265. United States War Department 1897b:558.
266. Wikipedia 2016f.
267. Madley suggests that the dispatch "may have been mere political insurance against future criticism" (Madley 2016:318).
268. Orton 1890:828,830. Company C was mustered in on August 28, Company E on August 31.
269. Orton 1890:425-426. The mention of the "Humboldt Reservation" is confounding, since no reservation by that name existed. Perhaps this is a garbled reference to Fort Humboldt, where Indians were sometimes taken prior to their transfer to the Smith River Reservation.
270. Smith 2001:284-286.
271. Eggenberger 1985:416, 474.
272. Seidner 1939[?]:2; McLean 1917:137.
273. Kinman 2010:31.
274. BlackPast.org 2016. Not all sources agree that the Confederates massacred garrison soldiers after they surrendered, but it appears that a preponderance of the evidence endorses that conclusion (Wikipedia 2016g).
275. Spartacus Educational 2016; History Vault 2016; Encyclopædia Britannica 2016a.
276. New York Times 1864a.
277. Madley 2016:321-322.
278. Humboldt Times 1864a:3.
279. Daily Alta California 1864a:1.
280. Madley 2016:323-324; Nelson 1988:88-89; Humboldt Times 1864b:2, 1864c:2.
281. Coy 1982:192-193.
282. United States War Department 1897b:963.
283. Orton 1890:830.
284. United States War Department 1897a:391-392; United States War Department 1897b:963.
285. United States War Department 1897b:1068.
286. Orton 1890:827-831.
287. Smith 2001:523.

Endnotes

288. It should be noted that although Grant started his presidential administration with a "peace policy" towards the Indians, he eventually yielded to pressure to remove Indians from locations such as the Black Hills, where gold had been discovered. In 1875 Grant indicated that that the army would no longer enforce the 1868 Treaty of Fort Laramie, which reserved the Black Hills and surrounding areas for the Indians "in perpetuity." Further, he instructed General Phil Sheridan to force non-reservation Indians onto a reservation. Soon Sheridan had three columns of soldiers in the field. One was led by Colonel George A. Custer, part of whose column came to a dead halt at the Little Big Horn on June 25, 1876. Before the sun had set, the column ceased to exist (Smith 2001:472-473, 538-539; Cozzens 2016a:252-265). Elsewhere Cozzens alleges a Grant-led "conspiracy" to remove the Northern Sioux from the Black Hills (Cozzens 2016b). I have tried to locate a key document that Cozzens cites in support of this contention, but have been unable to do so. My thanks to Bob Libershal for alerting me to the Cozzens article. Another reviewer of Grant's policy towards the Indians concluded that "Grant as a President . . . made some promising initial attempts to strike out on a new course, but lacked the drive and sense of direction to make continued headway against the obstacles that soon emerged" (Waltman 1971:342).
289. The Chilulas were actually the northernmost members of the Whilkut tribe, having received their distinguishing name from the neighboring Yurok tribe. Since most of the accounts used in this narrative identified these Indians as Chilula, the nomenclature will be kept here.
290. Monroe 1962:2.
291. Humboldt Times 1862c:2.
292. Surveyor General's Office 1876d.
293. Monroe 1862:6; Goddard 1914a:268.
294. Impr. 1858:2.
295. Humboldt Times 1858b:2. The Times also railed at the white murderers for being "degraded . . . by habitually living with squaws . . . ."
296. Humboldt Times 1858c:2.
297. Humboldt Times 1857a:2.
298. Humboldt Times 1858c:2.
299. Humboldt Times 1858d:2.
300. Humboldt Times 1858e:2.
301. Humboldt Times 1858f:2.
302. Humboldt Times 1858g:2.
303. Humboldt Times 1858h:2.
304. Surveyor General's Office 1858b.
305. Humboldt times 1858i:2.
306. Humboldt Times 1858j:2. Another article in the same issue repeated the suggestion that genocide was an option: "Removal or extermination now being the watchword . . . ." (Humboldt Times 1858a:2).
307. Humboldt Times 1858k:2.
308. Humboldt Times 1858l:2. The Eureka Board of Trustees subsequently determined that they lacked the authority to levy the tax (Humboldt Times 1858n:2).
309. Humboldt Times 1858m:2.
310. Monroe 1962:7.
311. Works Progress Administration 1940a:239.
312. Works Progress Administration 1940a:240.
313. Works Progress Administration 1940a:240.
314. Works Progress Administration 1940a:240.
315. Madley 2016:264; Humboldt Times 1858p:2; Trinity Weekly Journal 1858a:2.
316. Humboldt Times 1858p:2.
317. Humboldt Times 1858q:2.
318. Humboldt Times 1858r:2. The article claims that the ranch "had been vacated on account of being surrounded by hostile Indians," but fails to explain how the Trinity Rangers, operating in the neighborhood, had let this happen.
319. Humboldt Times 1858s:2.
320. Goddard n.d.f.:114-115.
321. Humboldt Times 1858s:2.
322. Humboldt Times 1858t:2.
323. Humboldt Times 1858u:2.
324. Humboldt Times 1859b:2.
325. Humboldt Times 1859c:2.
326. Goddard 1914a:274-275, Plate 38; n.d.f.:81-83.
327. Humboldt Times 1859d:2.
328. Humboldt Times 1859d:2.
329. Humboldt Times 1859e:2.
330. Humboldt Times 1859d:2.
331. Bledsoe 1885:273-274.
332. Bledsoe 1885:274-275.
333. Goddard n.d.f.:110-111.
334. Goddard n.d.f.:63, 65.
335. Goddard 1914a:265.
336. Goddard n.d.f.:114-115.
337. Humboldt Times 1859f:2.
338. Goddard 1914a:269.
339. Essene 1942:89-92.
340. Goddard n.d.f.:116.
341. Goddard's field notes state: "they were all killed." (Goddard n.d.f.:116). His monograph on the Chilulas says that the Lassiks killed "all but one or two" (Goddard 1914a:269). His notes do not seem to contain all the information present in his published works on the Chilulas. Perhaps some notebooks are missing. The June 4, 1859 edition of the Weekly Humboldt Times contained an article stating that 20 Redwood Indians, who had escaped from the Mendocino Reservation, had tried to obtain food at an Indian ranch in Long Valley, in Mendocino County, and that they were all killed by the local Indians except the one who gave the report (Humboldt Times 1859j:2). This may have been a second group of escapees or it may have been a corruption of Lyons's story.
342. Goddard 1914b:351.
343. Goddard 1914a:269.
344. Goddard 1907b:18.
345. Goddard 1903a:56.
346. Goddard n.d.f.:117-120. According to a report in the Humboldt Times, the first whites to arrive at Albee's after the murder "found all his fine improvements, the labor of years, in ashes . . ." (Humboldt Times 1862d:2).
347. Goddard n.d.f.:120.
348. Goddard n.d.f.:121.
349. Goddard 1914a:269-270.
350. Nelson 1988:187-188.
351. Goddard 1914a:265, 272.
352. In this chapter, Goddard's information is cited more often than all the other sources combined.
353. This was the land held by the Bear River (Nekanni) tribe, which included all of its namesake river, the lower end of the Van Duzen, and a short stretch of the main Eel.
354. Golla 2015b.
355. Kroeber 1962:29-38.

356. All the southern Humboldt Indians spoke some form of what are called the "California Athabascan languages," part of the widespread Athabascan language family that also includes numerous tribes in Alaska, Canada, southwestern Oregon, New Mexico, and Arizona. Among the best-known members of this group are the Navajo, Apache, Cree, and Ojibwa.

357. Goddard 1903a, 1907b, 1907e, 1908a, 1908d, plus other notebooks not used in this book. Goddard did record a notebook full of information from Pete's wife, Minnie, but she was from a neighboring tribe, the Mawenoks, whose language resembled that of the more northerly Whilkut tribe (Goddard 1908c; Golla 2015a). The other two Nongatls who were interviewed by ethnographers, Nick Richard and Susie Burt, supplied very little language information. Richard spoke with Harold Driver, describing "cultural elements" of Indians from the Van Duzen (Driver 1939) and also with Gordon Hewes, where the main subject was fishing practices (Hewes 1940). Susie Burtt was interviewed by C. Hart Merriam as a sort of adjunct to his more extensive recording of information from her husband, George Burtt. Susie provided Merriam with 94 names of plants and animals and a few other words (Merriam 1993:(30)346, 508, 582, 584;(52)179-207).

358. Kroeber 1925:142-154.

359. "Let the reader beware."

360. Baumhoff 1958:162. Baumhoff shows Kroeber's mapping in greater detail than the original depiction in Kroeber's Handbook.

361. Merriam 1993:(9)281. Other ethnographers name the tribe by its primary geographical location, Bear River. Goddard refers to the "Bear River people" and a "Bear River Athabascan dialect" without ever specifically mentioning a Bear River tribe (Goddard 1929:292). Nomland writes of the "Bear River Indians," which she indeed refers to as a tribe. She also indicates that "the Bear River people called themselves and the Mattole by the same name, Níekení," but she chose not to use this name to designate the Bear River tribe (Nomland 1938:91-92). Others also conflated the Nekanni with the neighboring Mattole tribe. Kroeber claims that the Mattoles "held the Bear River and Mattole drainages" (Kroeber 1976a:142). Elsasser refers to the Mattoles as one of "five groups collectively referred to as the southern Athabascans," along with the Nongatls, Sinkyones, Lassiks, and Wailakis. He notes, however, "that the case of the Mattole and their neighbor to the north, the Bear River people, presents a quandary," since they spoke dialects that "were recognizably distinct and they were slightly different in culture." Nonetheless, he concludes lamely, "because they at least shared a continuous section of coastline and because they are not separated in the earlier literature, being simply called Mattole . . . , they will be considered here a single unit" (Elsasser 1978:190-191). By now the use of the name "Bear River" for the Nekanni tribe has become so ingrained that it will (reluctantly) be continued here in order to avoid confusion.

362. Goddard 1929:291; Nomland 1938:91-92, Map 1.

363. Nomland 1938:104.

364. Nomland 1938:105.

365. So Merriam renders the name. A more plausible version might be Klah-tel-kos-tah.

366. Merriam 1993:(31)336.

367. Merriam 1993:(31)336. One of John P. Harrington's Mattole informants corroborates this, indicating that the gulch where the wagon road from Petrolia reached the beach, which would have been at Oil Creek, "was the line betw[een] the Wiyot tribe and the Bear River tribe" (Harrington 1983:(2)575).

368. Loud 1918:287, Plate 1.

369. Loud 1918:Plate 1; Nomland 1939:Map 1; Baumhoff 1958:161-163; Merriam and Talbot 1974:26; Nomland and Kroeber 1936:39-40, 47; Kroeber 1976a:113-114, 142; Goddard n.d.a:74; Hewes 1940:34; Powers 1976:101, 122). None of these sources is in exact agreement with any of the others regarding the boundaries. The exact course of this boundary line, while uncertain, is subject to informed speculation. Knowing that the western end was at the mouth of Oil Creek, it seems most likely that the line ran southeastward along Bear River Ridge through the later Mazeppa Ranch, turned north near Big Hill to skirt the headwaters of Price Creek, and then followed the ridge immediately north of Price Creek to its terminus at Weymouth Bluff. This would bring the boundary to a point nearly opposite the mouth of the Van Duzen, where there was a Bear River village. There was a known "Indian trail above Grizzly Bluff" (Edeline 1978:7) that apparently followed this ridgeline and which would have connected the village at the mouth of the Van Duzen with Bear River Ridge. Another possibility is a boundary line running north from Bear River Ridge along the ridgeline between Price and Howe Creeks. This is the line shown by Loud (Loud 1918:Plate 1), but he incorrectly shows another section of the Wiyot-Bear River boundary as running east of the mouth of the Van Duzen, rather than at the mouth itself, which could mean that his line up onto Bear River Ridge is also too far to the east. With the Bear River tribe claiming the Eel between the mouth of the Van Duzen and Rio Dell, it is likely that they also controlled the drainages of the streams that entered into that section of the river. On the west side of the Eel this would include both Howe Creek and Price Creek; the boundary I propose would run along the northern side of the Price Creek drainage.

370. Harrington 1983:(2)575.

371. Goddard 1919:325.

372. Goddard n.d.a.:74.

373. Loud 1918:273.

374. Loud 1918:273, Plate 1.

375. Merriam and Talbot 1974:10.

376. Harrington 1983:(1)447.

377. Edeline 1978:7.

378. While Goddard calls it this (Goddard 1929:291), Nomland gives the name as Itc'alkó (Nomland 1939:Map 1), and Merriam refers to it as Chal-kó-chak (Merriam 1993:(31)336).

379. Goddard 1907a:140.

380. Merriam 1993:(30)265; Nomland 1938:91; Harrington 1983:(2)606. The Mattole Indian Joe Duncan told Goddard that there was a camp called Set-co-be-nin-do-din "north of [the] lighthouse" (Goddard 1907a:139), which implies that it belonged to the Mattoles, but elsewhere Goddard indicates that there was a Bear River village called Setcodan "by the lighthouse," which was "a popu-

Endnotes

lous place" (Goddard 1929:291). Thus it appears that the camp that Duncan mentioned, being north of Setcodan and north of the Davis Creek border, was in Bear River territory.

381. If an Indian was killed, his or her family was paid an indemnity by the family of the person responsible for the death. In this instance, the indication is that so many Indians were killed that only a massive indemnity (a whale) sufficed.
382. Harrington 1983:(2):707-708.
383. Nomland 1938:106.
384. Nomland 1938:104-105.
385. The only conflict I have identified with more than two battles was the one between the Lassiks and the Chilulas described in Chapter 3.
386. Merriam 1993:(14)228.
387. Cozzens 2016a:47.
388. Cozzens 2016a:47-49.
389. Goddard 1929:292.
390. Merriam 1921a:32; 1922a:40; 1998:(31)247.
391. Nomland 1938:91.
392. Milota 2003.
393. Nomland 1938:92.
394. Duncan indicated that he was "10 or 12 years old" when he first saw whites (Merriam 1993:(9)140), who had arrived in the Mattole Valley as early as 1854 (Humboldt Times 1854a:2). He was thus of an age that allowed him to clearly comprehend the tragic events that soon befell his people.
395. Goddard 1907a:139. Baumhoff, when mapping the Mattole tribe's territory, relies on Goddard's village notecards, but five cards that apparently refer to the tribe's northernmost villages were missing from the set. What Baumhoff has labeled as Mattole village number 1 actually has the number 6 on Goddard's notecard. Goddard's field notes with Joe Duncan indicate several village and camp locations north of village number 6 that may have been described on the missing notecards (Goddard 1907a:136-142). Goddard's village numbers are in the upper left corner of each card; numbers that correspond with Baumhoff's sequence appear in the upper right corner of the cards, which suggests that they were written in later by Baumhoff (if so, this constitutes a serious breach of scholarly etiquette). When I attempted to view the original notecards at the Bancroft Library, the cards could not, even after three days of searching, be found.
396. Ethnological Documents 2002:12(4)95-96; Goddard 1907f:4-5). In the latter reference Joe Duncan indicates that: "a house and barn on higher beach John Mackey. This far [south] Mattole people lived." Another section of Goddard's field notes are less precise: "Joe's [Duncan] country as far as Kooskie and the light house" (Goddard1907a:130), but these two locations are more than three miles apart. Harrington, interviewing Joe Duncan's son, Ike, and Johnny Jackson, indicated that "Kooskie Mt. was disputed & was being paid for," which suggests that the Mattole tribe was attempting to settle a boundary dispute there (Harrington 1983:(2)649).
397. Goddard indicated that the last Mattole village upstream on the Mattole River was near Conklin Creek, while the most downstream village of the "Upper Mattole people" was near Indian Creek. Thus the most probable location for the boundary between the two tribes would be the barrier that separates the two villages, Shenanigan Ridge (Ethnological Documents 2002:12(4)112-113).
398. Except for the boundary points on the coast given by Joe Duncan, I have been unable to locate any precise description of Mattole territory in the primary ethnographical record. The boundary I propose follows the ridgelines that enclose drainages I believe were held by the Mattoles. Baumhoff, using the limited information available to him, maps a similar boundary for what he believed was the northern tribelet of the Mattoles but which was actually the entirety of the tribe's land. He differs chiefly by drawing a nearly straight line for the southeastern boundary, whereas in point of fact it almost certainly wriggled around the headwaters of the various creeks that his line intersects (Baumhoff 1958:197).
399. Driver 1939:415.
400. Driver 1939:415.
401. Coy 1982:152-155.
402. Goddard 1907f:16.
403. Legier 1958:18.
404. Murphey 1941:351-354.
405. Belcher 1921:4.
406. Ethnological Documents 2001:12(4):86-87.
407. Belcher 1921:4.
408. Goddard 1907f:94-96.
409. Merriam 1993:(9)140.
410. Goddard 1908b:42; 1907c:129.
411. Hodge 1910a:576, 874. Elsewhere in Hodge's books Goddard referred to the tribe as "Sinkine," (Hodge 1907a:735, 761) which is closer to the word Charlie gave him, but with the main entry for the tribe using "Sinkyone" it was this latter name that stuck.
412. Hodge 1910a:576.
413. It is possible to confuse this Sally Bell, who lived near the coast at Four Corners, with another Indian woman, Sallie Bell, a member of the Wailaki tribe, who lived in Round Valley (United States Bureau of the Census 1910a).
414. Merriam and Talbot 1974:10-11; Merriam 1993:(1)64, 78. Merriam, who collected almost no information from Smith, apparently decided to accept his Lassik informants' claims that their tribe's territory extended westward over Mail Ridge all the way to the South Fork Eel (Merriam 1993(31)19), which led Merriam to place Smith's To-kub-be ke-ahs within the Lassik tribe. Nomland suggests a boundary somewhat similar to Merriam's, but it is unclear how this determination was made (Nomland 1935:149-150). Goddard's various Sinkyone informants describe their tribe as controlling both sides of the South Fork Eel. None of them mention a Lassik presence in the South Fork drainage.
415. Nomland 1935:150.
416. Baumhoff 1958.
417. Baumhoff 1858:186, 189, 190.
418. As opposed to Merriam's belief that it included only the west side of the river.
419. Merriam 1993:(30)420, 422.
420. Goddard 1903a:1, 1907c:138-152; Merriam 1993:(30)346, 419-420, 422. Merriam's papers, unlike Goddard's, do not contain notebooks that provide verbatim records of what the interviewees actually said. Instead, Merriam filled out vocabu-

lary lists on preprinted forms, made rough notes of important information, and created summaries or paraphrases of Indians' statements in his own words. The material cited from Merriam 1993 is from his collected papers, while Merriam and Talbot's 1974 account is a summary of Merriam's findings prepared by his daughter, Zenaida Merriam Talbot, under his supervision (Merriam and Talbot 1974:i-ii). Near the end of his career it appears that Merriam was eager to tie up some of the many loose ends that existed in his research. In doing so, he reached certain conclusions not fully supported by his interview information.

421. Merriam 1993(1)322. He states here that the "Lo-lahn-kok . . . [claimed] main Eel from Shively to Scotia." Elsewhere Merriam indicates that the group held the main Eel "from Shively to Dyerville" (Merriam 1993:(9)153). I have taken the two statements together as indicating Lolahnkok control of the main Eel from Scotia to the mouth of the South Fork at Dyerville. Merriam also believed, without any apparent substantiation, that Lolahnkok territory continued up the main Eel past the South Fork to McCann, but Briceland Charlie provided detailed information to Goddard showing that a series of other Sinkyone tribal groups occupied this area (Ethnological Documents 2002:12(4):46-56). On the other hand, Charlie's information is vaguer than Burtt's for the main Eel downstream from the mouth of the South Fork. Charlie named several places on the main Eel in this area, but the locations Goddard recorded are imprecise, unlike the descriptions that George Burtt provided Merriam (Ethnological Documents 2002:12(4):42-45; Merriam 1993(9)153).

422. United States Department of Agriculture 1920a. The map resolves conflicts in Merriam's textual boundary descriptions, since Merriam and Talbot are inconsistent in assigning territory on the northeast side of the Eel. At one point they claim that the Lolahnkoks held this area "a few miles" back from the river (Merriam and Talbot 1974:10), while a page later they indicate that both sides of the Eel "from junction of Van Duzen to Dobbin Creek" belonged to the "Ket-tel or Lassick" (Merriam and Talbot 1974:11) a bizarre claim that reflects a faulty understanding of basic tribal nomenclature and ethnogeography. Merriam's notes on the Lolahnkoks contain a sort of compromise between these two extremes, indicating that the group claimed the west side of the river, while "on the east side of main Eel River it [their claim] is confined to a narrow strip along the river . . ." (Merriam 1993:(9)153). Nowhere does Merriam explain the rationale for any of these assertions. This leaves his working map, which reflects the usual pattern of tribal land control, whereby a particular group claimed the entirety of a section of a stream or river canyon, from one bounding ridgeline to the other. It is the map that guides my description.

423. Merriam and Talbot 1974:10; Merriam 1993:(9)153.
424. Loud 1918:273, Plate 1.
425. Harrington 1983:(1)637.
426. Merriam 1993:(9)153, 169-170.
427. Ethnological Documents 2002:12(4):42-45. One place is described as being near "a big rock [that] is said to project there in the river pointing down-stream" which is probably High Rock.
428. Goddard 1903a:55. The name is rendered as "Itcunta dun" in Goddard's village notecards (Ethnological Documents 2002:12(4)57).
429. Merriam 1993:(9)170.
430. On the South Fork, Goddard's village notecards indicate that a string of Sinkene villages began south of the mouth of Bull Creek and extended upriver to the vicinity of Fish Creek, which is located between Phillipsville and Miranda (Ethnological Documents 2002:12(4):61-91). Goddard also states that the area at the mouth of the South Fork was Sinkene (Ethnological Documents 2002:12(4):57), but this assertion apparently comes from Charlie's statement that the inhabitants of the Dyerville area were "our kind people," (Goddard 1903a:57), which Goddard seems to have thought meant "my kind of people," i.e., Sinkene. I have given this a different interpretation, believing that the "our" generalized the reference to mean all the Sinkyone people regardless of tribal group. If this was the case, then Merriam's claim that the lower South Fork was Lolahnkok is accurate.
431. Merriam and Talbot 11974:10.
432. Goddard 1903a:19; 1908b:52-54; Ethnological Documents 2002:12(4):46-56, 186. Goddard's 1903 notebook entry is difficult to decipher, but the order of the tribal groups listed there has been harmonized, as much as possible, with the information provided on his village notecards in the Ethnological Documents. In addition, Goddard renders some of the names he received from Charlie in 1908 differently than in his 1903 interview. The 1908 names appear in parentheses after the 1903 names.
433. Ethnological Documents 2002:12(4):186-187.
434. Ethnological Documents 2002:12(4):186-195.
435. Goddard 1908b:20.
436. Goddard 1908f:24. Redwood Creek flows through the Briceland area on its way to the South Fork Eel. It is not be confused with the better-known, more northerly Redwood Creek that runs northwestwardly between the Mad and South Fork Trinity rivers.
437. Ethnological Documents:12(4):61-91; Goddard 1908f:65.
438. Ethnological Documents:12(4):61-91.
439. Merriam 1993:(30)422.
440. Harrington 1983:(2)697.
441. Ethnological Documents 2002:12(4):129; Goddard n.d.d.:10.
442. Ethnological Documents 2002:12(4):136.
443. Goddard n.d.d:12.
444. Goddard 1907c:55; Ethnological Documents 2002:12(4):138.
445. Sam's last name was spelled variously. His death record refers to him as Sam Solto (Milota 1993b:711); he lost an "l" in the 1900 Indian census, which lists him as Sam Soto (U. S. Bureau of the Census 1900a:234b); the 1911 Denny map uses Soltos (Denny 1911); the 1921 Belcher map has it as Solto (Belcher 1921:3); a news article about his death calls him Indian Sam; and Pliny Goddard's field notes have him as Sam Suder (Goddard n.d.d:1). Goddard's rendering is used here, since he interviewed Sam and had the best opportunity to accurately record his last name.
446. Ethnological Documents 2002:12(4)136.
447. Goddard 1903a:13.
448. Goddard n.d.d:5.

Endnotes

449. Lentell 1898; Denny 1911; Belcher Abstract & Title Co. 1921:3.
450. Goddard n.d.d:4.
451. Goddard n.d.d:5.
452. Merriam 1993:(52)117.
453. Ethnological Documents 2002:12(4)91, 129-130, 136, 139, 141-146.
454. Milota 1993b:711.
455. Van Kirk n.d.a.
456. Humboldt Standard 1908a.
457. Milota 1993b:711.
458. Merriam 1993:(30)422.
459. Merriam 1923a:59.
460. Ethnological Documents 2002:12(4):138.
461. Goddard 1903a:19.
462. Goddard 1903a:39, 49.
463. Ethnological Documents 2002:12(4):139, 141.
464. Ethnological Documents 2002:12(4):142-146.
465. Goddard 1907c:33.
466. Goddard 1907c:48.
467. The interviewees and their renderings of this tribal group's name are as follows: Bill Ray, a Kato: Nahs-ling-che ke-ah-hahng (Merriam 1993:(9)308); George Burtt, a Lolahnkok: "Nahs-lin-ko ke-ah" Merriam 1993:(30)422; Sally Bell, a To-cho-be ke-ah: "Nahs-lin-che ke-ah (Merriam 1993:(30)503).
468. Merriam 1993:(31)417.
469. Goddard 1907c:48.
470. Goddard 1907c:47. Albert calls him "Charlie John Smith" (Goddard 1907c:47), and Cook and Hawk have him as Jose "Chandler" Domingo Smith (Cook and Hawk 2001:192), but his 1889 land patent gives his name as Joseph D. Smith (Bureau of Land Management 2018b).
471. Goddard 1907c:46.
472. Goddard 1907c:35-48.
473. Goddard 1907d:9.
474. George Burtt calls them the "To-kub-be ke-ah" (Merriam 1993:(30)422), while Sally Bell gives the nearly identical "To-kub-be ka-ah" (Merriam 1993:(30)503). Merriam and Talbot list three versions of the name (Merriam and Talbot 1974:93), while Merriam, on his master map of the region's Indian tribes, has it "To-kub-be keah" (United States Department of Agriculture 1920).
475. Goddard n.d.d:10.
476. Merriam 1993:(9)303; (31)102. Merriam affiliated the To-kub-be ke-ahs with the Lassik tribal group called the Set-ten-bi-den ke-ah, which occupied the Alderpoint area. He appears to have done so based on statements from the Set-ten-bi-den ke-ah informants Yellowjacket and Lucy Young, who claimed that the western boundary for their group was the South Fork Eel (Merriam 1922a:32). Information from Goddard's interviewees, however, suggests that various Sinkyone tribal groups along the South Fork claimed all of both sides of the drainage (Goddard 1903a:56, 58; 1908b:42-43, 45, 56; N.d.d.:10). Albert Smith, Goddard's To-kub-be ke-ah informant, describes in detail sites on the East Branch from the South Fork Eel eastward all the way to the top of Mail Ridge (1907c:36-46). The usual pattern was for a tribal group to control land in a drainage from the stream up the ridgeline. Essene, in describing the Lassik "round of year," indicated that after a long summer trip to the east, the people traveled "southwest in the early fall until they got back to their home on Eel River," more specifically mentioning that "about the time the acorns ripen, most of the Lassik return to Alderpoint" (Essene 1942:84). His information came "primarily" from Lucy Young (Essene 1942:2). Goddard, although lumping the Lassiks with the Nongatls in his statement, indicated they occupied "a portion of the Main Eel r[iver]," and that on the west they bordered "the Sinkyone on Southfork of Eel r[iver]" (Hodge 1907:761). Merriam adds to the confusion by mapping the east side of the South Fork between its mouth and Rocky Glen Creek as being in Sinkyone territory all the way from the river up to the ridgeline at Mail Ridge (United States Department of Agriculture 1920a).
477. Goddard 1907c:40-46.
478. Goddard 1907d:10; Goddard 1907c:43.
479. Goddard 1907c:37. Goddard's interview notes with Smith state "Nun lives there where was born," leaving it unclear as to whether Smith or someone named "Nun" was born at the location.
480. Goddard 1907c:51.
481. Goddard 1907c:25.
482. Goddard 1907c:50-51, 53.
483. Goddard 1907c:50.
484. Goddard 1907c:44-45.
485. Goddard 1907c:57.
486. Goddard 1907c:107-108.
487. Goddard 1907c:97.
488. Cook 1997:(3)117.
489. Goddard 1907c, 1907d.
490. Cook 1997:(3)117. Cook incorrectly refers to the couple as "Alfred and Sally Bob."
491. Goddard 1907c:24; Denny 1911; Belcher Abstract & Title Co. 1921:3.
492. Swanlund-Baker 2018a, 2018b.
493. Humboldt Standard 1920a.
494. Merriam 1922a:40; 1993:(31)102.
495. Baumhoff 1958:194.
496. Cahto Dictionary 2024.
497. Merriam 1993:(9)250, 258.
498. Merriam 1993:(30)422.
499. Kroeber 1919:346.
500. Goddard 1907d:27.
501. Asbill 1953:81ff. This rambling but revealing account was written by the son of Pierce Asbill, one of the massacre perpetrators. Much of its information is suspect or patently incorrect, but it appears that certain sections describe actual, unsavory events not reported elsewhere.
502. Raphael 1992:97-98.
503. Nomland 1935:166. Bell's account is probably inaccurate. In 1907 she had told Goddard that "her father was killed by Indians (she thinks) when she was little" (Goddard 1907d:39). In her 1928-1929 statement for Nomland, Bell claimed that "some white men . . . killed my grandfather and mother and father" and also her little sister. Nomland noted at the time, however, that Bell appeared "senile" (Nomland 1935:149). It seems likely that Bell indeed witnessed the massacre of most of her family, but not that of her father.
504. Moungovan 1964:7; Humboldt Times 1939a:12. The accounts differ in some details, and the summary given here uses parts of both.
505. A phrase I once read but can no longer attribute to its author.
506. Asbill 1953:108.
507. Goddard 1908b:61.
508. Goddard 1908b:59.

509. Goddard 1908b:57-58, 60.
510. Goddard 1907a:136. Goddard writes: "Up as far [as] John Evarts were his [Joe Duncan's] people." Evarts's ranch straddled Conklin Creek (Denny 1911).
511. Ethnological Documents 2002:12(4)98; Goddard 1907f:5.
512. Ethnological Documents 2002:12(4)96-98.
513. Goddard 1907f:6.
514. Goddard 1907a:131.
515. Ethnological Documents 2002:12(4)96.
516. Goddard 1907a:131.
517. Goddard 1907f:14.
518. Goddard 1907f:6-7.
519. Davidson 1889:302-303.
520. Goddard 1903a:21.
521. Merriam 1993:(30)428, 503.
522. Goddard 1907d:39.
523. Goddard 1903a:21.
524. Merriam 1993:(9)143.
525. Merriam interviewed Bell in 1923 (Merriam 1993:(30)428-503), collecting only a small amount of information. Nomland interviewed Bell in 1928-1929 and described her then as "blind, senile, sees spirits in rafters, etc. Information unreliable" (Nomland 1935:149).
526. Gifford 1965:14,78. Gifford indicated that Tom Bell was Coast Yuki (Gifford 1965:78-80), but Bell's obituary states the he and his brother were found, as children, after a massacre at Shelter Cove and taken to live with a white man, Samuel Bell, in Mendocino County (Humboldt Times 1939a:12.) This raises the possibility that Tom Bell belonged to a Sinkyone tribal group rather than to the Coast Yukis.
527. Merriam 1976:96.
528. Merriam 1993:(32)105.
529. Gifford 1965.
530. Merriam 1993:(30)501.
531. Goddard 1907d:27.
532. Goddard 1907d:13; 1907c:28.
533. Calisphere 2018a; Gifford 1965:78-80.
534. Gifford 1965:1-2.
535. Humboldt Times 1939a:12.
536. Gifford 1965:14.
537. Merriam 1993:(9)196.
538. Powers 1976:114.
539. Asbill 1953; Evans 2007. Ike Duncan, a Mattole Indian, indicated that "Waylaeki is a whiteman name" for a certain group of Indians (Harrington 1983:(2)699).
540. Goddard 1923. In this monography Goddard fails to disclose the identity of his Wailaki informant(s). His notebook(s) for most of this area have not been located. One untitled notebook from 1922 contains information from the Wailaki known as Good Boy Jack (Goddard 1922a:70-110). Goddard worked with at least one other Wailaki, Captain Jim (Link, et al. 202a:401).
541. Goddard 1923:108.
542. Merriam 1993:(31)181.
543. Curtis 1970b:21.
544. Curtis 1970b:22.
545. Curtis 1970b:22-24.
546. Curtis 1970b:25.
547. Merriam 1993:(9)274.
548. Hodge 1910a:893.
549. Goddard 1923:107.
550. Merriam 1976:81-82.
551. Goddard 1923:107.
552. Merriam 1976:90-91.
553. Belcher 1922:11-12.
554. United States Department of the Interior, Geological Survey 1949a.
555. Goddard 1923:107.
556. Goddard 1923:107.
557. Goddard 1906b:40.
558. Merriam 1976:90.
559. Roscoe 1985a:18-19.
560. Merriam 1993:(9)44.
561. Merriam 1922a:30-31, 1993(31)80, 84; Goddard 1906b:29, 39, 40.
562. Goddard 1906b:43-44.
563. As indicated earlier, Merriam's Lassik informants claimed that their tribe's territory extended over Mail Ridge all the way to the South Fork Eel, which, however, "they were not permitted to cross" (Merriam 1922a:32). If fact, the Lassiks "had many camps but no winter villages on . . . South Fork Eel . . ." (Merriam 1922a:33). The informants' knowledge of South Fork area appears severely limited, as they gave only one tribal name for all the Indians "from Bridgeville to the coast" (Merriam 1993:(31)84). Furthermore, their geographical claim is challenged by the statements of several Indians from the South Fork Eel itself, including Briceland Charlie, Sam Suder, and Albert Smith, all of whom indicate the presence of Sinkyone tribal groups along the South Fork that were linked to both sides of the river, rather than just the western side, as Merriam would have it. This suggests that at most the Lassiks spilled westward over the top of Mail Ridge, perhaps as part of their extensive annual migration cycle, and temporarily occupied areas on the eastern side of the South Fork Eel's drainage. There they would have had to contend with various Sinkyone tribal groups that had permanent winter villages along the eastern side of the river.
564. Hodge 1907a:761.
565. Merriam 1993:(9)216; Essen 1942:84.
566. Goddard 1907b:90-91. Van Duzen Pete told Goddard that the southern boundary for the Nongatls on the Mad River is in the middle of the southeast quarter of Section 27, Township 1 North, Range 6 East, Humboldt Meridian.
567. Merriam 1993:(31)93, 97. Merriam twice listed the location as "Blue Rock," but in each case he has crossed out the "Blue." Once he replaced it with "Gray" and the other time with "White." No rock of any designated color appears on maps of the general area.
568. Essene 1942:89.
569. Essene 1942:v, 2.
570. Essene's account does not disclose the time of year when tanoak acorns ripen, but the event occurs in the fall (United States Department of Agriculture 2015b).
571. Essene 1942:84.
572. Essene 1942:84.
573. Essene 1942:84.
574. Murphey 1941:361.
575. Essene 1942:84.
576. Essene 1942:84; Jones 1981a:359-360. As late as 1955 Soldier Basin was accessible only by trail (United States Department of the Interior, Geological Survey 1955a.
577. Jones 1981a:359-360.

Endnotes

578. Murphey 1941:350.
579. In his thesis about Young, Eric Krabbe Smith refers to her as T'tcetsa (Smith 1990a). It is unclear how Smith determined that this was Young's Lassik name.
580. Murphey 1941:351.
581. Murphey 1941:351-354.
582. Murphey 1941:355-358.
583. Essene 1942:89.
584. Merriam 1922a:30.
585. Essene 1942:89.
586. The Sinkyone Sally Bell was interviewed briefly by Goddard, Merriam, and Nomland; the accuracy of what she told Merriam and Nomland is questionable as it appears that at the time of these interviews her memory was failing. Jenny Young, a Sinkyone, gave information to Merriam, Driver, and Nomland, but its accuracy is questionable. Susie Burtt, a Nongatl, provided material for Merriam's vocabulary sheets but even this basic information may reflect the many years she spent away from her people while living in Sinkyone territory as the wife of George Burtt. Minnie Pete, Van Duzen Pete's wife, was interviewed by Goddard. However, she was not Nongatl but Mawenok, a tribe more properly connected with Indians in the northern part of the county. Sarah Carrol (Carl) apparently provided Merriam with a single sheet of vocabulary when he interviewed her in Garberville. Mary Major, a Lassik, gave Essene some material that supplemented what Young provided, but it is unclear what this consisted of.
587. Merriam 1922a:30-31.
588. Essene 1942; Encyclopedia.com 2015a; Smith 1990:104-105.
589. Essene 1942:84, 89-92.
590. Essene 1942:2.
591. Murphey 1941:349-364.
592. Murphey 1941:358.
593. Merriam 1922a:30..
594. Merriam 1922a:30-31; Merriam 1993:(31)19.
595. Merriam 1993:(9)295. The author of the original article was congressman William Kent.
596. Goddard 1906b:39.
597. Goddard 1906b:39.
598. Goddard specifically referred to the North Fork Dobbyn Creek as "little Dobbin," and to the South Fork as "Dobbin." He only used the term "big Dobbin" in reference to the tribal group that occupied it.
599 Goddard 1906b:39.
600. Goddard 1906b:29.
601. Goddard 1906b:40.
602. Goddard 1906b:40.
603. Ethnological Documents 2002:12(4)221; Goddard 1906b:24.
604. Goddard 1907b:90-93.
605 Elsasser 1978:192; Kroeber 1925:143. Merriam, however, believed that the name was "supertribal . . . covering all [the] . . . tribes between Round Valley and Iaqua" (Merriam 1923:276-277), but much of the information he collected contradicted this claim.
606. In both 1907 and 1908 Goddard spent several weeks in the company of Pete, traveling through the Indian's homeland and recording information about various locations, tribal groups, and related topics. Goddard's notes from these trips are voluminous. They often appear to be hastily written and sometimes are difficult to understand. What emerges, however, is a detailed geography of the Nongatl people that includes the names and locations of a score of Nongatl tribal groups. Goddard also obtained a few scraps of information from Minnie Pete, Van Duzen Pete's wife.
607. Although Goddard spent more time with Pete than with any other southern Humboldt Indian, he was unable to get a clear understanding of two key terms—Nongatl and Se-nun-ka. It appears that Pete used the words to distinguish between two dialects—Nongatl being spoken on a section of the Mad river and Se-nun-ka being spoken in the Larabee Creek and Eel River drainages. Goddard, however, seems to have sometimes treated the words as names for tribal groups, despite Pete never attaching the "kai-ya" suffix that means "people of," to either word. At one point, when Pete mentions "Nongatl" while traveling along the upper Mad River, Goddard adds opaquely that "the distinction Pete indicated always as linguistic never political although it may have been that also" (Goddard 1907b:120-121). In the same notebook Goddard states that "Pete's language and stories are nongal, not kit-tel kai ya, not se-nunk"(Goddard 1907b:21-22). In the south, Goddard repeatedly labels villages "Senunka," even though his notes sometimes indicate they belonged to either the Ye-lin-din kai-ya or the Bus-ta-dun ki-ya tribal groups. To further confuse the nomenclature, Goddard eventually decided that the name of one of the dialects should be used as the tribal name for all of the groups that Pete had spoken of. In a letter to C. Hart Merriam, Goddard stated that "my Indian's [Pete's] name for his people was Nongatl which I adopted."
608. Ethnological Documents 2002:12(4)176-195. Goddard 1907b:17, 19; 1908a:60-61.
609. Goddard 1908a:60; Ethnological Documents 2002:12(4):176-195.
610. Lentell 1898.
611. Ethnological Documents 2002:12(4)185.
612. Goddard's first "Senunka" village notecard has "Blocksburg" written at the top. The location he gives for the village is several miles north of there but he also notes that it is "the most northerly village of the Senunka on Laribee Creek" (Ethnological Documents 2002:12(4)176).
613. Ethnological Documents 2002:12(4)186-194; Goddard 1908a:70, 125.
614. Goddard 1907b:17.
615. Goddard 1907e:5.
616. Essene 1942:90.
617. Merriam 1993:(31)97.
618. Ethnological Documents 2002:12(4)185.
619. Ethnological Documents 2002:12(4)182-185.
620. Goddard 1908a:61.
621. Goddard 1908a:61-62, 64-66.
622. Goddard 1907b:31-40.
623. Merriam 1993: (9)153.
624. Hewes 1940:34.
625. Turner and Turner 2010:217.
626. Ethnological Documents 2002:12(4)186-195.
627. Goddard 1908a:125.
628. Goddard 1908a:46-48. Goddard's notebook states: "Pete had been told by Nick's father that kos dun [is the] place kos dun kai ya [are] the Indians [that] used to live there." Although no last name is given, "Nick" almost certainly refers to Nick

Richard, a Nongatl who provided information to ethnographers Harold Driver (Driver 1939:307) and Gordon Hewes (Hewes 1940:32).
629. Goddard 1908a:46-54; Ethnological Documents 2002:12(4)174-175.
630. Goddard 1907b:20.
631. Goddard 1907b:19.
632. Goddard 1907b:21. This last statement is confusing, since it seems to indicate that Kos-dun is a sort of sub-dialect of Se-nuka, which is itself a dialect. Adding to the confusion is another statement by Pete, who says that the Kos-dun ki-yas "talk like us," apparently meaning the Nongatl dialect. Perhaps Kos-dun was a hybrid of the other two dialects, as the location of its use lay between the areas where the Se-nun-ka and Nongatl were spoken. Kos-Dun is listed here as a Se-nun-ka dialect on the strength of the two statements quoted in the text.
633. Goddard sometimes confusingly refers to the dialect itself as "Kit-tel ki-ya."
634. Pete tells Goddard that "This side Hydesville talk like mi tol [Mattole—actually the Bear River language]. Kit tel tcit tel on V[an] D[uzen] above" (Goddard 1907e:3).
635. Goddard 1908a:48.
636. Goddard 1908a:24. At one point Goddard records Pete as saying "tcit tle kai ya all people way down Griz[z]ley [Creek] & Iaqua including Pete's country," noting that this statement is "not very clear" (Goddard n.d.a.:77. If by "Pete's country" he means not where Pete grew up, which was on the Mad River, but where he now lived (near Fort Baker), this statement would make sense.
637. Goddard n.d.a.:74.
638. Goddard 1919:323.
639. Goddard 1907b:40-48.
640. Goddard 1907b:46.
641. Goddard 1907b:45. Goddard's notes sometimes refer to "kon tel ki," which seems to be the same as "kon tel dun."
642. Goddard n.d.a:73.
643. Goddard 1907b:26-27.
644. Goddard 1907b:23-25.
645. Goddard 1907b:26.
646. Goddard 1907b:16; n.d.a:83.
647. Goddard 1907b:21.
648. Goddard 1907b:25-27.
649. Belcher 1922:13.
650. Goddard n.d.a:49-50.
651. Goddard n.d.a.:56-57. Merriam interviewed Susie Burtt but received only a small amount of vocabulary (Merriam 1993:(30)508, 582, 584).
652. Goddard 1907b:49-50.
653. Goddard 1907b:19.
654. Goddard 1907b:50.
655. Goddard 1907b:53.
656. Goddard n.d.a.:76-77, 82-83; Ethnological Documents 2002:12(4)232.
657. Goddard 1908a:48.
658. Hewes 1940:34.
659. Compare this with Pete's statement that about 25 Kos-dun ki-ahs stayed in the area all winter (Goddard 1907b:20).
660. Hewes 1940:51.
661. Hewes 1940:51.
662. This probably occurred after the white invasion dislocated various tribal groups, since the area Richard refers to reportedly belonged to the Lolahnkoks, a Sinkyone tribal group.
663. Hewes 1940:49.
664. Hewes 1940:44.
665. Hewes 1940:51.
666. Hewes 1940:41. In 1879 the first Bridgeville bridge washed out during a flood (Brown 1879:3).
667. Hewes 1940:51.
668. Hewes 1940:49.
669. Hewes 1940:42.
670. Essene 1942:91. Elsewhere Young states that the "Ni i che" were a "small tribe on Post Creek and So[uth] Fork Trinity north of Auto Rest [Forest Glen]. Ranged west over South Fork Mt. to Mad River" (Merriam 1993:(31)84).
671. Merriam 1993:(30)422.
672. Golla 2011:141-142.
673. Goddard 1908a:7. Ethnological Documents 2002:12(4):160-165.
674. Ethnological Documents 2002:12(4):164. I have taken the liberty of syllabicating this 19-letter word, which Goddard left whole on his village notecard.
675. Essene 1042:91.
676. Goddard 1908a:24.
677. Goddard 1908a:25.
678. Goddard 1908a:29-30; Ethnological Documents 2002:12(4):147-152.
679. Goddard n.d.a.:61.
680. Goddard 1908a:24.
681. Goddard 1907b:21-22. The groups on the Big Bend on the Mad River, the northeastern part of Kneeland, and the northernmost part of Iaqua probably all belonged to a related Athabascan-speaking tribe called the Mawenoks, which claimed the drainage of the middle section of the Mad River (Merriam and Talbot 1974:9).
682. Goddard 1907e:3.
683. Ethnological Documents 2002:12(4):166-170.
684. Goddard 1907b:120.
685. Goddard n.d.b:5. At one point Pete tells Goddard that his father was from "Old Fort Baker," which was the domain of the Kit-tel ki-ya tribal group. Pete's grandfather on his father's side, however, was from Mad River, and Pete's mother was a Se-nun-ka, which would place her in the upper Larabee Creek or Eel Rock area (Goddard 1908d:92).
686. Goddard 1907b:90-93.
687. Goddard 1907b:119-122.
688. Goddard 1907b:98.
689. Merriam 1993:(9)87.
690. Goddard 1907b:16-17.
691. Goddard 1908a:32.
692. Goddard 1907b:134.
693. Goddard 1907b:139.
694. Humboldt Standard 1934a:9.
695. Merriam 1976:125-126.
696. Goddard 1908a:70, 91; Scott 1997a:22-23.

Epilogue

Yi-dan-din-nun-dun Creek

From the old road to Iaqua Butte this view of the North Fork Yager Creek drainage is visible through a screening of Oregon white oaks. The trees lead down to a gulch that contains a small stream known as D*gger Creek. This name was meant to disrespect the local Indians and should have long since been removed from the maps. For just once, let us honor the Nongatl tribal group that lived here and use their name for themselves by calling it Yi-dan-din-nun-dun Creek.

About the Author

Jerry Rohde has been researching Humboldt County history and writing about it for over 30 years. He has been the ethnogeographer and historian for Humboldt State University's Cultural Resources Facility for over 20 years. He has authored or co-authored six previous books and written more than 500 reports for state and local agencies and various Indian tribes. His History of Humboldt County People and Places series is planned to include seven books, of which *Southern Humboldt Indians* is the second. Jerry and his wife Gisela live in South Stumpville, a Eureka suburb.

Made in the USA
Monee, IL
04 March 2025

05bee005-cd64-4eef-93ce-7f13fc1a7781R01